A HERITAGE OF CANADIAN HANDICRAFTS

A HERITAGE OF CANADIAN HANDICRAFTS

EDITED BY

H. GORDON GREEN

McCLELLAND AND STEWART LIMITED TORONTO / MONTREAL

The Canadian Publishers
McClelland and Stewart Limited
25 Hollinger Road, Toronto 16

"Published on the occasion of the Centennial of Canadian
Confederation and subsidized by the Centennial Commission".

"Ouvrage publié à l'occasion du Centenaire de la Confédération
Canadienne, grâce à une subvention de la Commission du Centenaire".

PRINTED AND BOUND IN CANADA

Contents ❦

Illustrations ❧

A HERITAGE OF CANADIAN HANDICRAFTS

Foreword ❧

As President of the Federated Women's Institutes of Canada, it is a very great honour to write a brief foreword to this, our Centennial Project – A Heritage of Canadian Handicrafts.

The decision to carry out this project was made in 1961, bearing in mind that Canada's Hundredth Birthday is an occasion to remember our Canadian history in all its bi-cultural and multi-cultural aspects. The Federated Women's Institutes of Canada felt that in no more fitting or lasting manner could it aid in the preservation of a very important aspect of our ten provinces – their crafts and the people who brought them to our shores. We hope that in so doing we have succeeded, in some measure, in recording the traditions of the past as a recognition of our proud heritage.

In 1897 the first Women's Institute in the world was founded at Stoney Creek, Ontario. From this beginning has grown an organization that is truly national in scope and outlook – the Federated Women's Institutes of Canada. Our seventy thousand members, in branches in many parts of the ten provinces, the Yukon and Northwest Territories, have as their primary aim and objective, adult education for Canada's country women; in fact, our organization is known as the "Rural Women's University." It has made a unique contribution to community development across Canada.

Our motto is "For Home and Country." Among the many phases of our program is our deep and lasting interest in, and our love for the crafts. We feel that the preservation of these crafts can, in great measure, be attributed to our homemakers. It is only natural, therefore, that we should wish their history to be preserved.

It is our sincere hope that, as you read this history of the crafts of our ancestors, you will catch a glimpse of the hopes, the dreams, the faith, the talents and especially the struggles which must have been theirs at many times – struggles which we cannot conceive but which have so magnificently enriched our lives, and which have produced priceless treasures wherever the work of their toil-worn hands has been preserved. It has taken many hours of research to assemble what is recorded between the covers of this book. Our humble thanks go to those dedicated women in communities from the Atlantic Ocean to the Pacific Ocean, who have given so unstintingly of themselves to this labor of love, that this book may be a living memorial to the early pioneers of our great nation – truly A Heritage of Canadian Handicrafts.

FLORENCE I. MATHESON

President,
Federated Women's Institutes of Canada,
Oyster Bed Bridge, Prince Edward Island.

A Word from the Editor ✍

For nearly twenty-five years now I have been promising my wife that I will someday write a novel about that part of New Brunswick which is her home. I must admit, however, that there is something more selfish in that promise than a mere desire to give her a personalized anniversary present. For in all the geography of America, there are few places more richly beautiful than the Upper Saint John, and in all the history of America there are few chapters more dramatic than that of the desperate Danes who, in 1872, hacked a hole in the tangled woods for the colony of New Denmark. And since no writer, so far as I know, has ever tried to make a book out of the New Denmark story, I have long felt that it might be good business to write one.

I have the uncomfortable habit of feeling so guilty about posponing a job that on occasion I am actually impelled to do something about it. So it was that I finally went down to New Denmark a few summers ago for the prime purpose of gathering material for the long projected book. I spent days talking hopefully to the oldest Danes I could find in the colony. But some of these admitted sadly that their memories were beginning to fail; others never seemed to have known much of the early struggles; still other oldtimers were obviously trying to make my trip interesting by regaling me with colourful half-truths or sheer imagination.

And then one evening when I was feeling rather empty about the whole effort, one of the neighbour ladies dropped in to see me. "I really cån't understand why you feel you must go through all that trouble," she said. "Why don't you just ask our Women's Institute to help? They've been working on a history of this place for the past two years, and really, I don't think you're going to uncover a thing that they don't already have in that book of theirs!"

I am ashamed to confess such an ignorance now, but I found it hard to believe that a group of rural women could ever get very serious about such a scholarly pursuit as the preservation of this nation's history. Well, what does a mere man ordinarily associate with a women's club anyhow? Quilting bees, perhaps. Church suppers. A strawberry festival to buy a new carpet for the parsonage. . . .

I was utterly astonished at the research and detail which had gone into the book which my lady friend had recommended to me, and I was even more amazed to discover that projects for the preservation of local histories were common to Women's Institutes all across Canada. The idea began back in 1945 with Lady Tweedsmuir as its chief sponsor. Furthermore, these community histories are but one of many equally ambitious programs which have been begun by the Women's Institutes. Here is a partial list of what the Institutes are doing at this very moment: establishing scholarships, giving aid to rural hospitals, promoting art and music festivals, giving assistance in adult education programs, helping to welcome new Canadians, studying how to care for the aged, assisting mental health research, promoting conservation, campaigning to abolish salacious literature. They also played an important role in the establishment of the Peace Garden on the Manitoba-North Dakota border and originated a gift coupon scheme to help establish training centres in Ceylon.

Small wonder that in 1959 our Postmaster General authorized a stamp in honour of the Institute, and that the Ontario Government has now erected a plaque at the old homestead of the Institute's founder at St. George, Ontario. The National Historic Sites and Monuments Board has also co-operated in the preservation of the founder's home and has named its former owner a National Historic Figure.

The name of the unique woman to whom that honour has fallen was Mrs. Adelaide Hoodless, born Adelaide Hunter, and the story of how she conceived the idea of the Institute provides a dramatic revelation of the kind of woman she must have been. As a young mother, she suffered the tragedy of watching her infant son die of an intestinal affliction then known simply as "summer complaint." The cause of the contagion, so Mrs. Hoodless discovered too late, could be traced directly to the drinking of impure, unpasteurized milk. And when she became certain of this, she made a solemn promise to herself that she would do everything in her power to help other mothers avoid similar loss. She began her campaign with Household Science classes in nearby schools, and gradually there evolved the idea of organizing rural women wherever possible "to improve physical, intellectual and cultural conditions in the home, and to raise the standard of home-making."

Finally, with the help of Erland Lee of the Farmers' Institute of Ontario, the first Women's Institute was organized at Stoney Creek, Ontario, on February 18, 1897. It was only natural that one of the first localities to follow suit was that of nearby St. George, where Mrs. Hoodless had grown up. And if I seem more effusive in praising the Women's Institute than is proper for an editor, one of the reasons may lie in the fact that my oldest daughter, Mrs. Herbert German, now happens to be the president of the St. George group.

One of the most remarkable things about the Institute is that it has a fine disregard for politics, religion and race. It has grown out of mother love and nothing else, and in the broadest sense, it has always had but a single aim – that of giving our children a better land and a better life than our parents were able to give us.

What of the future?

It is true that the rural population of our Dominion is but a fraction of what it was in Mrs. Hoodless's time, and that it is still decreasing. And at first sight it might seem that since the Institute is still rural and small town, it must inevitably lose prestige and importance as Canada becomes increasingly urban. But I do not think this is so. For while modern techniques now enable more and more city dwellers to be fed by fewer and fewer farmers, it is also a fact that these remaining farmers are taking on new stature. They must be capable of sound thinking today, or making quick, sure decisions, of anticipating progress. And the wife of such a man will, I think, be much better informed than her mother was. I do not doubt for a moment that the farmer of tomorrow will assume a new importance, and that we will be glad to look to him and his wife for much of the leadership which the future will demand.

Finally, a word about this book. As you will see, it is just one more of the ambitious projects undertaken by the Federated Women's Institutes of Canada, and I hope that my part in it will help to make it as successful as so many of the others have been. I must congratulate the members for the essential idea of this work. It is an undertaking which has taken an incredible amount of research and labour, but it is surely a book which had to be done sometime, and I can think of no one better qualified to attempt it than the Institutes and no more fitting time for it than Centennial Year.

I must hasten to add that my own part in this has been relatively small. I have corrected, subtracted substantially and added very little. The work is mainly that of the members themselves, and especially of those whose names appear on the credit page.

H. GORDON GREEN

Acknowledgements

We would like to thank the following for the contribution of material for this book:

Mrs. Arthur Bagnall for the chapter on Prince Edward Island.

Mr. Arthur Pratt for the chapter on Newfoundland.

Mrs. W. A. Turner for the chapter on Nova Scotia.

Mrs. A. R. Ayling for the chapter on New Brunswick.

Mrs. Arthur Coates for the chapter on Quebec; Mrs. T. C. LeBeau for the material which appears on page 114; and the *Canadian Geographic Journal* for material on "The Renaissance of Handicraft in Quebec from 1930," which appears on page 113.

Miss Ethel Chapman for the chapter on Ontario.

Mrs. Elva Fletcher for the chapter on Manitoba.

Mrs. S. J. Hill and the Extension Division of the University of Saskatchewan for the chapter on Saskatchewan; and Mrs. J. H. Maduke for the material on the Ukrainian handicrafts.

Mrs. J. L. Richards for the chapter on Alberta.

Miss D. Geneva Lent for the chapter on British Columbia.

And we extend special thanks to all members of all branches of the Federated Women's Institutes of Canada who contributed to the research and writing of the book.

A HERITAGE
OF CANADIAN
HANDICRAFTS

1 ❧

Newfoundland

IT IS REASONABLE TO SUPPOSE that all handicrafts, as the term is now accepted, were begotten of necessity; that the sense-pleasing beauty of design or texture we find in hand-wrought production has evolved from the stern demands of an earlier, less affluent way of life. Beyond doubt this is the case in the province of Newfoundland and Labrador, where, due to centuries of severely restricted economic growth, crafts have been slow to reach maturity, either as regards quantity of production or widespread quality of product.

But, if it has been late in achieving stature, craft work in the province has had in recent years, the great advantage of painstaking care and wholehearted devotion lavished upon it by those responsible for administering specialized training in the subject. The results are correspondingly good; quality now is excellent by the most exacting standards, and this is an achievement of surpassing merit, since only lately have handicrafts become anything more than one of the basic semi-skills required for existence in remote areas.

There have always been notable bright spots in the general picture of crafts in the province, of course. Produced many years ago and still to be seen are carefully guarded examples of woven goods, hooked rugs, wood carvings and ship models, for instance, which for purity of design and consummate workmanship are practically flawless. But by

1

and large, lack of materials, training, or opportunity prevented production of anything but the most basic articles for home consumption, in which appearance was a far less important consideration than utility.

The early history of the island of Newfoundland and its huge Labrador dependency is eloquent of conditions that helped bring about this situation. Settled first as a mere fishing station, "like a huge ship moored on the Grand Banks", Newfoundland missed out entirely on the eager colonization which later took place in other parts of North America. In fact the first settlers here had to hide away in remote bays and coves because English law forbade permanent settlement – a measure designed to protect the interests of English merchants who were amassing huge fortunes from the cod fishery in Newfoundland waters.

The French-English wars, piracy around the coasts which caused settlements to be razed time after time, and the difficulties of existing in winter isolation also helped discourage colonization. But the land and sea resources were a powerful magnet to the adventurous types of the sixteenth century; and they defied the laws by taking up residence in places where authority was hardly likely to reach them. The result was more than one thousand tiny settlements strung along six thousand miles of coastline, most of them implacably cut off from their neighbours by many miles of often-stormy sea. In these communities life was basic indeed – nothing but complete self-sufficiency permitted existence.

This meant that the people lived almost in the manner of remnants of lost tribes – preserving what they could recall of old cultures but drawing nothing from the world's progress because they had little or no contact with it. In those years, the island of Newfoundland did in fact harbor one such authentic lost tribe – the Beothic Indians. Obscure as to origin, the tribe was wiped out of existence by the white settlers and by the mid-nineteenth century none remained. But enough evidence remained of their way of life to classify them as Newfoundland's earliest handicrafts workers.

A pitiful reminder of this is seen in the museum in the provincial capital, where the skeleton of an Indian boy is shown with child-sized eating utensils and a primitive carved wooden toy which were buried with him. Research has shown that the Beothics, said to be not akin to other North American Indians but of later Asian origin, were adept at utilizing animal skins and decorated their leathern garments with a profusion of fringes and patterns of vegetable dyes.

The Nascopi Indians of northern Labrador made similar garments, but the Montaignais tribe of the more southerly part of that land have no record of any particular skills beyond the manufacture of skin clothing and of primitive weapons of war. They used to be a highly warlike people who hunted down the Eskimos and forced them to move northward from their traditional homeland.

The Eskimos of Labrador are a people of remote Asian origin and of extremely primitive culture. Until recently when they made contact with other races, their only hand-wrought production was confined to the very simplest of utensils and clothing from bone, stone, and skins. But they proved highly adaptable to instruction and are now productive in a range of handicrafts.

The Micmac Indians of Newfoundland are of comparatively recent tenure, having first landed here from Nova Scotia about 1792. History has it that they were sent by the French as saboteurs, to wreak what havoc they could to English installations in the island at a time when those two powers were warring over North America possessions.

Regardless of this rather unpatriotic beginning, the Micmacs quickly adapted to their new home. For a livelihood they augmented hunting with the manufacture of baskets from "witherods" (presumably the small branches of alder bushes), which were durable and serviceable and formed a good medium of exchange with the white settlers. Having integrated with other races, they do not now exist as a tribal entity.

As for Newfoundland's original colonists, they came, almost without exception, from Great Britain. The English counties, Scotland and Ireland contributed their shares of culture to the new-found-land. In a few places people of French descent, mainly deserters from the warships which were then thick upon the waters, settled and formed communities which had their distinctive heritage and mode of life.

These settlers eked out a hazardous existence from the sea, augmenting it mainly with hunting and primitive cultivation of a few vegetables. They had to make, generally from the most scanty materials, practically everything they used. Occasionally a ship from Europe would land a few manufactured articles but such visits were rare indeed in the remote settlements.

There exists today some evidence that the wooden furniture (including intricately carved sea chests), eating utensils, clothing and footwear made from available materials were often of superb craftsmanship, their design varying as widely as the many localities from which their makers had come. Great ingenuity was displayed in fashioning serviceable articles from the most sparse odds and ends of leather and cloth. It was a case of "fine bricks from very little straw," a handicrafts instructor was to remark many years later.

At this time also developed the particular knitting craft for which many Newfoundland women (and some men) were to become renowned. Mittens and socks of home-spun in a traditional double-knitting pattern were (and are) ideally suited for wear in the rugged and mostly frigid environment of North Atlantic fishing from small boats.

These knitted garments were worked of black and white wool in the most intricate geometric patterns — perhaps the first evidence that despite the starkly utilitarian reason for their production, the women who made them were aware also of the need to bring to their work whatever they could of beauty. The double-knitted garments were commonly worn everywhere for many years; but they gave way to the inevitable competition of shoddier factory-made goods and now they are practically collector's items. The few women who still produce these articles in the real traditional style can command good prices for them. In the years of Newfoundland's great economic depression they became practically the only cash-producing commodity in some fishing villages, and the beautifully patterned mittens were brought by the men to St. John's, where they went on sale under the familiar name of "Torbay mitts."

The fisherman of Newfoundland have much to thank their womenfolk for. The wives help on the fish-curing stages and in the home gardens and they supply the bountiful meals demanded by voracious sea-whetted appetites. But not the least of the assistance they give the fishery is the production of warm clothing, for nothing is more important to the fishermen. Many women are still adept at knitting the "long-johns" underwear that keep a man comfortable throughout long days on the water; these are not made of home-spun, of course, but of soft, imported wool.

These arts, then, of manufacturing household articles and knitting family garments, existed in the earliest and hardest of times in Newfoundland. Such of them as still exist were handed down through generations but only the pioneers knew the real necessity of them.

As years passed conditions grew easier. By the middle of the eighteenth century trade with the outside world opened up as restrictive laws were relaxed, and the standard of life improved. Here can be traced the first instance of the rule of necessity which governed handicraft production in Newfoundland from the beginning.

With some of the rigorous need for self-sufficiency removed, the old arts and skills from Europe gradually faded out. They were no longer vital to daily life and the generations no longer carefully handed them on. Where they continued to exist, they did so as individual labors of love rather than of everyday occupation, and so they passed almost beyond recall.

Meanwhile the barter or "truck" system held a great many of the people in continual economic thralldom. Merchants supplied the fishermen with equipment for the yearly operations, and with food for their families; then they paid for the fish with goods in kind. Very little cash was therefore in circulation and the people were gripped by perpetual debt. Such crafted goods as were produced belonged automatically to the local merchant in payment for fishery supplies and there was little incentive to make them.

When a bitter depression hit the island many years later, leaving the fishermen in a state of "dazed desperation", the need for resumption of the old skills was starkly apparent. They were necessary to avert actual disintegration of communities and families; but except in isolated cases at a limited level, the people were helpless to revive them. It took long periods of training under instructors from "outside" before the small settlements could respond to the morale-building lift given by the positive force of self-industry.

To accomplish this — and it has been accomplished, in a spectacular manner — several agencies, working entirely for the common good, took upon themselves the big task of helping raise a distressed people from the slough of despond. To do so, they turned first to handicrafts as a means primarily of restoring communal self-respect, and incidentally as a means of securing some small economic aid.

In the main, four organizations devoted to public service are responsible for the record of success in restoration of crafts. In order of their creation they are the Moravian Brethren, operating their five mission stations in Labrador; the justly world-renowned International Grenfell Association, also in the north; the Newfoundland Outpost Nursing and Industrial Association, and the Jubilee Guilds of Newfoundland (both of the latter operating throughout the province and both strong proponents of the "dignity through industry" scheme) .

MORAVIANS

The Moravian missionaries first came to Labrador from their native country in 1752, and they found a land rugged and forbidding beyond telling, peopled by pagan and largely hostile bands of Eskimos.

But the first Moravian Brother who landed on the coast astutely noted that natural resources existed which could be used to further the cause of Christianity by improving the common lot. He saw bears, wolves, foxes, seals and birds, and reported that "hares are tolerably plenty". From these wild creatures, he reasoned, not only food to sustain the missionaries could be obtained, but skins and feathers which could be used in a variety of ways to aid the savage natives, once they had been taught handicrafts.

But the Eskimos weren't too susceptible to teaching. In fact, they killed four of the first Moravian missionaries, along with the captain of their ship and an interpreter.

The missionaries who bravely followed in 1754-56 had to battle sorcerism, age-old superstition, plagues, killing storms and indescribably foul living conditions as they settled in with the Eskimos and strove heroically to better the lot of Labrador's stone-age people.

Their first success came when they persuaded the Eskimos to relinquish their heathen gods, having first had to dissuade the white traders of northern Newfoundland from totally exterminating the savage tribes; their second was to get the Eskimos to live peaceably together in the neighbourhood of the mission stations; the third was teaching them to be productive with their hands.

For more than two centuries now the Moravian missionaries have been successfully training Eskimos while leading them spiritually. Theirs was established as a "trading" mission, with the idea that the natives could turn their innate skills to account with the mission acting as the market for the products of their hands and supplying their material wants. It was designed as a practical form of Christianity in which God-given resources are utilized to improve the common lot and gain a more fruitful way of life both spiritually and materially.

Once the basic requirements of food and shelter had been provided, there was an opportunity to extend the work by helping the natives become self-supporting. The Moravians supplied equipment and taught new methods of hunting and fishing, for a start. Then they trained the Eskimos in various handicrafts, at which the people were naturally adept but possessed of a very limited range of ideas.

Obviously, the materials found ready at hand were the only ones available for this purpose. From the skins of seals, the ivory tusks of walrus, the pelts of foxes and the feathers of northern grouse, the first hand-worked articles that were not strictly utilitarian were produced.

The Eskimos were, and still are, natural craftsmen and crafts-women. Their ivory carvings in particular are superb, and the most popular of these are intricately fashioned replicas of a dog team and sled, so cunningly worked that the tiny animals seem to be joyously speeding across the snow while a beaming, whip-cracking Eskimo rides the komatik behind them. Handicrafts fashioned of sealskin are also very well made, and a favorite item is soft, warm footwear gaily decorated with beads to add colour.

Many years passed between the landing of the Moravian Brethren in Labrador and the time when the opportunity arose to display Eskimo crafts to the outside world, to any large extent. Doubtless some of the earlier missionaries had brought samples of the work to their homes in Europe when they went on their rare holidays, and the crewmen of occasional visiting ships would have seen the work, but apart from this there would have been no means to distribute Eskimo crafts widely.

But the demand for them grew as surely as it did slowly, and towards the end of the last century they were becoming quite widely sought as curios. There is evidence that the Eskimo crafts so carefully nurtured by the Moravians in Labrador as a means of exchange to produce better living standards antedated by about two hundred years the recent interest in production of shop-window curios by the natives of the more westerly Canadian Arctic.

There is an effort now in Newfoundland to expand production of Eskimo work for commercial purposes. Particular emphasis is being given to hand-embroidered items, this being a skill at which Eskimos have shown themselves to be remarkably adroit. Embroidery on linen for tablecloths, bed clothing and sportswear, using the Arctic motif, has proven quite popular, as have Eskimo productions of hooked mats and wall decorations and skin footwear. Marketing of these items is being done by the International Grenfell Association under a recent arrangement made by the Newfoundland and Labrador government.

The Moravian Mission having flourished in Labrador without interruption for 215 years, it is obvious that the Brethren and their wives are unique among exponents of original Canadian handicrafts. They continue their interest in this field today, and the Labrador missions they conduct are centres of considerable production of hand-worked goods, which still are fashioned mostly from materials grudgingly yielded by the bleak land and bleaker sea.

The name of Dr. William Thomasen Grenfell is acclaimed internationally, and beloved as well throughout Newfoundland and Labrador. His self-chosen avocation among the people of the north has ranked him high among the world's great humanitarians, and from the time he first found his life's work in northern Newfoundland and Labrador in 1892 until his death in 1940, he never lost sight of the fact that handicrafts formed a most important part of the magnificent results he achieved. He once aptly summed up his feeling that this was so: "Training of hand and eye fosters the larger development of the mind," he has written.

Dr. Grenfell found appalling conditions of poverty forcing an almost brute existence on Labrador's people. Dominating all the immediate efforts to relieve distress by way of medical care, provision of necessities of food, clothing and housing was the premise that to achieve any sort of independence whatever the people must be taught to develop their own resources, however meagre those resources might be.

The doctor noted that the natural aptitude of Newfoundlanders, reared in the hard school of privation, and pitting their strength and wits against boisterous sea and inhospitable land, made an excellent starting point for a handicrafts project that now has world-wide ramifications.

His own early records of life among the northern fishermen reveal that he instituted wood carving, first as "good therapy" for convalescents denied their normal activity, then as a means to produce a marketable commodity. This was followed by ivory carving, for which the materials — walrus and narwhal tusks — were bought from Eskimos and distributed to patients in many Labrador settlements. Basket-work was another craft which was early introduced, the baskets being made from northern sandgrass, a singularly tough, coarse and wildly-flourishing plant from which the Norse Vikings once ground their grain.

These handicrafts, first done by convalescent patients, quickly gained vogue among the fisherfolk of the tiny settlements of northern Newfoundland and Labrador. In 1907 the Grenfell Mission began its industrial department, a highly significant development in the slowly unfolding picture of handicrafts in Newfoundland.

The first supervisor of Grenfell handicrafts as an organized department was Miss Jessie Luther, a devoted instructor who served faithfully for many years to help the people of the desolate northern coasts. The industrial department rapidly became a resounding success and has been an integral part of the Grenfell Mission's wonderful humanitarian work ever since.

The people whom Grenfell came to doctor and remained to love and admire were as courageous and hard-working as any on earth, he reported. They were God-fearing, loyal and good-humoured, but their material advantages were so pitifully slim that they existed in a condition bordering at all times on extinction.

Isolation, storms, fishery failure, the barter system and resulting malnutrition had combined to beat down their eagerness for life; they were destitute, and worse, hopeless, wrote the deeply sympathetic Grenfell.

But the cure was not to be found in either pity or medicine, he decided. With characteristic determination he began an immediate program of cottage industry. He first asked the women of the settlements to utilize such natural materials as they could come by to make warm garments, and the Mission supplied some animal skins to the communities for this work. Most of the women needed only the encouragement, and soon a trickle of results in the form of coats and boots beautifully worked from pelts began to flow into Mission headquarters at St. Anthony, Newfoundland.

These were desperately hard times for the struggling Mission as well as for the people it served, and the supply of materials for handicrafts just wasn't sufficient. Grenfell turned to his friends in Canada and the United States, appealing for old, cast-off garments or cloth that could be used for clothing, rugs, and bedding. Used silk stockings for rug making were particularly needed, he told audiences during lecture swings through the eastern United States.

The women of more fortunate climes responded nobly to the missionary's appeal, and large consignments of stockings and garments were collected and sent to St. Anthony. Dr. Grenfell noted: "Now, when silk stockings run, they run to Labrador!"

This friendly support gave the Grenfell handicrafts a life-saving boost, and the donated cast-offs, distributed in a hundred small outports, returned to the Mission in the form of saleable mats and rugs and other articles. These had been wrought with loving care and represented an astonishing fund of patience and unexpected creativity of design on the part of their makers.

Handicrafts continued to grow in importance in the Grenfell organization's plan of things to come, and a large industrial centre was constructed at St. Anthony in the early 1930's. It served as a training establishment for women of Newfoundland and Labrador fishing communities, and highly skilled instructors from England and the United States gave freely of their time to serve with the Mission.

Grenfell underlined the importance of crafts in the effort to rebuild the lives of destitute people when he noted "an absolute necessity exists of increasing production of home-made goods to offset an economy dependent on the fluctuating industries of furring, fishing and lumbering."

There has never been any thought behind the Grenfell Association's sponsorship of handicrafts beyond its power to provide a new and cheering way of life for many persons who formerly merely subsisted. Hence the project's name of industrial department. Industry is seen as the answer to conditions that were de-humanizing; but only home industry was possible and that had to be a genuine and satisfying work capable of restoring human dignity, with an appropriate return for labor given.

On these lines, Grenfell handicrafts have been markedly successful. Insistence upon quality of exceptional standard has made the Grenfell imprimateur respected in world markets. To provide an outlet for the products of its workers, the Association operates gift stores throughout the eastern United States as well as in Canada, and these are able to offer an astonishingly wide range of home-produced goods.

The famous Grenfell parkas are made from a pattern developed by Dr. Grenfell himself, as a result of his experiences in northern travelling, and they are generally made of the equally renowned Grenfell cloth, a light-weight, wind and water resisting material ideal for arctic use. Garments of fur are produced as well, and footwear made of the tough hides of seals, after the age-old Eskimo fashion, are in constant demand.

Knitted goods with the Grenfell label also are known for exceptional quality, but probably the most widely popular articles are ornaments and keepsakes fashioned from seal fur, an extremely versatile medium, now so widely used as to be found covering cocktail bars and cigarette lighters as well as in coats, stoles and footwear. Miniature seal pups, the appealing "whitecoats," made of the genuine fur have been popular for many years. Nevertheless, ivory work, produced mainly by the Eskimos living within the Grenfell mission's range of operations, has always been regarded as one of the leading handicrafts, and still ranks as a top prestige product among the array of attractive goods produced in the desolate ice-bound hamlets of the far northern coasts.

A great deal of the credit for the development of handicraft activity in Newfoundland must go to the Vice-Regal representatives who served in Government House at St. John's before the island became a province of Canada in 1949.

Indeed, records show that as far back as 1750, Governor Sir Hugh Palliser was interested in improving the lot of the Labrador Eskimos (whom he had never seen, but pitied anyhow), and did all in his power to further the prospects of the Moravian missionaries who undertook to teach the natives handicrafts.

Various colonial governors and their wives thereafter took an equally keen interest, and though naturally they served at different periods, seemingly they were united in the conception that cottage industry in the form of handicrafts was the solution to many of the ills caused by a desperate economic plight.

As a result of the efforts of Lady Harris, wife of Sir Alexander Harris, Governor of Newfoundland in 1920, the Newfoundland Outport Nursing and Industrial Association came into being. The title admirably summed up the organization's aims and objects, and though cumbersome it possessed the advantage of being easily contracted to the attractive name NONIA, which has since become a highly honoured trademark wherever good quality hand worked goods are discussed.

Lady Harris had been perturbed by the almost complete lack of nursing care in the Newfoundland outports, and formed a committee charged with hiring and financially supporting nurses willing to serve in the isolated districts. Small government grants were forthcoming, and contributions from the people whom the nurses served were supposed to pay part of the costs of the plan. But times were so difficult that the women of the outports just couldn't raise the cash to give as their share, so NONIA had to survive some real crises.

In 1924 Sir William Allardyce was Governor, and Lady Allardyce worked out a plan whereby the women in the fishing communities might knit and weave in their homes, selling the products of their hands and looms through a retail store to be established at St. John's.

In common with other public service projects of its type, NONIA's aim was two-fold: to provide a cash source to pay for nursing care, and to raise the standard of living generally in the remote areas.

In 1934, NONIA was relieved of the nursing aspect of its program, which was taken over by the Newfoundland Department of Public Health and Welfare. The organization was then able to concentrate

fully on the handicraft side, which was succeeding admirably in helping to maintain at least a subsistence if not comfortable standard of
living during the depression years.

For the past thirty-two years NONIA handicrafts has been a venture
that could be described as inspiring. It has grown with each succeeding year, though faced with severe difficulties in war time when
supplies of materials were drastically curtailed. Thousands of Newfoundland and Labrador women work part-time for NONIA, and some
of them full-time, in villages large and small throughout the province.
NONIA has three hundred and fifty knitters and six weavers in one
community alone, turning out the attractive garments and housewares
which have become so renowned for quality.

The work they do consists mainly of hand-knitted garments of all
descriptions and hand-woven material which has gained an enviable
reputation for its fine texture and durable qualities. Much of the
work is produced on looms manufactured by the fishermen of the
outports for use in their own settlements, making the community
project a self-starting one from the ground up, so to speak. Finely
worked hooked mats and rugs, in designs considered by connoisseurs
to be outsanding, are also an important part of the NONIA range of
homecrafts.

The organization maintains a headquarters office in St. John's
from which materials are sent out and payments made, and operates
a most attractive gift shop which is a popular stop for visitors to the
city, who report that NONIA articles compare favorably with those
produced by handcrafters anywhere in North America. In the line of
ladies' sweaters particularly, NONIA workers have developed their art
to such perfection that their organization's label on these garments
has become emblematic of the last word in quality.

In 1966 Lady Outerbridge, the president of NONIA, said recent
reorganization of handicraft activities in Newfoundland will strengthen
the work of the Association immensely, designed as it is to further
encourage crafts in the smaller settlements.

JUBILEE GUILDS

In Newfoundland and Labrador, no name is more widely honoured
as a force for good than that of the Jubilee Guilds, and certainly the
organization has well merited the acclaim.

Begun in 1935 by Lady Anderson, wife of Governor Admiral Sir David Murray Anderson, it is modelled along the lines of the Women's Institutes of Canada and Great Britain, though it was established to include men in its ranks of workers as well as women.

The name was taken to honour the Silver Jubilee of the reign of King George V and his Queen, and the Guilds' motto was part of the King's Jubilee speech: "Confidence, Courage, and Loyalty."

Certainly the first two attributes had to be deeply ingrained in the Guilds' workers of 1935, and although Newfoundlanders have always been intensely loyal to the Crown, it is something of a wonder that the crushing series of misfortunes which had overwhelmed them had not disposed of the third part of the slogan!

However, all three traits were found intact when Lady Anderson and her helpers set up the scheme to aid the people of outport Newfoundland. Those people, in far too many cases, had been left almost destitute by a savage monetary depression, a devastating tidal wave, and the tragic failure of the basic economic mainstay, the fishery.

Miss Elizabeth MacMillan, a trained handicrafts worker who formerly had been director of Women's Institutes in Prince Edward Island, was the first supervisor of the Jubilee Guilds. She was succeeded in 1939 by Miss Anna Templeton, B.H.Sc., a Newfoundlander who joined the Guilds as organizing secretary and remained as its guiding light until her appointment as director of the newly established handicrafts division of the provincial Vocational Education Department in 1965.

The first step in developing the meagre local resources of the affected districts was taken by the Guilds in setting up a program of weaving and knitting so that the people could at least have warm clothing. Other classes, in dress-making, home economics, preserving, soap making and related crafts followed, but only after the basic necessities had first been met.

Supplies of wool for weaving were scarce; there were few sheep, and those that did exist "seemed to be half starved" investigators reported. The government of the day responded to this need by importing some high grade ovine stock and distributing it where the need seemed greatest and where the Guilds recommended. This made a small beginning, but the women of the outports took up the work enthusiastically and set about learning the crafts with which their forbears had been familiar but which had fallen into disuse.

The men of the communities were no less keenly interested in this new chance to improve their circumstances. They copied the first imported Canadian and Norwegian looms, and did a fine job of it, making an article that performed just as well at a quarter of the usual cost, and awed the instructors who had come from Canada.

Difficulties just weren't allowed to stand in the way. In one fishing community, perched on the bare rocks at the sea's edge, wood was a precious commodity and practically unobtainable. So the men dismantled an organ to make parts for their loom. In another place they had no adequate space to install a loom, so they set it up in the local church, and weaving and praying then became the common order of the day.

The men found too that the work started in the communities by the Jubilee Guilds had certain material, not to say bodily, advantages. For example, women's slips in the Princess pattern made fine, warm nightshirts; and windbreakers of woven wool proved comfortable at sea. There was some mild astonishment reported when the first gaily coloured placemats appeared under the dishes of traditional fish-and-brewis, it was said; but male rebellion occurred throughout the land when the women began fashioning underclothing from sackcloth. The fishermen drew the line there; they said it itched!

Meanwhile the work of the Guilds expanded rapidly. Lady Anderson left Newfoundland in 1936, and Lady Walwyn, wife of Rear Admiral Sir Humphrey Walwyn, the succeeding Governor, took over the direction with zest. She was an indefatigable worker in the cause, and under her aegis the Guilds flourished. She had a loom installed in Government House and proudly set the example by turning out some excellent work on it. She was able to report that when the King and Queen visited St. John's in 1937, they used, and apparently were quite impressed by, two cushions that had been hand-made by the Guilds' president.

The Guilds held their first exhibition in that year, showing a fine range of good quality handicrafts, and arousing a great deal of interest in weaving throughout Newfoundland. The Guilds' effort was seen as conducive to breaking down "the innate reserve that is characteristic of many of our people, and changing rugged individualism into warm-hearted co-operation." This was an editorial accolade that is still standing the test of time.

All is never perfect, of course. In the early training period, apparently there were difficult times for some Guild members. One local secretary reported wryly: "Mrs. ———— is still at her blankets, and if by our mistakes we learn, she will be an infinitely wise woman by the time she gets them finished." Another local reported it had just re-opened, not having worked during the winter, and was now about to close down for the summer months!

But the overall activity was highly impressive. In 1937 the first field workers were hired and sent to the districts and Guilds objectives received a fine boost, with extension of the work on a new dimension being made possible. A weaving school established at St. John's that year was described as "a school of enthusiasm."

Glove making, using dressed sheepskin, became a fairly important part of Guilds' production and continued so until the outbreak of the Second World War, when supplies of material became scarce.

The war had other effects on the Jubilee Guilds. Repeating the pattern of economic influence, boom times caused by defence expenditures in Newfoundland saw some reduction in the number of outport Guilds. But it was a slight and temporary effect, mostly, and the real worth of the Guilds' basic philosophy remained, so that the work has gone from strength to strength ever since. In war time, too, the Guilds' members turned their attention to helping the Allied cause and much of their energy was expressed in making warm clothing for servicemen, in providing treats for men on leave, and donating to the Women's Patriotic Association.

In 1945, a provincial exhibition revealed the amazing extent of production of which the Guilds were capable. There were 106 local Guilds at the time, and the exhibition display included blankets of homespun, measuring 90 inches by 72 inches, travelling rugs, woollen floor rugs, tablecloths, luncheon sets, napkins, handbags, scarves, drapes, baby blankets, crib covers, upholstery, sash curtains, pile rugs, lace curtains, pocketbooks and samplers – all of washable and colour-fast materials. It was an impressive indication of what could be done with local handicrafts and gave impetus to the work throughout the island.

In 1946 a National Handicrafts Centre for training was established, and this worked closely with the more experienced agencies for several years, capably directed by the late Frank Templeman. The Government asked the Jubilee Guilds to combine its efforts with those of the Centre and this was done. It was not too successful an alliance, however, mainly because of factors of duplication of effort, and it terminated after a couple of years. The Guilds' organization was then left free to devote all its energies to further promotion of its highly successful program.

Meanwhile the Handicrafts Centre continued for some time to sponsor training courses, and gave valuable impetus to the overall handicrafts program by offering financial assistance to crafts students while training. The Jubilee Guilds expanded its own program, adding to the original projects news ones such as training in pottery, leather-work, beadwork, copper tooling, aluminum etching and jewellery making, with instructors holding classes throughout the province.

Weaving, however, has remained a basic craft with Guilds workers. In the small outports weaving groups operate as knitting groups do in more sophisticated centres, with patterns exchanged and regular get-togethers being held. But where knitting groups meet mainly for pleasurable social intercourse, weaving is a reminder that the purpose of the group is actually to achieve a reasonably comfortable way of life. One of the original purposes of Jubilee Guilds was expressed by the first president as an effort to "relieve the dull monotony of life in the small outport." It has certainly accomplished that end.

GOVERNMENT AID

Newfoundland, the first of Britain's overseas colonies, had been granted self-government in 1855 and attained, in 1918, the proud status of a Dominion within the British Commonwealth of Nations. But by 1933 financial difficulties, caused mainly by over-extension of resources to aid the war effort, had become insurmountable and the government of the day applied to Great Britain for aid.

The "home" government's answer was to appoint a Royal Commission to investigate the Dominion's affairs. It reported a shocking collapse of economic security, and strongly recommended, among other remedies, the prompt implementation of an adequate program of cottage handicrafts. A Commission of Government was appointed by the British Colonial Government to administer Newfoundland's affairs until she should again become solvent, and this body endeavoured in various ways to carry out the recommendations on handicrafts promotion. But funds were short and not a great deal could be accomplished. Co-operation with the Jubilee Guilds, NONIA, Grenfell Mission and other agencies was freely given, however, and one of the most solid supports given the handicrafts program was the sponsorship of rural exhibitions by the Commission of Government.

Attempts were made to create interest in furniture making and other crafts, taught by imported instructors, but these were mostly spasmodic and were sometimes met with derision, particularly an effort to teach Newfoundland fishermen how to make bows and arrows!

Alliance of efforts by the government and existing agencies was probably the most successful pattern produced by the Commission.

The provincial government taking office after union with Canada in 1949 was strongly favourable to expansion of the handicrafts program as an integral part of the over-all development plan for the province. One of the first decisions made by Premier J. R. Smallwood, who took a keen interest in this aspect of affairs, was to reorganize completely the existing crafts set-up. For this purpose he wisely appointed Jubilee Guilds to handle the reins, resulting in interest in handicrafts reaching a peak never before attained.

One particular handicraft which is solely indigenous to Newfoundland is the production of Labradorite items. Labradorite is a feldspar mineral originally found on an island off Nain, northern Labrador, but since located in other areas. It is beautifully veined with green and takes a high polish to make a most attractive material for rings, bracelets, brooches and a variety of other jewellery and ornaments. One Labradorite hobbyist has even succeeded in producing miniature ship models with the mineral. Outgoing presidents of the Canadian Authors' Association are traditionally presented with a two by four inch "tombstone" of Labradorite.

Grenfell first experimented with Labradorite in 1900 and was convinced it could be made the basis of a sizeable industry if it could be located in large enough quantities. But only recently has Labradorite production reached any noteworthy proportions. It is a fascinating handicraft, but the cutting and polishing processes are highly intricate and the necessary equipment is costly for the beginner. Labradorite is customarily cut with diamond saws in an oil-bath and polished with graduated silicon grits under running water.

The government has taken some interest in the larger possibilities of Labradorite production and endeavoured to establish properly equipped craftsmen. This has succeeded in a relatively small way, with Labradorite costume jewellery now being produced on a scale where it can be marketed commercially. It meets a ready demand.

Pottery is another craft in which the government, through its national Handicrafts Centre, displayed considerable interest. The Jubilee Guilds has continued the experiment and brought it to fruition. A number of locations have been found where clay of excellent quality for pottery making is available, and Guilds groups are now turning out hand-fired and hand-glazed pottery of most attractive appearance. This is a recent development which seems certain to grow into one of the more important Newfoundland handicrafts.

Facilities for training in copper tooling, aluminum etching, textile and china painting, basketry, metalwork, wood carving and pottery are provided by government as well as the regular classes for weaving, knitting, dressmaking and home economics conducted by Jubilee Guilds.

Newfoundland handicrafts received considerable impetus during the Second World War and in the years afterwards through the interest displayed in locally made goods by members of the armed forces, particularly those stationed at United States bases in the province. As a result, orders for work are commonly received from, and completed articles sent to, places as distant as British Columbia, Texas and Greenland.

A notable contribution to Newfoundland crafts was production of a book on weaving by Miss Anna Templeton. This contains all the weaving patterns, with instructions, and is regarded as a veritable bible of the weaving art. Local handicrafts authorities have received orders for it from as far away as Australia.

Besides the organizations mentioned, there have been notable contributions made in the field of Newfoundland handicrafts by a number of individuals. One such was Rev. Hugh MacDermott, a missionary of the Congregationalist faith who came to Newfoundland in 1904 to a particularly poverty-stricken section in Fortune Bay. He worked closely with the original designers of cottage industry plans, and largely through his efforts and those of his wife, the area where he ministered during a pastorate of thirty years became invested with a new dignity of living and a degree of financial independence.

This was achieved almost solely through the introduction of handicrafts, particularly weaving, and as an example of the zeal with which "Doctor Mac" infected the district, the people of one community once hauled an abandoned telegraph office seventeen miles in order to set it up as headquarters for the village looms. Furniture making and the working of splendid hooked mats and rugs were also introduced by Mr. and Mrs. McDermott, and the good results of their work in this field are today strikingly evident in that part of the province where they laboured and became beloved.

Ship models have always been a popular form of handicrafts in Newfoundland and Labrador, as would be expected in so completely a maritime environment. Even in this respect, however, and though it could be said ship models serve no useful practical purpose, the art of model making owes its strength of perfection to everyday necessity in the first instance. Practical and not aesthetic considerations governed the early model builders.

Since fishermen need full-size boats and schooners, and since the only way they had to get them was usually to build them, ship models started out as just that; they were carvings of half a vessel done on a flat board which reproduced one side of the proposed construction. One side only was necessary since the opposite one would naturally be identical.

Although this sounds a most prosaic undertaking, these half models, as they were called, had real beauty of design. Centuries of dealing with the ocean's more savage moods have given fishermen an inborn knowledge of what will best meet and withstand them; a fraction more sheer to a bow, an inch more of freeboard 'midships can make all the difference between sailing and sinking in a blow. And the preparatory half-model was one way to ensure that the ship when built would have thoroughly seaworthy lines.

So, from these working models developed the superb examples of miniature ships for which Newfoundland is noted. Built with the patience of sea love, many of them were produced in lamp-lit fishermen's cottages during the long nights of ice-bound winters; twenty years, if necessary, was not too long to make sure that a model when completed was worthy in all respects of the craftsmanship and sea lore of the sailor who built it.

Many Newfoundlanders are adept still at producing the "ships in bottles" which have fascinated landlubbers since the first sailor thought of the idea of laying a model's masts flat and pulling them erect by the forestay after the little ship was safely set afloat in a "sea" of putty inside a bottle. These were made more as curiosities than as attempts to produce accurate scale models; nevertheless some of the old-time ships-in-bottles display amazingly accurate design and detail. There are many of them still extant in Newfoundland, the prized possessions of families who may today have little contact with the sea.

A Newfoundlander who gained international acclaim for his marine scale models was the late Ernest Maunder of St. John's. Examples of his handicraft, done with almost unbelievable accuracy of detail, have been shown at world exhibitions, have appeared as designs on stamps and coins, and have brought special recognition from craftsmen all over the world, as well as an award from the Master of the Royal Canadian Mint. Best known are the Maunder historical models of ships, which include the *Great Eastern* of cable-laying fame, the valiant racing schooner *Bluenose*, and the *Matthew*, John Cabot's tiny ship in which he discovered Newfoundland. All are crafted from the genuine original plans of the actual vessels.

Among visitors, tourists, and landlocked Newfoundlanders themselves, one of the most popular of all locally produced handicrafts is the familiar scale model of the ubiquitous yellow fishing dory. Models of "killicks," the fishermen's home-made anchors, of lobster traps and fishing stages, and tiny replicas of oilskin-coated fishermen are high on the list of the more common crafts sold as mementoes and curios, testifying to the distinctively maritime trend of life and labor among the province's artisans. But newer products are taking their places also in the ever-increasing stream of articles that flows from the hands of craftsmen and craftswomen in Newfoundland and Labrador. There are foamcraft, shellcraft, chenille work, jewellery, felt pictures, crochet work, wood carving, all with the Newfoundland motif expressed in the form of representations of Newfoundland dogs, fish, trees, caribou, seals, and ships.

The 1965 decision by the provincial government to establish a division of crafts training in the educational set-up of the province was one of the most important developments in the history of handicrafts in Newfoundland. This allows further expansion of activities on the part of existing agencies that have accomplished so much in this field.

The crafts training division puts first emphasis on teaching to increase production, with special attention to the most readily marketable handicraft items. The marketing is being done by Jubilee Guilds, NONIA, the Grenfell Association, and by private enterprise. Training is given through regular courses in the province's modern vocational schools, and leadership training courses are set up for instructors who then hold classes in small centres throughout Newfoundland and Labrador.

Education Minister H. R. V. Earle declares that "crafts training is now an integral part of the province's educational curriculum," and he foresees "considerable increase" in the future demand for the products of spare-time workers. Handicrafts production in Newfoundland has now "come of age," the training director has remarked. Born of dire need, fostered in soul-searing adversity, handicrafts have emerged as a clear symbol of the resurgence of human dignity in a proud land that has met fate's buffetings boldly; handicrafts form an important part in that same land's exciting future.

2 🖎

Prince Edward Island

THE ANCESTORS OF MOST OF THE PEOPLE living in our province today, not including our native Indians, came from either England, Ireland, Scotland, France or the Guernsey Islands and a few from Wales. There are also many descendants of United Empire Loyalists whose ancestry is either English or German-Dutch.

But, over the years, due to the small size of the province, and to our close association with each other in closely knit neighborhoods, we have long ago forgotten our geopraphic origins. We are all Prince Edward Islanders – a fact of which we are so proud that other Canadians sometimes make jests about us.

In the early settlements of the province, poverty, tragedy and distress were daily visitors, and our history is the story of a fearless, loyal, deeply religious and proud people, who bore their burdens, changed their minds without excuse and always had faith in the future. Above all, they were incurably industrious.

Some historians say that John Cabot landed at what is now Malpeque in 1497. Certainly Jacques Cartier sighted the Island in 1534 and referred to it as "the fairest land it's possible to see." The first known inhabitants were the Micmacs, who as far as we know were a peaceable people who roamed the forests and fished the streams from time immemorial. They were a branch of the great Algonquin tribes who inhabited the north east part of the continent. It has been said by some historians that a kindred race, the Abenaki, also used to visit the Island.

The Indians called the Island "Abegweit" meaning "cradled on the waves." The French colonist called it Ile St. Jean. The British named it St. John's Island, then changed to Prince Edward Island in honour of Edward, Duke of Kent, Queen Victoria's late father in 1799. Today we are likely to call it the "Garden of the Gulf," or "Our Million Acre Farm," and our crafts are still those of people who have always lived close to the sea and the soil. Many items of genuine Island craft are still to be found in the Fathers of Confederation Centre, in our Museums and in many homes.

INDIAN CRAFT

Indian crafts were for a time fast disappearing in our province, but of late are being revived and there can be seen at various public centres excellent examples of beadwork embroidery and basketry, and striking ornaments made from birch bark. There are also several authorities in our province who make a special study of early Indian crafts. Among these are Mr. Arthur Gallant, Dr. J. H. Maloney and Mr. Byron Burns all of Charlottetown. Exhibits of their collections of stone arrowheads, flint tomahawks, stone axes, beautifully mottled stone scrapers and part of the bowl of an ancient clay pipe may be seen by the public at the Fathers of Confederation Centre, at the Miscouche Museum and at other public as well as at private exhibitions. While many of these items were used by the Micmac tribe on the Island before Jacques Cartier landed in 1534, it is thought that some of the pieces may pre-date the Micmac and were used by whoever was here in the sixth or seventh century B.C.

Today most of the Indians live on the reservation on Lennox Island – a small Island in Malpeque Bay where they fish and farm to a small degree, but many have taken the wider horizons of the white man's world as their way of life and are filling positions which are a credit to them and to our province.

KNITTING

Knitting, like many of the other crafts such as hooking, quilting and weaving, is very ancient. It has been said that the first knitting originated on the far-away hills of an ancient land. A shepherd "watching his flock by night" felt the bite of a keen wind, and gathered little tag-ends of wool from the bushes where the sheep had left them as they moved from pasture to pasture. The action of the wind had formed the wool into crude lengths of yarn. The shepherd, using sticks from the bushes as needles, fashioned a scarf or head piece for his comfort from the rude wool.

In the early history of our province, knitting was one of the most essential crafts, essential indeed to the Islanders very survival. Now in our more affluent society it still is a very popular craft. During World Wars I and II the contribution that Prince Edward Island made in the way of knitting through the Canadian Red Cross Society was tremendous. Many women still carry on the practice of knitting for the Red Cross Society who use the articles which are donated for the alleviation of distress among children and adults in countries torn by disaster and war.

Mothers of earlier years knit by the light of their fireplaces such articles as socks, long stockings, mittens, underwear, scarves, shawls, bedspreads, petticoats, caps and babies' wear. Our young mothers of today knit practically the same articles omitting the petticoats, the long stockings and the underwear, but they often knit by the light of a movie screen at a drive-in theatre or while viewing a television show. But knit they do, just as their great grandmothers did.

With the exception of bedspreads, fancy lace for pillow cases, petticoat edgings and diverse fancy articles such as doilies, which required cotton, most of the women of a century ago knit exclusively with wool. This wool was sheared from their own flock, washed and picked by hand, carded by hand into rolls, and then spun into yarn on a handmade spinning wheel. The yarn would then be dyed in a great pot over the kitchen fire and dried, ready for use.

The women of today are much more favoured. They buy their yarn in any desired colour in wool or in many of the synthetic materials, such as nylon, of which our pioneer mothers never dreamed. The result of the knitting however is much the same – their families are well and happily clothed and cared for and their households are beautified. There are many homes throughout the Island where knitted articles such as bedspreads, afghans, cushion tops and many samples of lace, which were made long before Confederation, are treasured heirlooms. The patterns of bedspreads and lace edgings are much the same today as they were in years gone by but there are of course many new patterns.

While many of the old crafts are not practised here as they once were, knitting seems to go on and on, ever gaining in popularity. The patterns become more intricate and modern and the resulting articles more beautiful but it all goes back to that cold night on a faraway hill when a shepherd lad knitted for his own comfort – a woollen scarf.

POTTERY

A well known pottery plant was located on what is now the Experimental Farm, Charlottetown, on the land where the lily pool now is. Mr. Oswald Hornby, an Englishman and a skilled workman, owned the plant after 1887. He first settled near Shearwater, Nova Scotia where he ran a pottery business, but moved to this province about 1880.

According to information received from George A. Leard, Souris, the Charlottetown Pottery, with Fred Hyndman as secretary, was advertised for sale in 1886. It had been established in 1880 and Oswald Hornby bought it in 1887. They made flower pots, milk dishes, umbrella stands, brown glazed tavern kegs, smoking sets, butter crocks, wine and vinegar jugs, and smaller preserve or jam crocks. It is a curious fact that while early P.E.I. pottery was known as the Hornsby Pottery, the man who owned it was a Mr. Hornby. It is said that his wife, a Miss Hornsby, came from England and he named the pottery after her.

Thomas M. Burns operated a pottery on Spring Park Road in 1863. He advertised on page twenty-eight of the *Prince Edward Island Directory* of 1864 that he had "Earthenware of every description and size . . . constantly on hand." James A. Joyce, Spring Park Road proprietor of City Pottery told people (*Islanders* of June 19, 1868) "that he had built a new kiln and had got better workman and is now making a much better article than formerly . . . . . . in all kinds of earthenware."

There can still be seen in St. Paul's Anglican Church, Charlottetown, embossed tiles, designed and modelled by W. C. Harris (a relative of Robert Harris the artist) and made by Hornby at the Prince Edward Island Potteries in 1895, from good old Island red clay. Those tiles are in the panelling in the chancel of St. Paul's Anglican Church.

24

The first inhabitants, the Indians, didn't have much furniture as such, apart from a sleeping bag, a basket or two and a cooking pot. The Acadians, who occupied huts and cottages from the period of 1720 to 1728, had wooden chests, tables and benches, and doubtless cradles, and probably settle beds which opened out to make a snug bed and could be closed to make room in a small cabin in the daytime. Those beds, vintage of 1820, were used long after the French lost control of the Island and can still be seen. Some were in plain pine and some were ornately carved, which suggests that carving goes back a long time.

Some of the settle beds had a high back which served as heat reflectors for the aged. Those high-backed settle beds, when folded for day use and sitting before the fire, were sometimes referred to in a facetious manner as "sparking benches."

The early furniture was from necessity crude and primitive – this did not reflect on the cabinet maker's craft but upon pioneer conditions. But time mellows civilization as well as the individual, and the country people had to have furniture even if they had to make it themselves, which is exactly what they did. There arose in our province a long line of furniture builders whose skill and versatility was unsurpassed, and one of the foremost of these was Benjamin Chappell.

Chappell, who was a man of considerable ability and integrity, left for posterity a wonderful diary which set forth the daily doings of the years around 1774. This diary is a classic. Friday, November 17, 1775, he records that he "finished a bed for Mrs. Allen." The next day he was working at a "Windsor chair for his wife." It well might be one of the first Windsor chairs in all Canada. November 27, he was busy "finishing a great chair." In 1777 following the birth of his son Richard he records that he "made a cradle."

Later on a son, Offie, became a cabinet maker. It is recorded that in 1780 he made a wooden leg for a lady, Mrs. Baker. Another most unusual item in Offie's records concerning his wood-working is that he was busy "turning a damsel." Could it have been a figure-head for a ship?

Later on Benjamin Chappell became the first postmaster on Prince Edward Island. He went into partnership with Samuel Bagnall, a United Empire Loyalist who was also a cabinet maker, and in 1806 they made tables for the House of Assembly at a cost of one pound fifteen shillings each.

William Schurman, another Empire Loyalist came to this province in 1774. He sold Island-made chairs in his store for four dollars (in our present currency) for a set of six. One set that he sold in 1811 to Mrs. George Linkletter of the Summerside vicinity is still in existence.

George Tanton of Darby's Corner near Summerside made four poster beds around 1819. The first Cutcliffe of South East Prince made chair and church pews. But perhaps the most famous chairs of early vintage on P.E.I. were those made by Mark Butcher, who died in 1883. On February 22, 1835, when Butcher was twenty-one, he advertised that he was in the business of wood-turning. He was a finished craftsman.

It is thought by some that he made the chairs in the Colonial Building in 1847, but this fact has not been proven as the committee who furnished the Government Offices used payment warrents that did not specify the makers. However it is established that Mark Butcher did supply a sizeable amount of furniture for the Colonial Building in 1848 to the value of seventy-six pounds. Later in 1854 Butcher made twelve and a half chairs (according to records) for the Legislature at a cost of thirty six shillings each. This consisted of eleven side chairs and one arm chair. His furniture is most distinctive, having a regency flavour.

In the Museum of the Fathers of Confederation Memorial Building, a display of miniature furniture made by Mark Butcher can be seen. This wonderful collection has been donated to the Museum by Mrs. R. R. Bell, wife of Judge R. R. Bell.

There are several collections of his furniture in different Island homes. Mrs. Kathleen Hornsby has a cabinet and Mr. A. H. Duvar, North River Road has an extensive collection.

Arthur Wadman (1836) of Crapaud also was a wood-worker. He made ladder-back kitchen chairs of pine with thin seats, reminiscent of Acadian Chairs. He also made Captains' chairs of heavy graceful turning with a seat that slanted backwards.

Samuel Sherren, another finished cabinet maker, made a communion table which is now in the Crapaud United Church. It could be called "Late Empire." It has ornately carved legs which signifies that Sherren was also a carver.

The Wilt chairs are much prized in this province. The 1864 directory lists Barnard Wilt of Lot 65, as a chair maker. This man and his descendants made chairs in this province for over one hundred years. The earliest sample of his chairs still extant was made in 1856. It is known as a Wilt Windsor Chair with dovecot curved back. Most of his chairs were simpler, like a side chair (still extant) of birch. It has a heavy one piece seat, curved on the sides, and scooped for saddle effect. It is indented around the top of the seat, with bamboo turning, and H stretchers – all which denotes a good Wilt Chair. The Wilt Captains' chairs were good and took a lot of wear. One is still in use after holding two hundred pounds of Captain for forty years.

A child's chair made in 1836 is still to be seen. It has the initials of the child's uncle T. P. (Thomas Pleadwell) on the bottom of it. The child was Henry Seller. Kirkland of Summerside was also a chair maker and he made rabbit-ear chairs, which were painted black, for Frederick Moyse's parlor in 1859. In the Miscouche Acadian Museum there are samples of Acadian Chairs made around 1836 by Joseph (Jessie) Desroche.

There are still today on Prince Edward Island several fine chairs and other pieces of furniture made by more modern craftsman. Ernest Duchemin was a splendid craftsman with all the joy of an artist. Ben Gallant did excellent work around 1920 to 1930. Daniel McCaskill and Golden Barrett made different types of church furniture and cabinets, and Spurgeon Hickox who died a few years ago was an outstanding finished craftsman. There were many other furniture makers in our province. But furniture making could not have been a paying business, for in 1902, one maker advertised his work for newlyweds which was as follows:

1 bedroom suite, 7 pieces, birch finished in light oak	$17.50
1 sideboard, birch finished in light oak, high back, mirror and shelves	$15.00
1 extension table (elm finished as dark walnut)	$ 7.00
1 lamp (Gone With the Wind) purple and white milk glass	$ 6.00
1 health mattress	$ 4.00
1 spring mattress	$ 4.00
1 parlor suite (birch and walnut finished as mahogany with multi-coloured velours, consisting of settee, arm chair, platform rocker, corner chair and side chair. The five pieces . . .	$25.00

With a cash discount it all came to $70.00

Carving, which is now a lost art in our province, was at one time a noted craft. Barney Wilt, the chair maker who specialized in Windsor chairs around 1864, had four sons, one of which, Ned by name, was a carver of beautiful snuff boxes. Another noted carver was James Alexander Stewart who in 1901 carved the frieze still to be seen in Hughes Drug Store, Charlottetown. Alexander Stewart was one of Mark Butcher's craftsman. He also carved the pulpit now in use at Central Christian Church, Charlottetown.

There were several other noted carvers of this era who specialized in altars and pulpits. One of those was Barney Creamer. Another was Billie Dick Dingwell. Compton at Summerside made pulpits of elm trimmed with black walnut, but whether he himself was a carver, is not clear.

Mark Wright was another. He was a nephew of Mark Butcher, and a chair made by Mark Butcher, carved by Mark Wright can still be seen in the Oddfellows Lodge. Then there were two Hobbs, James and John. One of them – it is not clear which – was an excellent carver. He made a bedroom suite, exhibited in London at one of the great expositions under the name of his boss, Mark Butcher.

A most imposing suite in heavy mahogany Gothic, it was owned by the late A. E. Morrison of Charlottetown before his death about ten years ago.

Charles Newson of 177 Euston Street, Charlottetown, whose father John Newson was born in 1840 and died in 1916, had five brothers all interested in some phase of furniture making. Mr. Newson, interviewed on January 20, 1960, remembered well the carvers employed by his father, namely Bill Jury and a Mr. Pike. Mr. Pike had worked at his trade of carving in Paris and later at Trafalgar Square in London. One of the articles which he carved, recalled Charles Newson, was a table for Judge Alley.

A furniture maker whose name has become famous for his carvings is Caleb Jesse Whitlock (1862 – 1929). All his furniture is built of such woods as walnut, oak and bird's eye maple, and he had an artist's eye for the lovevly designs in the grain of the wood used. One of his bedroom suites is of quarter oak, consisting of bureau, vanity and seat, complete with a man's dresser. The sides of the vanity seat are in fretwork in a tulip design. The lines of all those pieces are straight, uncluttered and clean. But in everything he made there is a touch of exquisite carving. The fixtures he used were always of brass or copper.

A large cabinet was used for the first radio the family owned. It was run on batteries and they used earphones. A panel which concealed the hidden speaker is done in carving and fretwork with the family initial "W" and musical symbols in the shape of clarinets.

A sewing stand with brass fixtures made by Whitlock is a beautiful example of his skill. Made of oak, it has ends carved like musical lyres. In one home there is a parlor floor lamp, about six feet high, made entirely of oak. The shade is of opalescent blue glass with a bead fringe, and one of his sons owns a grandfather clock which was made by him.

A china cabinet of quarter oak is about seventy years old, and a wall cabinet or whatnot is of bird's eye maple. All mirrors used in his furniture are of french bevel and after all these years are as clear as crystal. One of the most beautiful of his pieces of carving is a small table about two by one and a half feet in size and one and a half feet high. It has fourteen legs, each carved in an intricate design. The table is oriental in design and can best be described as a piece of wooden lacework. There are Whitlock carvings in St. Peter's Anglican Church chapel, and in the many homes of his family can be seen the clever work of their father and grandfather, Caleb Jesse Whitlock.

HOOKING

Mat hooking, like weaving, is an ancient craft practised so long ago by our ancestors that its actual origin is lost in the mists of antiquity. Mat making was a most fascinating craft and in the years around 1867 scores of mats were hooked. It was indeed a poor housewife who could not boast of a new mat or two come spring housecleaning time.

The earliest mat hookers must have been most creative and imaginative as they were obliged to make their own designs with but little knowledge of the skill of designing. Even so, they planned and hooked marvellously worked rugs which are heirlooms to-day. Some of the designs so skilfully created and hooked were passed down from mother to daughter and are even used by mat makers of today.

For use in their kitchens they usually made mats of an all-over design such at Tea Box, which was a series of cubes, Shell Pattern, Hit-and-Miss, Thunder and Lightning, Elbow pattern, and Cucumber pattern. One which has been revived in our province recently is the Marilla or Anne of Green Gables pattern. This design was one much used in the area of which L. M. Montgomery wrote in her "Anne" Books.

The mats were made mostly of rags cut into strips from discarded clothing. Sometimes the yarns from worn out blankets were used to make roses and leaves for the more superior mats. Many of these old rugs with their allover patterns were true mosaics of the family life of that era, a hundred years ago. They were a composite of the various aspects of a family's everyday life.

In the early days not too much new or virgin yarn found its way into a mat. Strips of rags were used which would perhaps have been at one time grandfather's shirt or father's old underwear or grandma's or mother's wedding coat. This was a matter of economy as few families could afford to use new yarn for rugs.

Some of the patterns used for mats for the parlour, bedrooms or front stairs and hallways were more elaborate but not more beautiful than the allover patterns. Many were of floral designs such as ferns, scrolls, leaves; many were geometric designs such as Boston Sidewalk and Abraham's Puzzle. One pattern called the Key was a repeating pattern much in use for the borders of hall runners and stairs. Another beautiful pattern was called Sunshine and Shadow. One also which at one time was considered quite striking and used in the same manner as the Key, was the Swastika. Needless to say this design fell into the taboo class during and after the Second World War. There was, however, another Swastika of Indian origin which continued to be popular.

The mats provided warmth in the homes and lent charm and dignity to the most humble abode. Although most of them were hooked by the mother, grandmother or aunts in a home, or by girls of marriageable age with an eye to filling their hope chest, some beautiful rugs were designed and hooked by men.

It was also a general custom to hold hooking bees. Women and girls would gather of an afternoon to hook and the men would join them in the evening for a party. It was an old saying "that many's a good match was made at a hooking bee."

Stair carpets were the result of long hours of bending over a mat frame but the results were most satifying. One particularly interesting design was made by hooking the steps in Hit-and-Miss or scrap with beautiful designs of posies or pictures on the risers, but generally stair carpets were made with a plain middle and had a border in the Key, Swastika or some other repeating geometric pattern.

Our great grandmothers who let nothing go idly through their hands, also braided lovely rugs from strips of discarded material which was too heavy or too coarse to hook. It has been said by some that the United Empire Loyalists brought this craft to this province. This may be so, but like mat hooking, the art of braiding is one of our oldest handicrafts. In the making of these rugs they used a balanced colour scheme, using both bright and subdued colours – a row of dark and a row or two of light and so on, finishing with a dark border. Some of these braided rugs were made so carefully and with such pride in workmanship that it was almost impossible to tell the underside from the upper.

Little bedroom mats were also popular a century ago. They were made from very heavy material or later from felt in brilliant greens, yellows and reds. The material was cut in about three inch circles, each of which was blanket stitched. When all was prepared they then were arranged in diamond shaped patterns and sewed by hand to a heavy piece of backing. They were very effective but not as substantial as the hooked or braided variety.

Braided mats were also made from used binder twine or the twine used to bind sheaves of grain. Part of this they would dye, in red or green shades, and the remainder would be used in its natural hue. When they began to braid, they'd drop the ball of twine into a pail of warm water. This softened the twine and made it more pleasant to work with. These little binder twine mats were excellent to use at a doorway to keep sand and dirt from coming in on the feet of the menfolk. These, however, were not of early vintage, but obviously were made after the introduction of binder twine.

A beautiful rug which was commonly found in many of the parlours or dining rooms a century ago was known as a crumb-cloth. These were generally square, about nine by nine inches, had borders of roses, leaves, scrolls and ferns, and were finished with a plain background. Many still adorn the floors of the homes of Prince Edward Island.

Certainly our forbears of a century ago have left much for us to remember them by. Their artistic ability, their ambition to make things better, their perseverence in face of scarcity and their resourcefulness in using what was at hand has left us much to admire. But nowhere do we see the spirit of those times so plainly portrayed as when we stop to admire a piece of their handicraft, a quilt, a rug, a piece of wrought iron or a knitted or crocheted bedspread.

There is a hand hooked rug on display in the Fathers of Confederation Memorial Building which, while not antique, is a present day continuation of one of the most outstanding crafts of our province.

This rug was made by the late Mrs. Brennan, Summerside, using a crochet hook instead of a mat hook. It measures nine by twelve feet and took two years to complete. It contains at least a million stitches. The mat was designed by Joseph Smith of Margate and Stanley Bridge and typifies our Island life where love of beauty, of the fragile delightful things of nature, butterflies, song birds and ferns and a love for craftmanship go hand in hand. The colours used are the soft yet bright hues peculiar to our Island scenery.

An unusual sample of present day hooking was done by members of the Oyster Bed Bridge Women's Institute, and this display took first prize at the Second National Convention of Federated Women's Institute of Canada which met in Vancouver in 1961. It consists of an entire set of chair seats. The design on each individual piece is that of a different shaped snowflake. The background of all is a soft green shade. It could well symbolize a late fall day on Prince Edward Island — when the work on the farms is about completed and everything is quiet and relaxed after a busy summer's toil. The grass is still softly green and great snowflakes flutter lazily down. Two members did the research on authentic snowflake forms. They also made the designs, stamped the canvas and dyed the wool. Another member hooked the entire set which was done with two ply Island yarn.

The hooking of twenty-eight chair seats for the dining room chairs of Government House by the Women's Institutes of Prince Edward Island as a Centennial Project was begun in the winter of 1962. The suggestion for this project came from Mrs. Walter Hyndman, wife of the Lieutenant Governor at that time, with the suggestion that the motif be the Island crest. This suggestion came following a television display of the Island's entries in the National Tweedsmuir Handicraft Competition in the spring of 1961. This consisted of six hooked chair seats and resulted in the first prize coming to Prince Edward Island.

The Provincial Board enthusiastically accepted the suggestion and a committee was appointed: Mrs. J. Philip Matheson, Mrs. Wilfred Pickering and Mrs. N. A. Cutcliffe, with Mrs. Robert Schurman added later. The provincial Government was contacted and the project explained. It was accepted with enthusiasm. Although Mrs. Hyndman was not a member of the committee, she was a tower of strength to us, giving us a welcome to Government House on more than one occasion when we went to measure the chairs and get other help. She gave us the address of the College of Arms, London, England, to which we wrote to resolve some points of protocol. Hon. Walter and Mrs. Hyndman donated four chairs of the same style to add to the twenty-four of Government House. To the Hyndmans we owe a debt of graditude and publicly express our grateful thanks at this time.

Mrs. Wilfred Pickering, Clinton, was asked to do the hooking. Materials were bought and the project was underway late in 1962, and continued the two following winters. The two-ply yarn was bought at Condon's Woolen Mill in Charlottetown, the designing and all the dyeing was done by Mrs. Pickering, whose good husband held the many skeins while she wound it into balls.

A visit was made to Government House after the appointment of the new Lieutenant Governor W. J. MacDonald to acquaint him with the project. He was very pleased.

The last of the hooking was completed before the end of March 1964, but the official presentation took place January 23, 1964, at Government House in the presence of His Honour Lieutenant Governor W. J. MacDonald and Mrs. MacDonald, Hon. Walter Hyndman and Mrs. Hyndman, Premier Walter R. Shaw and Mrs. Shaw and the Provincial Board of the Women's Institutes of Prince Edward Island. Premier Shaw accepted the seats on behalf of the Government, and Lieutenant Governor W. J. MacDonald spoke in appreciation of the planning, work, and creativity which the Women's Institute had devoted to the project.

CROCHETING

Crocheting, which is really a form of knitting done with a hooked needle, is a craft which has always been practised by the women of Prince Edward Island. While its value as a utilitarian craft is not as great as that of the similar crafts of weaving, hooking, and knitting, yet it has its uses and gives much pleasure to the women who work at it. It is considered more for its artistic value than for any particular need.

Women have in years gone by crocheted from wool such articles as afghans, petticoats, large doilies in colour with many roses and leaves, and babies' wear, besides shawls for grandmother and scarves for grandfather and the children. From cotton thread they made belts, handbags, collars and lace to be used on pillow cases and on milady's lingerie, as well as deep valances for parlour, kitchen shelves and drapes for the piano. Many made fine drapes in a cobwebby effect from silken threads, which were used to decorate the huge gilded – framed likenesses of the dear departed. Some very thrifty housewives saved the string which came around parcels from the grocery store and crocheted dish cloths of excellent quality.

There are still today many samples of crocheting which are heirlooms, while many of the women of today still crochet bedspreads, doilies, tablecloths, place mats and babies' wear.

TANNING

Many women of the era around 1867 were adept at tanning skins, and luxurious rugs of great beauty were made from the skins of sheep and lambs. Generally the skin of the lamb was left white and brushed and combed with great care and energy. Sheep skins were sometimes left white but were generally tinted in pastel shades of rose, pink, green, yellow or blue. This craft is still practised in our province and often one may see beautiful sheep skin rugs on display at our provincial and county exhibitions.

WEAVING

Weaving, which is one of the most ancient of crafts, was for obvious reasons one of the earliest crafts practised here. All the women of a hundred years ago were expected to know how to manufacture the wool of their sheep into comforts for their household. Even as that good and virtuous woman mentioned in *Proverbs* clothed her household in scarlet, so the women of early Prince Edward Island clothed theirs in "drugget."

One of the earliest pices of weaving, which we now know was done in 1792, was owned by Mrs. Edison Storey of Millview. This was woven by a Mary MacMillan, called Mary Fortune. Since she could count only to ten, this beautifully designed blanket is made in a series of coloured yarns in tens. It was put in the loom the day the first hanging took place on Prince Edward Island, which was then the Island of St. John. We were informed by George A. Leard of Souris, well known Island historian, that he believed this hanging was in 1791. Further information from Chief Justice Thane A. Campbell places the date on July 30, 1792.

Flax was used in weaving as well as wool. This flax was homegrown, and after being processed — all by hand — was spun into thread. At first all the weaving done with flax provided sails for the boats. Then later for utility's sake, seed bags, tableclothes, bedspreads and personal linen were woven. Some beautiful examples of bedspreads and table linen are still to be found, many of them still in use in various homes throughout the provinces. They are now treasured as precious heirlooms. The patterns woven into the various articles are diversified and intricate. Many of the weavers had their own particular pattern such as Church Windows, but it is obvious they were woven with pride and much loving care, and they grant us a glimpse into the lives of the women of a century ago who though poor in worldly goods were rich in spirit.

They also wove material both from wool and flax for men's and ladies' suits. A garment for an adult required nine yards of material approximately thirty inches wide. Some of these suits, whose material was woven over a century ago, are still preserved. They were beautifully made, both in their manufacturing and precise tailoring. Needless to say the styles are a bit out of date.

Scarves and shawls of exquisite taste in colour and design, winter underwear for all the family, and men's work shirts and trousers were made on the loom. In many cases these were sewn by hand by the mother in the home or a grandmother or aunts.

As many of the articles which were produced required coloured yarns of both flax and wool, it was of the utmost importance that a variety of fast colouring dyes be obtained. In 1820 Walter Johnstone came to Prince Edward Island from Dumfriesshire, Scotland in the capacity of a missionary to organize Sunday schools. He published an account of his visit, which has been accepted by historians as correct. One remark he made which has considerable bearing on weaving and dyeing is "that the women were dressed mostly in homespun druffles, stuffs, and druggetts, dyed blue," and that "a wife who is a good spinner, knitter and sewer (dressmaker) is an acquisition here."

They solved the problem of colouring by manufacturing their own dyes and this in itself became an early craft.

DYES

Golden red blossoms set with alum made *yellow*.
Bay leaves set with alum made *dark green*.

White maple bark set with alum made *light brown*.

Ferns set with ammonia made a *gray green*.

Beet juice set with vinegar made *garnet*.

Onion skins set with alum made *yellow*.

Blueberry juice set with alum made *purple*.

Common yellow wall lichens were used to make *brown*. (It was called *crottle*.)

Bitter vetch set with alum made *violet*.

Ragweed bramble set with alum made *orange*.

Dandelion set with alum made *magenta*.

A particularly harsh blue but one which was absolutely a "fast" dye was made as follows:

Indigo Dye: 2 gallons human urine

1 pkg. indigo dye powder.

Place this mixture in a large iron kettle. Mix, stir and add wool material and allow to soak for a fortnight.

This dyeing job is better done in summer in the out-of-doors since it is important to keep the liquid warm.

If the mixture is stirred every morning and kept warm the resulting colour will be a beautiful blue which will never fade. Material dyed this way is in great demand for making carpets and rugs. (Taken from an old scrapbook.)

Before the growing of cotton became common in the United States, flax from which linen is made was the world's most important fibre crop. In the nineteenth century, cotton became the world's leading fibre crop.

The production of linen flax today on the Island is insignificant, though at one time every family cultivated and prepared its own flax from which the people manufactured their linen. Flax grows from two to three feet high with long narrow leaves and pale blue flowers. The flowers are followed by five round-chambered capsules, each containing two seeds. The seeds were sown broadcast and when the plants were about two inches high they were carefully weeded by the women who knelt at their work.

When the flax is ripe it is pulled by hand because the fibre, which is contained in the stem, loses the spinning value if cut with a sharp instrument. As the flax is pulled it is piled in bundles. In order to save the seeds, care must be taken to have the heads of the plants together. To dry the flax, it is spread lightly in rows, a few inches apart, on a stubble field or meadow. When the flax has been exposed to the sunshine and rain for several days, it becomes quite brown and dry; then it must be turned and allowed to stay in the sun for another week or so till it becomes very crisp. When it is dry enough, it is gathered in bundles and ready for retting.

Before retting, the seeds are separated from the stalks. For this, a large cloth is laid on the ground and a bundle of flax laid across a plank over the cloth. The threshing is done by means of a flail. For retting, the women would usually go to the edge of a woods where they were well sheltered. A frame of light wood, about four feet high with a few sticks across the top, was placed over an open fire. The flax was spread over this rack to dry. By retting, the woody part of the stalks is broken in pieces and detached from the fibres which enclose it.

After retting, comes the scrutching which consists in beating the flax by means of a wooden blade. First we hold the flax by one end and beat the other end violently for a few minutes; then the same process is repeated, in scutching the other end. This separates the fibres and makes them fine and smooth. By this process, a lot of the flax is broken and falls off. This can be spun into coarse thread and woven to make coarse linen.

This process is followed by the combing of flax. This is done with a heavy steel comb. In combing as in scutching a lot of the fibres are loosened and remain in the comb. These are afterwards picked and spun to make a finer grade of linen. When the flax has been combed, it is wound loosely on a distaff and spun. Spinning flax is not an easy task because it has to be spun very evenly. After the flax is spun, it is put into skeins for bleaching before it is woven, for if this is omitted, the linen will never become thoroughly bleached.

In bleaching, the skeins are steeped several hours in a weak solution of lye. Sometimes potash or washing soda are used instead of lye. After boiling, the skeins are removed and well washed in a weaker solution. They are then drawn separately over a washboard and well beaten with a wooden beater. When this is done, they are hung on a line for a few weeks, and the more rain, snow and frost the yarn can get, the better it will be because it will bleach well. After bleaching, it is woven into linen. The linen is then bleached by soaking again as before. Even after the linen is woven, it is left outside for a few weeks. In course of time, home made linen becomes as white as the finest linen and it is more durable than many finer fabrics that money can procure." (Copied from an article by Clarisse Poirier in Grade IX, 1927.)

One interesting item on the weaving of linen is that an eight-yard, finely made tablecloth was presented to Government House for use when the Legislative Council and the Legislative Assembly had their annual banquet there. It was given by James Thomson, a Scot and a former, British Army Officer. The entire cloth was the product of his farm where it was grown, prepared and completed. The date was 1840 which makes us realize, we think, that when we talk of developing handicrafts and other works of art now, we are merely trying to regain something we have lost in the last century, or perhaps in the last forty or fifty years.

The growing and making of flax into household linens was very common in the early days but from the turn of the century to 1960 it was an all but forgotten craft. But now it has again come into its own and women are beginning to grow, spin and manufacture flax into beautiful and long lasting linens for home use and for sale to tourists.

QUILTING

Quilting, like weaving, hooking and the other home handicrafts, is of ancient origin, and arises from the daily needs of humanity.

Some of the old designs handed down from mother to daughter in our province are Log Cabin (which sounds distinctly new world) Steps to the Lighthouse, Star of Bethlehem, Dresden Plate, Double Irish Chain, Drunkard's Trail, Double Wedding Ring, Rose of Sharon, Borrow and Lend, Lone Star, and a most economical one called Crazy Patch Work which consisted of patches of whatever was at hand. The quilts when made were interlined with sheeps' wool and lined with a plain material. They were quilted in quaint designs such as Fan, Feather, Scroll, Grape, Star and Double Ring, while some were quilted in diamonds or other geometric designs.

There are many quilts well over a hundred years old of quaint design still in use or treasured as heirlooms in many homes throughout the province. One antique bedspread well over a century old is owned by Mrs. Edison Storey of Millview. It is of an original design, presumably, as no one seems to have seen another like it. It is a bright red scroll pattern appliqued onto a white background. It was made by her grandmother Tweedy who came from England. The stitches are so fine that they are almost invisible.

The women of today who quilt do not of course use sheep's wool for padding as the women did a hundred years ago, but use sheets of cotton batting.

WROUGHT-IRON

Perhaps the most important of all the early trade crafts was that practised by the village blacksmith in iron and steel. As he stood leather-aproned by his flaming forge, he hammered and shaped the hot metal on the anvil into horse shoes (sometimes round the clock to keep up with the demand), plough shares and the parts for iron harrows and cultivators. Further, he used his imagination and crafts-manship to fashion ornamental fences to enclose grave plots; to build beautiful and useful iron gates: to embellish the seat backs and dash-boards of carriages and sleighs with fancy grille work; to shape grace-fully the iron braces which fastened wagon frames to wheels, sleighs to runners.

For the fisherman, the blacksmith made such implements as oyster rakes and quahaug drags. For the household, the craftsman fashioned mat hooks from the steel tines of stable forks and made iron mat clamps to hold in place the hooking frames for mats. The supreme artistic effort of one well-known blacksmith was a "rose tree" which he forged from iron and painted, so realistically — stem, branches, leaves, buds and full-blown roses — that no one could tell, unless quite close, that it was man-made. This "tree" and a miniature anvil and forge were displayed at exhibitions far and near, winning first prizes wherever they were shown.

Long before the day of official weather reports, versatile black-smiths turned out artistically constructed weathervanes. One outstand-ing weathervane was on the steeple of the present United Church at Malpeque. It is not now in use, as the steeple was torn down, but it stood there for all to see which way the wind blew for over a hundred years. It was made by the late John Crozier of Darnley.

A beautiful gate of excellent design was made by the late John Murphy of New Glasgow for the burying ground, and many mills had a bold Chanticleer perched atop their ventilator, the work of some local blacksmith. At Margate a wrought-iron Black Horse was the sign over a halfway house or early tavern. To this day this locality is still called "The Black Horse."

When the Crystal Palace Exhibition opened in London between the years 1850 and 1860, a Mrs. Hazard of Charlottetown sent a shipload of Island handicraft to be exhibited there. One of the persons who sent articles was Elisha Weatherbie of Pownal, a blacksmith.

A couple of centuries ago, items made of iron were valuable beyond price: the axe, the hoe, and the scythe in the field and forest; the crane, andirons and the pot over the fire. In 1783 William Schurman, a United Empire Loyalist, came to the Island. He, among other activities, ran a store. He sold hand made nails at sixteen cents a pound, hand made spikes at ten cents each and hand made tacks at thirty cents a dozen, all the handicraft of some local blacksmith.

3 🙰

Nova Scotia

THE HANDICRAFTS OF NOVA SCOTIA were developed by many different groups of people, and it seems best that we begin with the first inhabitants of our province.

THE INDIANS

The Indians were here to greet the Norsemen. When and whence came the Indians to North America is a very controversial subject, as well as when and where the Norsemen landed. But undoubtedly the Micmacs were the original inhabitants of Nova Scotia. Lescarbot, Champlain, and Diereville describe them as friendly and intelligent. A century before the founding of Port Royal (1504-1604), there had been dealings and acquaintance between them and the fishermen from Bretagne, Basques and other French who frequented the coast. Nicholas Denys states, "They were a clever people. They made kettles and canoes by burning log ends and hollowing the ash with bone knives. Robes made of moose skin were made by soaking and stretching the hides, then heating them so the hair could be removed with bone instruments. It was then rubbed with bird livers and oil, after which it was dressed over polished wood until it became supple. The moose robes were coloured red, violet and blue, with dyes applied in the skin by isinglass. Heated bones were placed over the colours, and once set they could not be washed away."

The art of dyeing was known to the Indians long before the French came. The flame colour, so liked by the Micmacs, was made from a plant called "bedstraw." The natives also displayed skill in making wigwams or tents of bark, canoes of birch bark, bows and arrows, fish spears both for salmon and for lobster, portable cradles for infants, shoes and moccasins, and snowshoes or requettes especially adapted to their use. "His gun, his squaw, his little dog and his bark canoe were his chief wordly goods" (*Jesuit Relations*). When the Micmacs wished "to put on the dog" they did just that. To kill a dog and serve the meat to a special visitor was a sure mark of friendship.

The Indians believed in a Great Spirit, the author of good; and an Evil Spirit, the author of evil. The Micmacs had several names for God, one of which means "Our Maker." An Indian youth approaching maturity would seek out a secluded spot in the wilderness and commune with his God. He would later return to his camp and describe his "vision." The visions were usually about some animal or voice that appeared to the youth and bestowed great powers on him in return for services rendered. The hunter then painted or carved the likeness of his vision, and included drawings of animals he sought to kill, bird or moose tracks, snakes and symbols. The rocks chosen for these carvings were usually inaccessible and were discovered many years later. These petroglyphs have been found in British Columbia, South America, and indeed in some islands of the Pacific Ocean. But it is to Mrs. A. Kelsall, Annapolis Royal, one-time District President of Women's Institutes of Nova Scotia, to whom we are indebted for the Micmac petroglyphs on the rocks of Kedgemakooge Lake, Queen's County, and on the rocks bordering George's Lake, a branch of Lake Kedgemajooge.

Indians handicrafts are symbols of an old, unique, and in many ways a previous civilization that preceded our own on this continent, and to which we owe more than most of us will ever know. It is a sign of our maturity that we are coming to prize a culture of those who lived here before any of us came and who have made tremendous contributions to American life and culture of to-day. Anthropoligists tell us that more than fifty percent of the agricultural products which we now raise are from plants which the

Indians of the Western hemisphere domesticated and improved before our forebears came from Europe. . . . This notable advance of the arts and crafts of the Indians is a part of what we commonly speak of as the handicraft movement in our country. It is not only a revival of many of the very old crafts, but it has elements as fresh as can be found anywhere. . . . The Indians more than any group in our population know the native plants and trees, and the useful and beautiful things can be made from them, and they know processes that were old before any of our forebears came here. To them as to all others who love to shape objects with their hands, handicrafts are both economy and culture. With all that has happened to our first Americans, the impulse to create has never been destroyed, and this response to shape things beautifully has been retained to a remarkable degree. (From "Smoke Signals" by Allen H. Eaton)

Food for Thought, February 1956, pages 193-205 contains another thought provoking article on the Canadian Indian. Of the traditional and temporary art of the Micmac and Maleseet, it says:

The Micmac (traditional) birchbark wigwams, canoes, and utensils. Fine patterned boxes and baskets embroidered with moose hair and porcupine quills or trimmed with wampum (beads from inner side of shells and used as currency) and shells, later with silks. Moccasins similarly decorated. (contemporary) baskets; clothes baskets, hampers, carriers, berry baskets, vegetable, shopping, sewing and food baskets, mostly of ash, poplar or maple splints, some splints brightly dyed. Sweet grass baskets and table mats from Hants County, Nova Scotia. Other articles include axe and pick handles, fishing gear and souvenirs. Only one old women (at Oldtown) is listed as doing fine beadwork.

The baskets exhibited at the 1954 Handcraft Exhibition were from the Millbrook Reservation near Truro, Nova Scotia; the pottery from the Shubenacadie Indian School; and the Micmac Indian cradle from the Bridgewater Museum, operated and cared for by the Bridgewater Women's Institute since 1938. The porcupine quill work on the cradle must be seen to be appreciated. The dyes, made from roots and leaves of various herbs, are fast colours.

A fine new museum is being constructed at Bridgewater as a centennial project. Thus, these examples of Indian relics and crafts will then be on display for the admiration and education of all visitors to the South Shore of Nova Scotia.

Although no complete record is given, we do know that only native plants were used for dye materials. Among these were bedstraw, now known as madder, goldenseal (Buttercup Family) also known as yellowroot, orangeroot and Indian dye. (A list of native vegetable dyes will be given in the Handcraft Section).

As far as can be learned the early Indians knew nothing of either cotton or linen, and used hides entirely in their dress. The sewing of these was very primitive, their only tools being a knife of stone, a bodkin of bone, and thread made from the twisted sinew of the back leg of some animal. Both women and men did sewing and they did not use patterns to guide them, but cut and sewed according to their own ideas.

There were some attempts made to decorate costumes even with these humble tools, although, prior to the coming of the white man, these were entirely managed through trimmings of porcupine quills, goose quills, moose hair, and a knowledge of painting and dyes. Robes of important chiefs were sometimes painted with crude scenes depicting escapades in the lives of the wearers.

The Micmacs had some talent for shell work and traded this with some of the Indians in the interior. Samples of their bead work have been found in two colours — white, which means peace or happiness, and a reddish-purple, which means war or death. The teeth of animals were also used for decorations, and they made a form of leather article — later called lace leather — by currying the sides of skins and then painting them.

All evidence points to early Indian designs being geometrical in design, but it is difficult to unravel the old art forms from those developed through contact with the white man. Most Indian work now shows designs of flowers and leaves, but this is believed to have developed from contact with the French.

ACADIANS

By the terms of the Treaty of Utrecht in 1713, all Acadia except the Island of Cape Breton was ceded to the English. The settlement at English Harbour in Cape Breton was renamed Louisbourg and during forty-five years of work and great expense, it became known as "The

Dunkirk of America." In 1758 Louisbourg fell to the English and two years later the fort was destroyed and the French scattered to other settlements. But now the fort at Louisbourg is again a scene of activity as the reconstruction of some of the buildings is one of Canada's Centennial Projects. The restoration of the King's Bastion is in itself a tremendous undertaking, and the Louisbourg National Park, after its official opening in 1967, will certainly be one of the most educational and interesting parks in the nation.

The sad story of the expulsion of the Acadians in 1755 is familiar to the whole English-speaking world. In 1955, the Acadian Bi-Centennial Celebration was held after months of research into the various types of authentic costumes worn by their Acadian forefathers. Two centuries before the Acadians had come back to Nova Scotia and settled on the shores of St. Mary's Bay and in the Metaghan area where their descendants still dwell. They are an industrious people, skilled as farmers, fishermen, tradesmen, craftsmen, and seafarers, and their talent for shipbuilding is renowned. They produce fine hooked rugs which are completely made by hand, even to the preparation of the wool and dyeing of the yarns, and they have won the reputation in rug-making of the Aubusson of America.

THE SCOTS

The craft history of Nova Scotia is closely connected with the Scots who arrived in the province in 1629. But when Nova Scotia was returned to the French in 1632, the Scots returned home. So it was not until 1773, when the *Hector* arrived with Scottish settlers, that the Scots really made an impression on the life of Nova Scotia. The Scots came well ladened with spinning wheels, looms, and smithy tools to make life possible in their new homes. The weaving of the Scottish tartans is a very old craft and one which came to this country with the Scottish settlers. Knitting is another of the most ancient crafts at which the early Scottish settlers were greatly skilled. These early settlers also made three types of floor coverings – rugs woven on the looms, hooked rugs, and braided rugs.

The Gaelic College of Celtic Folk Arts and Highland Home Crafts was established in 1939 at St. Ann's, Cape Breton, and there has been a great increase in the production of authentic clan and family handwoven tartan by students and graduate weavers since that time.

THE ENGLISH

John Cabot and his sons sailed from England in 1497 and made their first landing on the continent of America. Whether Cabot came to Newfoundland or Nova Scotia is still a controversial subject.

After years of war with France, all of Nova Scotia came under the British rule in 1763. Nova Scotia is the only province of Canada and the first colony of Great Britain to possess, through Royal Charter, a flag of its own. The founding of Halifax was carried out at Government expense under the Honourable Edward Cornwallis on June 21, 1749. Citadel Hill, rising 350 feet above the harbour, was fortified to defend the base against the Indians. Today, our Maritime Museum is situated atop Citadel Hill and here are preserved for posterity many fine nautical and military relics. There are also examples of the early crafts of the settlers at this interesting old city.

THE GERMANS

Between the years 1750 and 1753, there was an influx of German Protestants to Halifax. Plans were made in Halifax to settle these colonists in a town of their own further south along the coast. The excellent harbour and site of the chosen location we now know as Lunenburg. These former farmers soon became sea-faring people famous for the Lunenburg fishing fleet, sea products, ship-building, and the world's fastest fishing schooner, *Bluenose*.

THE UNITED EMPIRE LOYALISTS

In 1781, the peace treaty between Great Britain and her former colony, the United States was signed. The main exodus of the British Loyalists began in 1783, though after 1776 small bodies of Loyalists had already found their way to Halifax. By the end of 1783 the total immigration amounted to thirty thousand and the population of Nova Scotia had been trebled. The resources of the province were unable to sustain so many so there was keen contention between the Old Settlers, or "Bluenoses," and the Loyalists. The most interesting

Loyalist settlement was at Shelburne. The United Empire Loyalists contributed much to the crafts of our province and it is to this group that we owe the art of quilting which had been very popular in the United States.

Immigrants from Ireland settled in New Dublin in Lunenburg County in 1762. In 1770, there were further Irish settlers in Amherst, in Londonderry townships, as well as the area around Onslow and Truro. The Charitable Irish Society was founded in Halifax in 1786, the founder and first president of the Society being Richard John Uniacke. The world-renowned Uniacke House at Mount Uniacke is now owned by the Government of Nova Scotia as an historic site.

In 1943, the Nova Scotia Department of Trade and Industry inaugurated the Handcrafts program. Instructions were given for home or for sale by Government instructors in weaving, spinning, leather tooling, wood carving, stone polishing and hand wrought silver jewellery. Groups of six or more were given eight lessons in a two weeks' course. A Handcraft Centre, library service and designing were provided. The Government never purchased articles, but made an effort to place buyer in contact with producer.

The booklet *Handcrafts in Nova Scotia* is published annually and copies are distributed to gift shops, Tourist Bureaus, and to any interested persons. A "Craftsmen-at-work Exhibition" is held annually in various parts of the province, and shows shearling rugs, unspun wool chair seats, and the famous "Welcome" mats, done in English, French, and Gaelic.

Handcrafts is the official bulletin and covers handcrafts on a local, national and international level. First published in 1944 with a subscription list of 250 is now appears quarterly and to-day has a mailing list of 4500. "Handcrafts" is available free of charge to any craftsman whether a resident of Nova Scotia or not.

Spinning of both wool and flax in Nova Scotia dates back to the days of the earliest Scottish settlers, many of whom built their log houses and cleared the land in the hilliest part of the country, probably because it seemed more like the highland country they had left. Sheep thrived on these hilly clearings and from these sheep all of the warm clothing for the family was provided.

Before 1788 all wool fabrics were woven in the home, and no manufacturer of synthetic fibres since that date has satisfactorily duplicated the miraculous qualities of wool. One hundred years ago, the little village of Minudie boasted the best breed of sheep in the province, or in America. But all Nova Scotian wool is of a very high grade. There is less shrinkage and a great demand for it, especially today at Stanfield's Limited at Truro, noted far and wide for the manufacture of woollen underwear.

The sheep were sheared in the spring. The wool was washed with soap made from the fat of the sheep butchered for the meat; lye came from the hardwood ashes burned in their fireplaces, and from the pile of carbon and ash left from burning the trees while clearing the land. The wool was rinsed in the running water of the brook near the home, and placed on logs or possibly fences to dry. It was then "picked," pulled apart piece by piece until all the small particles of spruce, bark and burs were removed, and carded into flat rolls with hand cards. Now the wool was ready for the spinner.

From the cards the wool was spun into a single thread. In the process of spinning or twisting the thread it was wound on a bobbin of the spinning wheel. This was then wound off on a reel which gave a resounding "crack" every time a "cut" was completed. Four "cuts" made a small skein.

The single thread skeins were placed on a home made affair called a "swift." This consisted of a three-legged stand, sometimes made from part of the trunk and the limbs of a small tree, the limbs making the legs of the stand. Two pieces of lumber about eleven and a half by two by four feet were crossed at right angles to one another, holes were bored through the centre and made to revolve on a spike driven in the trunk end of the tree trunk. Wooden pegs were placed in the ends of each cross bar. The skeins were then placed on this in such a manner that two threads would run at one time to the bobbin of the spinning wheel. Thus they got their doubled and twisted thread ready for knitting the socks, sweaters and underwear for the family.

The spinning was done on both large and small wheels. The first wheel was no doubt from the native land of the pioneer. In one instance we are told of a spinning wheel being given to the daughter as part of her dowry on coming to this country.

Our forefathers had to be ingenious and soon set about to make their own spinning wheels, reels, cards, swifts, and so on. Many small shops could be found scattered throughout the country. One such was between Mabou and Inverness operated by a Mr. MacIntyre. Another was at Earltown, Colchester County, operated by William McIntosh. Several of the Earltown wheels are to be found in the homes of today with such dates as "McIntosh 1831 and 1848" engraved on them. At Glendyer, in Cape Breton in the early 1830's a woollen mill was started by a Mr. MacDonald who came from Pictou. This proved a thriving industry until after the first World War.

WEAVING

Star of the Sea Handcrafts was not taken up as a hobby, but was put on a financial basis to assist a community in dire need. The late Hon. W. H. Dennis, Halifax, N.S., sensing the possibilities latent in the struggling people of Terence Bay to help themselves, sought to establish his 'pet project' — a subsidiary employment of industry to assist the fisherfolk.

Unsuccessful in obtaining assistance from several charitable organizations, he appealed to the Sisters of Charity, Mount St. Vincent. Senator Dennis sparked the idea of self-help but Sister Eucharia carried the torch. She decided weaving for girls and woodworking for boys would be a good beginning. To cope with the work the Sisters studied designing and weaving in Montreal and later in other part of North America. In Montreal, Sister Eucharia studied weaving under Karen Bulow, nationally known Danish expert. From her she got the Norwegian loom which she brought back for the Terence Bay men to copy. So skilfully did they copy the loom that the women of Terence Bay prefer their own to other Canadian types. There are now eleven of these looms in operation in Terence Bay.

Here housewives and girls turn out beautiful woollens, linens and homespuns under the supervision of the Sisters of Charity. Star of the Sea scarves interlaced with non-tarnishing gold or silver thread and fine table linens worked in gold and silver threads are guaranteed washable. Neckties for men and many other pieces of handcraft are all well known far and wide.

"Our weavers have beautiful capable hands that work unremittingly, inspired with the spirit of medieval craftsmanship to turn out a perfect product," say the Sisters. The Terrence Bay Weavers lent a hand in the early production of the now famous Nova Scotia Tartan designed by Mrs. Douglas Murray, for which ready markets are found in Halifax and tourist centres throughout the province.

A weaving guild has been organized at Main à Dieu under the supervision of the Sisters of St. Alexander's Convent. Several looms are in operation, and others are being added. The first interest is in blankets, homespuns and other household articles. As well, throughout the province, there are many women who weave for their own enjoyment or who sell their handwork at various gift shops. Some articles are of truly superior quality, such as the set of beautiful white linen place mats woven by Mrs. Dorothy Hill of Halifax, which was included in the exhibit of Canadian crafts at the Brussels Exhibition in 1958.

THE ORIGIN OF CANADA'S MOST FAMOUS TARTAN

How the nationally recognized blue tartan of our province was born, has been told in an article by Marjorie Major in a 1953 issue of the *Family Herald and Weekly Star*. Here is part of her description:

> In 1953 the Sheep Breeders Association asked the Handcrafts Division of the Department of Trade and Industry to show a collection of articles made of homespun wool. The idea of introducing such a collection in the display was to interest the farmer, and his wife and daughter, in the many uses to which his farm product can be put.
>
> The Handcraft Centre in Halifax, under the direction of Miss Mary Black, sent word to craftsmen all over the province, and many lovely articles came in for the display.
>
> Still, the more they thought about it, the more Miss Black and her associates at the Centre thought there should also be a completed project of some sort, which would serve as the focal point to dramatize the display.
>
> They started to work on this idea about the middle of June.

Mrs. Douglas Murray, Jollimore, designed a modest panel to illustrate the history of sheep raising in the province. And it acted like a fuse on the imaginations and enthusiasm of the whole group at the Centre, which resulted in a vastly expanded project.

The original purpose, to depict the history of sheep raising, was still the central theme. But by the time all the ideas were talked out and put down on paper, the whole project was expanded to include two additional purposes. One was to indicate the main geographical characteristics of Nova Scotia as a background for the theme.

The other purpose was to suggest the march of the seasons from left to right across the panel. This was an ambitious idea, and one which easily could have resulted in a jumble of unrelated subjects and effects. However the completed work is a triumph of imagination, art and skill; a new and original form of tapestry. . . . Woollen materials were hand-loomed especially for the panel. Original colour combinations were worked out to portray sky and sea, mist-covered hills, meadows and ploughed fields. Special weaving techniques were used to achieve the right texture for each area. These lengths of material were then cut, like the piece of a jig saw puzzle, into irregular shapes and sizes and then appliqued, with wool stiches to sturdy cotton backing.

In the foreground on the extreme left hand side of the panel a graceful birch tree flaunts its yellow catkins and extends the depth of the panel as a kind of frame. The background above has a church, woodlands, and an apple tree in full bloom. The focal point of this springtime section is a French-Acadian girl, in characteristic dress, with a spray of flowers in her hand, and woolly lambs beside her. At the base of the panel there are ferns and spring flowers.

The centre of the panel shows a United Empire Loyalist, with his wife and child, his hen, sheep and pet cat. They have paused to rest in an open field, against a background of purple hills and a tiny village nesting by the sea. A butterfly, daisies and other flowers along the base of the panel emphasize the summer season.

There is a hint of autumn in the colouring, as the eye travels to the right-hand side of the panel. It is accentuated in the Cape Breton Hills, where a Scottish shepherd tends his flock, his little sheepdog at his feet; the lone shieling in the distance. And here again there are flowers at the base. This time they include the thistle, fireweed and goldenrod. And to balance the birch at the left, the frame of the picture is completed by a sombre pine tree, also extending the full length of the panel.

The craftsmen struck a snag though with the Scottish herdsman. His costume had to be a "plaidie." But it couldn't be the tartan of any particular clan, without defeating the plan to make the whole scene typical of Nova Scotia. But Mrs. Douglas Murray proved equal to the challenge, and her solution of the problem is likely to have far reaching results. Far beyond anything the Sheep Breeders Association thought of, or the Handcraft Centre either, for that matter. For Mrs. Murray created a plaid especially for the panel! And in turn created such a new wave of enthusiasm it eventually was registered as the authentic Nova Scotia Tartan.

It has the dark and light greens, which represent the evergreen and deciduous trees of Nova Scotia, and the October blue of the sea. Against this background of green and blue, there is a white line of surf, the gold line for our Royal Charter, and the red line to represent the lion rampant, on the Nova Scotia crest. What could be more appropriate than such a tartan for this province of "New Scotland," the only one to foster a Gaelic College?"

HOOKED RUGS

Rug hooking as we know it in Canada is purely a Canadian art. No doubt the technique originated in England, but its application grew out of necessity, materials available for the work, and of course the all important desire to beautify. With little material available for floor coverings, the pioneer mother utilized the last fragments of worn out clothing to draw through a bit of hand woven linen to make a rug for the earthen or rough board floor.

The original type of hook was a large nail filed down to a hook and set in a wooden handle. The cloth was cut in widths of one-half to three-quarters of an inch, and folded as it was drawn up through the linen, or later burlap bottom.

Later sheep's wool was used in making mats. From the sheep to the rug, the wool is washed, carded, spun, dyed and hooked in wonderful designs and colourings. In particular the Cheticamp hooked rugs in Cape Breton are good examples of this type of hooking.

The Cheticamp hooked rugs of Cape Breton are probably the best known outside this province because of the early interest and enthusiastic assistance of Mrs. Alexander Graham Bell, and later her daughter, Mrs. Marion H. Bell Fairchild, and her friend of many years Miss Lilian Burke, an artist and teacher in Washington.

Miss Burke taught Cape Breton women the art of blending and combing colours, drawing designs, proportions of designs and many of the small items that combined to make the completed Cheticamp hooked rug an outstanding accomplishment which has added very materially to the economics of the community. More important than Miss Burke's practical teaching, she instilled an inspiration and ambition to achieve that has carried these French women even beyond their fondest dreams. Cheticamp rugs are in great demand by our tourists, and hooked mats, rugs and even carpets may be found in gift shops throughout the Maritimes, and even farther afield.

Geometric designs such as the familiar Hit-and-Miss of the South Shore were popular in the old days. Many of the old geometric designs are known by their names: Boston Sidewalks, Maltese Cross, Checker Board, Log Cabin. The floral designs are popular along the French Shore, but have reached the peak of excellence and perfection among the French-Acadian hookers of Cheticamp.

As in every other art, there are some craftsmen who excel, while others are content with the pleasure of accomplishment. Mrs. Daniel Wentzell of Pleasantville on the LaHave River, a few miles below Bridgewater, is an old lady past eighty years who has excelled in mat hooking. One of her rugs, nine by twelve feet, a floral design, is now in the Ford Museum at Dearborn, Michigan, and was sold to an institution for $4500. Another of her large rugs is on display at the Judge Haliburton home in Windsor. Probably one of the most unusual of her creations is a thirty-five by forty inch rug with the Nova Scotia coat of Arms as its only theme. The background is all white and the crest is in natural colours. Mrs. Wentzell used a printed copy of the crest that was about eight inches square. From the original, without even a drawn to scale plan, she made the larger pattern on the rug with everything in proportion.

As an indication of the fine art to which rug hooking has attained, about ten years ago Mrs. Wentzell began to hook picture rugs, as she calls them. These are mostly landscapes about twenty-four by thirty-six inches. To get a variety of colours worked into the design she may use ten or twelve colours in as many inches. The best effect is gained from a distance of about ten feet. Then the picture rugs resemble oil paintings. One of these rugs shows a log cabin beside a small stream with mountains in the background.

Mrs. Lillian Crewe Walsh of Glace Bay, C.B., is another rug hooker who has won laurels. Her "Hooked History" which shows John Cabot and his son Sebastian raising the flag of England on the top of Cape Breton Island following their landing in 1497, has won wide acclaim. A mat hooked about twenty years ago, known as the "Louisbourg Mat" showing the landing of General Wolfe's soldiers at Gabarus Bay in 1745, won first prize over one thousand entries at an exhibition.

Mrs. Matilda Hunter of Truro, with a hook made from part of an old pair of scissors, has also received much praise for her work. And there are countless others in this province who merit high honours for their artistry and craftsmanship in rug making.

WOODCRAFT

The study of the domestic woodenwares of the early settlers is an interesting one. When the early settlers first opened up the new country, limited transportation forbade the carrying of any but the most important household utensils. Once settled in their new homes it soon became apparent that these few utensils were inadequate to meet the needs of everyday living and that others must be procured from some source. As there were no stores or itinerant peddlers to buy from, they were forced to turn to the one material which was available — wood.

Still in use in many old homesteads of Nova Scotia are hand hewn butter trays, chopping bowls, butter paddles, milk skimmers, potato mashers, rolling pins, and bowls and spoons for table use. Boxes carved out of a piece of a tree trunk, with a tightly fitting cover were used for many purposes — the purpose usually being determined even today from a good sniff of the interior.

The earliest pieces were hand hewn; many of the later ones turned on crude wooden lathes. Maple, because of its fine hard grain, was the favoured wood in the east; the butternut further west. The constant impregnation of the fat oils into the grain of the wood built up a surface that made the wood almost as hard as metal. This probably accounts in part for the survival of these utensils until the present day.

The worker in wood, searching for some pure forms to give inspiration to his work, will do well to turn to some of these old pieces hewn out by his ancestors and study the fine lines of the old spoons, the trays, and bowls and the delicately carved designs on the butter moulds. Aside from satisfying a functional need at preserving time, a fine hand-hewn, beautifully polished maple spoon can well add a decorative note to our modern kitchens.

Our mention of wood carving should also include a brief mention of the artists who carved the figureheads on the vessels built by the shipbuilders of Nova Scotia. Benjamin Doane was one of the master carvers of figure-heads whose creative brain and skilled hands carved almost one hundred. The figurehead of the *Mabel Taylor*, built in 1878, was one of the very few two-in-one, a young girl atop the American bald eagle. His masterpiece, though, was on the *John Bunyan* and shows the immortal writer full length, with a copy of *The Pilgrim's Progress* in his hand.

Another master carver, George McLeod, won a diploma and three pounds for a figurehead of a ship at the Industrial Exhibition held in Halifax in October, 1854.

WITTENBURG CHAIRS

A quiet little village near Truro seldom found on any map of Nova Scotia, Wittenburg was formerly known as St. Andrews, so named by early explorers for the Patron Saint of Scotland. Over two hundred years ago St. Andrews was the centre of a slate quarry, owned and operated by an English company for building purposes in England. They quarried and made into shingles or tile a quantity of this slate and hauled it down through what is now known as Coldstream and West St. Andrews, to the wharf at Stewiacke. There it was loaded on scows and taken to South Maitland, on the Shubenacadie River, where again it was loaded on vessels bound for England.

The Sibleys were among the leading families when Wittenburg was in its hey day. It had two factories manufacturing Venetian blinds, shutters, slit blinds, rocking horses, wheelbarrows, and handsleds which found markets in Maritime homes and in the United States. It had eight mills including a grist mill, shingle mill and a tannery. Today only twenty families remain of the once-thriving community of two hundred people. Only one of the Sibley family, Mrs. Ramsey, still resides in Wittenburg and she proudly recalls the days when her father was one of the leading manufacturers. In her kitchen are chairs more than one hundred years old; she recalls that the chair factory was started in the first place because of the excellent supply of suitable hardwood so near at hand, and the water power available from the St. Andrews River.

She has in her possession a record book of Michael Sibley's dated 1855, which is priceless, as it is the only record of births, deaths and marriages in the community, and records of business agreements as well. One made September 9, 1869 between Michael and Benjamin Sibley reads as follows: "Benjamin Sibley has hired with me for two years, the first year for the sum of ten cents per day (or thirty-one dollars and thirty cents the year) and the second year for twenty cents a day . . . to work in the shop, to make chairs and whatever may come in the way that would be called shop work. Payment to be made at the end of each year or otherwise as may suit."

A year or two ago only one of the last industries of Wittenburg, a wood-working plant, was operating and only at brief intervals. Although the factories have closed and the hands that made the chairs are stilled, the wooden chairs made more than one hundred years ago are mute tribute to the craftsmanship of our hardy pioneers.

BASS RIVER CHAIRS

When a twenty-year-old land surveyor of Scottish-Irish ancestry, James Fulton by name, emigrated from Londonderry, Ireland, to the New World, he was engaged by the Government of Nova Scotia to make surveys and plans of Colchester County. In payment he was to receive a free grant of land wherever he might choose.

So it was by choice and not by chance that he chose Bass River in 1765, in the Township of Londonderry. His grant of land extending from Bass River to the Portaupique River and from the Bay back six miles, was of unbroken forest at that time. If he could have peered into the future he would have seen that few, if any, of his descendants would regret his choice. "Judge" Fulton had fifteen children and 107 grandchildren, so it is understandable that the "Fulton blood was spread fairly well over Colchester County."

His brother Samuel joined him in 1770, and thus these two were the pioneers of Bass River, although later three other brothers came over. He would have seen that ninety-five years later, in 1860, two Fulton brothers, George and William, built a saw mill utilizing the water power of Bass River to operate a home-made jack-knife saw which moved slowly up and down as the log was fed to it by means of a low geared ratchet. So slow and tedious was this process that brother George invented an automatic attachment that would reverse the carriage, move the log over sufficiently to provide for the cutting of another plank, and continue this way until the log was converted into lumber.

The time saved gave freedom for other work, and after installing a lathe, they began turning out finished pieces of wood for bedsteads. From such small beginnings, through good and bad times, through fire and flood the company, now The Dominion Chair Company (in 1903) continued to grow bigger and better. They now make about sixty chairs, with markets all over Canada and in a number of foreign countries. They make and sell five thousand rocking chairs yearly in the four Maritime provinces.

Throughout the province, there were other makers of chairs which have also stood the test of time. One of these craftsmen was George Cole of Rawdon, Hants County. His comfortable, durable chairs were marked "G. Cole, Warranted" and still may be found in Musquodoboit, Maitland, Rawdon, Mount Uniacke, and Windsor.

About 1859, George Gammon had a workshop on the road to Lawrencetown in Halifax County and made chairs and tables, rocking chairs, and spool beds. Where decoration was required, the cutting was done by hand with chisels. In his workshop, women and girls from the neighbourhood made eel-grass mattresses to sell to sailing ships.

In 1958, a most attractive splint bottom chair was made by the "Cape Breton Chairmaker," the late E. H. Hart of North-East Margaree.

There are also good examples of carved mahogany chairs made in Halifax in the 1850's. Some of these may be seen in the Red Chamber of the Province House. These chairs were made by George MacLeod, who has been mentioned previously as a carver of figure-heads. There are two other splendid chairs in the Red Chamber known as the Royal Chairs. The first Royal Chair was made in 1860 in New York for the state visit of the Prince of Wales, later King Edward VII. A second Royal Chair was needed for the visit of King George VI and Queen Elizabeth to Halifax in 1939. This was constructed and carved by Alexander Herman MacMillan. Mr. MacMillan has also made an oak carving of the Halifax coat of arms for the Council Chamber.

THE BLACKSMITH AND WROUGHT IRON

In an article published not long ago in a Scottish magazine, Mr. R. A. Robertson described a blacksmith's shop thus:

A smiddy is never in its natural element in a town and one feels that its proper setting is in the country. It is the core of village life with its picturesque heap of old wheels and scrap iron at the door, its resounding anvil, its roaring forge and glowing metal throwing up in dramatic high-lights the sooty cavern within. A smiddy gives continuity to life, for the craft has preserved much of the pagan splendor of its early beginning.

Certainly in the early days of Nova Scotia, the forge was of first importance. Ploughshares had to be made and repaired, oxen had to be shod, bars, latches and countless things had to be made for tilling the land, and for domestic use. The blacksmith was absolutely indispensable to the settlement.

As peace settled over the country, protection was not as vital, but nails, door latches, hinges, and other equipment necessary for building homes kept the forges roaring to capacity. There was little time for anything fancy in the wrought iron of those days — speed and serviceability were the watchwords. As time advanced oxen were extensively used in farm labour, horses provided means of transportation, and the smith was still hard-pressed to meet the demands on his time and strength.

With machinery gradually replacing horses and oxen in so much of the farm work, the labour of the smith has lessened, and he now has time to do some of the things that were not possible in the horse age. First, as a spare time project, or just as a hobby, many of our blacksmiths have turned their talents to making intricately designed door knockers, candle holders, magazine racks, table lamps, door hinges, fireplace accessories, coffee tables, stair rails, outdoor furnishings such as garden benches, bird baths, and many, many things limited only by ones imagination.

Arthur and Stuart Smith of Smith's Forge in Chester have been prize winners at the Canadian National Exhibition each years since 1951 with their wrought iron work, but few realize that this particular forge has a unique history of one hundred years of continuous service.

Blacksmithing is a natural background for wrought iron work, but a year or so ago the Halifax papers showed a picture of Joseph Kennedy of Inverness, a skilled blacksmith, sitting in a metal rocking chair that he fashioned in his privately owned forge, playing a tune on a violin he had repaired. Making and repairing violins is a far cry from blacksmithing, but it is apparently more evidence of Mr. Kennedy's artistry.

LEATHERCRAFT

By the time the white man arrived on the shores of Nova Scotia, Indians were old in the art of tanning and used articles made from skins and leathers for countless purposes in their everyday lives. Their clothes, moccasins, wigwams, arrow quivers, and blankets were made from the skins and leathers which they prepared. Most of the work, the curing of the leather and the making of the finished articles, was done by the squaw. She would take a deer which her brave had killed, remove the skin with a stone or bone knife, and bury it until the hair cells became soft. She then placed it over the trunk of a tree and scraped it with another crude implement until all of the hair was removed. Next she gave the raw hide a thorough rubbing with the dust of rotten wood, and applied fats and greases, or sometimes a mixture made up of the brain and liver of the deer. The dust of rotten wood was her tanning agent for it contained tannin, or tannic acid, a substance found in various vegetable products which converts raw hide into leather.

In our pioneer days, once a man started to till the fields and live in a house, the demand for leather rose sharply, and to meet the requirements tanning factories sprang up and thrived in many small communities.

Today tanning leather has become an art in itself. Different methods of tanning are used for particular purposes. For instance, leather to be used for handcrafts, tooling, dyeing, carving and embossing is tanned by a method quite different from leathers to be used for harnesses or footwear.

Since the last quarter century, leathercraft in Nova Scotia has become very popular, and some very beautiful work is shown at handcraft exhibits and gift shops.

LACE MAKING

It was no doubt through the French and English aristocracy that lace making was undertaken in Nova Scotia. Lace was in such demand by the courtly ladies of yester-year that they very often took lace makers along with them when the travelled.

Today the very delicate factory-made laces fulfil our everday needs, yet as an interesting handcraft, lace making in its simpler forms can be highly recommended as a hobby. In our grandmother's time, knitted and crocheted laces and tatting provided the trim for many garments – no under-garment or dress was quite complete without some lace. Later on, in our mother's day, Battenburg lace was the decoration used on both garments and household linens. Battenburg lace was made on a traced pattern on architect's linen. Very fine braids and rings were basted on the traced pattern, and then the spaces filled in according to direction by means of a needle and thread. Some of the work and braids were gossamer fine, and the needlework of most intricate design. The patterns were carefully used and passed along.

Pillow lace, so called because it is done on a pillow or soft pad as a working base, is a revived art, and it is fascinating to watch the swiftly moving fingers move the bobbins around as the resulting lace reaches a very high peak of artistic achievement. Mrs. Catherine Jensen, Willington, Yarmouth County, of Danish descent, and Mrs. Coli MacRitchie, Sydney, who came to this country from Holland, are two of the outstanding lace makers of the province.

SILVER

The craft of silver smithing is one of our real heritages. Original settlers brought silver and jewels with them when they came to settle in Nova Scotia, but as sons and daughters established new homes for themselves, imports were brought in from England or the New England States. Trained craftsmen came from Boston, Maryland, and Germany. Provincial Archives' collections show high standards of workmanship and use in simple design. Early craftsmen were satisfied only with quality; they could import quantity.

Hallmarks identified the name of the silversmith, the date and place produced, and the quality. John Frederick Herbin, Wolfville, was trained in the art by his father, John Herbin, a Huguenot jeweller from France; Richard Tweedell trained in England (pieces of his work are in Wolfville); James Eastwood, New Glasgow and Tully Brothers, Halifax, and M. S. Brown & Co., now Birk's — Mr. Brown being trained by Peter Nordbeck of Germany — all were noted Nova Scotia silversmiths and jewellers.

Today an estimated 120 individuals are interested in this craft. They are receiving their training through the Handcrafts Program, Department of Trade and Industry. They meet together in groups of six twice a year to receive instruction. In the interim they work together in groups or as individuals in their homes. Their motif is generally centred around the simple designs native to the province.

Among the most outstanding of Nova Scotia's artisans are C. H. and Winnie Fox whose work is now known all over America. Mr. Fox works with agate, a semi-precious stone found in the Maritimes. These he cuts and polishes to a gem-like finish. He and his wife then combine talents to give the stones proper silver mountings. Their jewellery has consistently won awards and special mentions in exhibitions sponsored by the Canadian Handicraft Guild. Early in 1957, an invitation was received from the National Gallery of Canada to submit "from two to four examples of original creations of jewellery" to the selection jury for the first National Fine Crafts Exhibition. Their entry won for them a special diploma and was subsequently selected for showing at the 1958 Brussels (Belgium) World Fair.

In 1951, the Nova Scotian government presented a matching set of an agate bracelet, ring and earrings to Princess Elizabeth when she and her husband were touring Canada. In addition, a pair of cufflinks and a tie clip were given to Prince Philip.

Another team of silver craftsmen is Madam Gabriel LeBlanc (one time President of Women's Institutes of Nova Scotia) and R. A. Le-Blanc, Director of Acadian Handcrafts (L'Artisane Maison Acadienne). It was from their studio the gifts of a handwrought sterling silver ring set with Nova Scotia agate, and a handwrought sterling silver bracelet of antique design were purchased and presented by the WINS to Mrs. Alice Berry, President of the Associated Country Women of the World, and Mrs. Nancy Adams, President of the Federated Women's Institutes of Canada, in 1955.

The top award for handwrought jewellery at the Canadian National Exhibition in 1965 was won by a Halifax School teacher, Miss Mabel Murphy. She uses stones cut by the skilled stone cutter, Mr. Earl Jollimore, then sets the beautiful agate in most intricate and artistic mountings.

QUILTS

From earliest times in America, as in the mother countries, it was woman's duty to supply her household with cloth for domestic use. Winters were cold and the accent was on bed furnishings. The job began with raising sheep, growing flax, preparing the fibres and exercising skill at the spinning wheel, dye-pot and loom. The function of the original bed quilt was warmth, but cheer and gaiety were as necessary to the pioneer woman as they are to the bride of to-day.

The quilt making era was about 1750-1850. The earliest bedcovers were designed with regard to the whole unit — a prepared homespun background, blocked, embroidered or appliqued — but these were hard to handle in the making. Then they were done in successive borders surrounding a medallion or motif. Pieced quilts worked around a central medallion are a traditional quilt style. Then there were quilts made in squares with repeat designs set together with strips or lattice work or with an alternate white block; this became a favourite method and was very popular through the 1800's.

Then there were Album quilts, also known as Friendship, Presentation, or Brides' Quilts, but at times some of these were not very beautiful. Lacy designs were obtained by folding a square of paper in half, then in quarters and eights: with a sharp pair of scissors motifs like snowflakes would unfold.

Quilting bees and frolics were a part of the social as well as the economic life of the pioneers. But even in this age of the atom and the rocket, quilting continues to attract many of our talented women. A quilt woven by Mrs. Michael McKim, Lower Five Islands, and now owned by her grand-daughter, was shown recently at an Exhibition. Woven in 1849, Mrs. McKim grew and spun the flax which is the linen white. The blue is wool from the sheep on the farm and is coloured indigo from the bark of trees.

Nova Scotia women have made and won prizes with many of their beautiful quilts. In the Star Weekly Dominion-wide Quilt-Makers Contest in 1956, the Women's Institute of Pubnico, Yarmouth County, and a New Waterford lady won prizes of $250.00 each for the third best "Canadiana" quilt.

The quilt designed by Mrs. Marguerite Gates and made by the Port Williams Women's Institute as a group project won honourable mention at the Canadian National Exhibition in 1955. The quilt design featured the two hundredth anniversary of the expulsion of the Acadians. This quilt has been donated to the Thomas Chandler Haliburton Memorial Museum at Windsor.

Mrs. Gates won a prize at the Canadian National Exhibition for a child's bed quilt which she designed and made herself. She chose the circus as her motif for this quilt, and it stole the hearts of children and adults alike. "The Stage Coach Quilt" made by the Coldbrook

Women's Institute was designed by Mrs. Winniferd Fox. This quilt was exhibited as Craftsmen at Work Exhibitions and won second prize at Orillia, Ontario, Quilt Exhibition in 1952.

A rather unusual handmade quilt is owned by Mr. and Mrs. James Langille, of Bigney, Nova Scotia. It is a quilt with a history, as it was made in 1910 by a Woman's group of the Methodist Church of River John. It has the embroidered names of many who lived in River John at that time, including the names of two prominent shipbuilders.

DOLLS

In the first century Roman girls had dolls as play-things, and in the fourteenth century Germany began making dolls for export, but they represented adults in the clothes of the period and it was not until the eighteenth century that England began making dolls that looked like babies and children and the idea soon spread over Europe.

In America the first dolls were brought from England and presented to the little Indian girls. When the settlers had none to give, the Indian mother made dolls of deerskin.

During Queen Victoria's reign, all the dolls had blue eyes as a compliment to the Queen, whose eyes were a real china blue. Indeed, the Queen had a collection of dolls to represent famous personage of the day.

To-day the trend to dress dolls to represent living people is very evident. To have appeal they should have a story behind them, or stand for an historical character. This has led not only to a hobby but to an economic venture.

To the late Miss Helen J. Macdougall, then Superintendent of Women's Institutes for Nova Scotia, belongs the credit for the souvenir dolls Evangeline and "La femme de Clare" as a Women's Institute project for the district of Clare. The dolls are about seven inches high; the head is made of white linen, and the body of black stockings. They have a very natural appearance with their black wool hair, can stand alone, and are hand painted. Great care is taken that the handmade costumes be accurate in every detail. The Evangeline doll has a bright blue skirt, black bodice laced across the front, and a cap, kerchief and apron of fine white cotton.

"La Femme de Clare" is dressed in the outdoor costume of the early Acadians: a black and white print dress, with little cape and kerchief of black. (After the expulsion, the older women never wore colors again.) Their names are printed on the hems of their aprons and each is stamped "WINS Hand-made." The workmanship is unusually fine.

Mrs. Marguerite Gates has won prizes for her character dolls, Scottish Highlander, Evangeline, Ulrica and Fisherman at the Canadian National Exhibition, and an honourable mention for her doll "Song of the Cloak," representing the days of privateering along the Nova Scotia coast. The women of the day wore blue pelisses with red lining. It is said that they defended their village by turning the pelisses inside out and shouldering their brooms. The raiders sailed away rather than tangle with an army of red coats.

Mrs. Bessie Murray designed the Lady Wentworth doll, depicting gay days of Halifax when Sir John Wentworth was governor and the dashing Duke of Kent held open house at Prince's Lodge. Miss Rosamond Pipes won wide acclaim for her character doll "Sam Slick the Clock-maker." The character, Sam Slick, was created by Thomas Chandler Haliburton for his historical novel of Nova Scotia. Miss Pipes also designed and made the soft rag doll, dressed in Scottish Highland costume with handwoven Royal Stuart kilts, presented to Princess Elizabeth for Princess Anne. Her hair of native Nova Scotia wool is dyed with vegetable dyes, and in her Balmoral there are feathers from a Nova Scotia partridge.

POTTERY

It is believed that the early French settlers made bricks at Mira, Cape Breton. Extensive brickwork has been uncovered in the ruins of the fort at Louisbourg. Mira residents believe the bricks were moulded from the blue clay found along the banks of the Mira River. An old deep-rutted French road has left a trail through the fields that leads directly to a spot where the earliest evidence of brick making has been found, along with odd tools thought to be French.

In 1900 the Mira Brick Company was formed by thirty venturesome Cape Bretoners. But the old method of brick making was outdated, and a man named Shaw was brought in from the United States to build a kiln. A thriving business which lasted until 1922 is seen in Glace Bay where the Town Hall, Post Office, Power House, and Central School are but a few of the buildings constructed of Mira brick. In

Sydney, Mira bricks were used in the construction of St. Andrews Church, the Post Office, and the Argyle Street School.

In Elmsdale, Hants County, brick and pottery making dates back before the turn of the century. Indeed there may have been a Prescott Brick and Pottery works early in the 1800's. Johnathon Prescott came to Nova Scotia from New England with the Sir William Pepperal expedition against Louisbourg in 1745. He was a surgeon as well as a Captain, and after Louisbourg was taken he granted land at Chester, Lunenburg, and Halifax. Captain Prescott was supposed to have defended Chester from the privateers (the doll "Song of the Cloak" commemorates this event). This information comes from Mary Allison Prescott, great-great-granddaughter of the Captain, and now living at Starr's Point, Kings County in the brick Prescott house built by her great-grandfather Charles Ramage Prescott. Other evidences of early Nova Scotian pottery are the urns, flower pots and jugs that are still found in Elmsdale to-day.

The buff-coloured clay deposits of the Shubenacadie River had been shipped in small quantity to a pottery located between Enfield and Elmsdale. The L. E. Shaw Company now lease the property and manufacture bricks and tiles at Lantz and New Glasgow.

Mr. and Mrs. Lorenzen of Lantz are helping to make Nova Scotia pottery famous. The Lorenzen Studio is situated on the site of one of the largest and best clay deposits in Nova Scotia. They dig and dry the clay and prepare it for the potter's wheel. After the pieces are moulded, dried and designed, they are given their first firing in an electric kiln. They are then cooled and ready for glazing. The material for glazes comes from all over the province.

Ernest and Alma Lorenzen have now earned international fame for their pottery. They are also becoming expert mycologists, because of the many unique pottery mushrooms which they manufacture. Collections of these pottery mushrooms have been shipped to many colleges to be used in Zoology departments. The Lorenzens were recently awarded a Canada Council grant for a study tour of famous potteries in Europe. Though what started over fifteen years ago as a hobby is now transformed into a business, the original artistic quality and skill has never been allowed to lessen.

The pioneer potter of Nova Scotia is Mrs. Alice Hagan who has her studio at Mahone Bay. Despite the fact that she is now eighty years of age, she still continues her art. As far as she knows there was no one making pottery in the Maritimes when she began her career. In fact she can lay claim to being one of the pioneer potters of Canada.

Mrs. Hagan is a ceramic artist whose work is Scotian pebble pottery. Her variety of style and technique is almost incredible. Her luster pieces are truly unique and should be preserved for the guidance of future artists, since luster painting is a rare and difficult art to learn. She is also renowned for her hand-painted china and her most prized possession is her "Moonlight Night in Lunenburg County" vase. Several of Mrs. Hagan's best pieces are on display in the Provincial Museum at Citadel Hill, Halifax. In February, 1966, the public was invited to a showing of more of Mrs. Hagan's excellent paintings and examples of her skill as a ceramic artist.

Foster and Eleanor Beveridge, who live at Mader's Cove, Lunenburg County, are two more Nova Scotian potters who have won renown for their artistic work. In the Brussels Exhibition in 1958, their exhibit was a cleverly designed bottle. At the Pottery Exhibition held in Montreal in 1963, Eleanor Beveridge won the honour of having a ceramic bowl on exhibit. This Exhibition was sponsored by the Canadian Guild of Potters and the Canadian Handicraft Guild. Mrs. Beveridge also received the seal of merit from the Canadian Government as well as a Nova Scotia Talent Trust Fund which was spent in study abroad.

Throughout the province, there are many classes held for the advancement of those interested in this craft. The Department of Trade and Industry has established a Handcraft Division where ceramics is taught; next to weaving, it is the most popular handcraft in the province.

GLASS

In July and August of 1964, members of the Provincial Museum staff conducted an excavation of the site of the old Nova Scotia Glass Companies in Trenton, where they were able to find samples of molten glass and a variety of bottle fragments. Seven district patterns of pressed glassware have been positively identified. These patterns have been named Nova Scotia Starflower, Kenlee, Raspberry, Raspberry and Shield, Victoria Commemorative (1837-1887), Diamond and Nova Scotia Gothic. These patterns appear on goblets, cake plates, spooners, compacts, water and cream pitchers, etc.

The Nova Scotia Glass Company was established in 1881. The

factory worked day and night making tableware, lanterns, globes and lamp chimneys. By 1884, the glass was much improved in style and colour, and over one hundred men and boys were employed. In 1886, the factory turned out a new and beautifully designed set of diamond flint crystalware; by 1887, chimney manufacture was curtailed so that more pressed glass and tumblers (engraved with Masonic and Odd-fellow emblems) could be made. New patterns in tableware were made during 1888. In 1890, the Nova Scotia Glass Company sold out to the Diamond Glass Company of Montreal, but in 1892 over eighty men were still employed. Local men were learning the glassmaker's art, for records show that James McKay of New Glasgow carved some of the molds used in this plant. But in 1892 the glass works were closed and the molds were sent to Montreal. The buildings were destroyed by fire in 1899.

In 1890, the Lamont brothers erected a glass house near the site of the Nova Scotia Glass Company. They intended to make coloured glass their speciality and soon turned out a superior type of lamp chimney for sailways and lighthouses. From 1893 to 1895 Lamont's was the leading glass house in the area, but due to high freight rates and competition with the larger Canadian glass companies, they too were absorbed by the Montreal Diamond Glass Company. The same fire that destroyed the buildings of the first glass company also destroyed one of their buildings, which contained the accumulated stock of the Lamont brothers.

The Humphrey's Glass Company also began operations in the same general area in 1890. In their new and commodious factory, they turned out from twelve hundred to fifteen hundred bottles daily as well as whisky flasks, medicine bottles, lamps, fruit jars, glass rolling pins, and fly traps. During the next decade the Humphreys were the leading bottle manufacturers in Nova Scotia; they weathered strikes, business depressions and the Gold Rush! Their plant was destroyed by fire in 1901, but they erected a larger one in 1906 and by 1907-1908, they were turning out twenty-five thousand pieces of glass per day. But in 1917, the Humphrey brothers decided to take advantage of the natural gas at Moncton, New Brunswick, and moved their plant to a site on the banks of the Petitcodiac River. Thus the Humphreys' Brothers Glass Works had the longest uninterrupted history of production in Nova Scotia.

Nova Scotian glass is now eagerly sought after by collectors. Visitors to the Provincial Museum may see beautiful pieces in attractive patterns and shapes, which are part of the heritage left to us by the early craftsmen.

NOVA SCOTIA FESTIVAL OF THE ARTS

The Province of Nova Scotia, over the years, has produced a great variety of talent both industrial and artistic, and has long been known as the province whose chief export is "brains." While such a reputation is flattering, and we are exceedingly proud of our compatriots who have made their mark and become famous outside our borders, we should realize there is probably more native ability in the arts and crafts per square mile in this small area than anywhere else in Canada.

In order to acquaint the public with this wealth, the idea of a Festival of the Arts which could be a "showcase" for the best we have to offer in drama, music, crafts, dancing and painting, came to a group associated with Guy Henson, Director of Adult Education Division, which has been staffing the School of Community Arts held in the Rural High School at Tatamagouche for the past four years.

So wrote Mrs. Lorna S. Grayston, Secretary, Provincial Program Committee, Nova Scotia Summer Festival of the Arts. This was its beginning in August 1956.

Thousands came to the first Nova Scotia Festival of the Arts last summer, the first of its kind on the North American Continent. They came from the rest of Nova Scotia, the rest of Canada, and from the United States. They crowded arts and crafts displays and brought out all six concerts. They sat in droves on the sunny grass slopes around the outdoor stage. They sunbathed and swam in the warm water of Northumberland Strait, and when the Festival was over, many of them continued by car along the lovely Sunrise Trail, the Festival of Arts an unforgettable interlude in an ocean-cooled Nova Scotia vacation.

And to Tatamagouche last summer came over three hundred Nova Scotia musicians, actors and dancers and the work of over seventy Nova Scotia artists and craftsmen. Everyone performing or exhibiting donated his time and effort, for the Festival began as a non-commercial venture and we are determined that it will remain a shining proof of the fact that in Nova Scotia we are still blessed with people who refuse to believe that the dollar is almighty.

4 🎋

New Brunswick

Historically, New Brunswick dates from 1784 when it was set apart by Royal Charter from Nova Scotia, to accommodate twelve thousand Loyalists forced into exile at the close of the Revolutionary War in the United States. The city they founded, Saint John, received its charter in 1785, and today is the oldest incroporated city in Canada. Factually, historians and archaeologists have traced New Brunswick's history back almost 4,000 years, in a dig at old Portland Point, a green mound jutting out into Saint John harbour.

The twentieth century archaeologists found more than the blackened palisades of the old Fort La Tour. They uncovered evidence of two phases of Indian life, the "Red Paint" Indians of the prehistoric period, so called because of their habit of sprinkling their graves with powdered red ochre, and a transitional Indian period when the aboriginals were coming into contact with the Europeans. They unearthed, among other things, a small red slate plummet, a fish effigy to which the carver had added eyes, mouth and an engraved pattern on the back and belly, typical of ancient Eskimo work. From the seventeenth century La Tour period came old glass, stoneware, dishes, pipes, Indian trade goods, cannon balls and several fragments of cloth of

69

European manufacture. The thousands of artifacts unearthed from old Portland Point are now in the New Brunswick Museum at Saint John.

Shortly after the turn of the century, the late Dr. William MacIntosh, first director and curator of the New Brunswick Museum, spent a portion of every summer, (until his death in 1950), paddling a canoe along the St. John river and its tributaries. Alone, or with groups of young campers, he searched for early examples of Indian crafts. How did he know where to search for aboriginal implements? He would say to himself: "If I were an Indian, where would I camp?" He would hunt for a good beach, pure drinking water and an unobstructed view of an approaching enemy. When the spring freshets had subsided and washed away some of the gravel beaches or muddy banks, the canoe parties found spear heads, arrow heads, knives, drills and scrapers of felsite or red jasper washed out of carboniferous conglomerates along the lakes and rivers in central New Brunswick. Chips of chalcedony, carnelian and milky quartz were discovered at many campsites and agates at an ancient quarry on the south side of Washademoak Lake.

Pieces of earthenware, implements and ornaments of bone, ivory, shell, horn, even wood and bark, came to light on these treasure hunts, and a few crude stone tools supported Dr. MacIntosh's belief that the Eskimos inhabited New Brunswick even before the Indians. He proved both races used the same camp sites. The artifacts gathered on one hundred and forty canoe trips number in the thousands and are all in the New Brunswick Museum, where they are considered the finest collection in the world of Micmac and Maliseet relics.

Another New Brunswick collector of similar artifacts is Dr. George Frederick Clarke of Woodstock, dentist, writer and historian. He has bits of cloth woven centuries ago from fibres of cedar bark, and Indian pipes predating the arrival of the first white man.

The real craft workers among the Indians were the women. They were obliged to build the cabins, sew and repair the birch bark canoes, stretch and curry the animal skins, make clothing and moccasins for the entire family. For their sewing they used pointed bodkins of bone, and sometimes adorned their work with pigments and porcupine quills. In many sections of the province shards of pottery have been found.

Probably made by the women, the shards are the remains of small bowls with conical bottoms, terra cotta, brown or grey clay on the outside, and permanetly black on the inside. Nearly all were ornamented with straight lines and indented patterns. Owing to the nomadic habits of the Indians their pottery was simple. Some of their larger vessels were of wood, others of birch bark.

The earliest observers of Indian life in New Brunswick, Nicholas Denys and Marc Lescarbot, mention "peschipoty," a general term for the finery worn by the Indians. Denys describes a textile woven with dyed porcupine quills on a warp made from thongs of moose-embryo skin, and dishes of birch bark ornamented with quills. Both Denys and Lescarbot mentioned the brilliant Indian dyes: the bright red made from the root of the common bedstraw particularly attracted them. The Micmac and Maliseet Indians of the Maritime Provinces carried the embroidery of quills on birch bark to a higher degree of perfection than any other Canadian Indian. They invariably covered the bark surfaces entirely with fine geometrical patterns so brightly coloured age has barely dimmed them. The edges of their boxes, birch bark cradles and other items were bound with spruce and fir roots, and the craftsmanship was excellent. Even today the lids of the boxes fit perfectly.

Seventeenth century textile weaving is one of the lesser known Indian crafts. The Micmacs and Maliseets did not use true looms. Instead they utilized convenient tree limbs, tied on the warp threads, and left them hanging to twist in the weft with their fingers. A small fragment of netting uncovered during the Portland Point excavations may have been part of a bag from grass or nettle fibres. The warp fibres were bound in alternating pairs to give a diamond effect. This twined weaving is characteristic of basketry made by many primitive peoples, and a similar weave has been found in drawings of fringed skirts in prehistoric rock shelters in Tennessee.

Denys is the only writer on the Acadian region who made any reference to the use of rushes by the Micmacs. He said their women plaited bags of flattened rushes, one within the other. Examples of bulrush mats from an excavation at Pictou, N.S., are now in the New Brunswick Museum and probably were made in the same way as the Portland Point netting. Matting fragments found in an Indian burial ground at Red Bank, N.B., and now in the Museum, were made from flat cedar bast fibre strips and woven in a twill pattern. Strand ends were rolled into cords and left loose to form a fringe. These fragments are the only known examples of Indian textile weaving in the Maritime provinces.

Also from the Red Bank excavation came a pair of ornamented leather and bark arm bands, the first seventeenth century Indian articles of that type to be discovered in the province. In Nicholas Denys' *Natural History of Acadia*, published in 1672, the Micmac method of treating leather is outlined. He said skins were soaked and stretched in the sun, then well heated on the skin side to remove the hair. The cleaned skins were rubbed with birds' liver and oil, then dressed over pieces of polished wood until they became supple. Finally washed, they were twisted with sticks several times, then spread to dry.

After their contact with Europeans, the Indians traded beaver, otter, muskrat, fox and other furs for commodities. Among the things they liked were white and coloured beads. During the early eighteen hundreds, Indian squaws became very proficient in beadwork and decorated moccasins, hats and garments for both men and women, with beads, using again their geometric motifs, and in many cases outlining their designs with white beads.

Both Micmac and Maliseet children played with dolls carved from wood. One Maliseet doll from the Kennebecasis river area, carved in 1825, represents a squaw wearing the clothing of the period. A Micmac Indian Chief with a finely chiselled aquiline nose sports a high-crowned hat, long black coat and red leggings above beaded moccasins. These and other Indian figures, together with a small birch bark cradle, from part of a collection in the Children's Museum in Saint John.

The Maliseet Indians have long had a reputation as fine basket makers, a craft they carry on to this day. Both the Indians of the Miramichi watershed area and the Micmacs of the Tobique reservations weave potato baskets, shopping baskets, handkerchief baskets bound with sweet grass, and laundry baskets. They also weave chair seats.

Their raw material is ash logs, and today several reserves are denuded of ash trees, forcing the craftsmen to hunt further afield. To prepare their material the Indians soak the ash and pound it until layers of wood can be peeled off in thin strips. The master basket maker is always a man, and he has male assistants to do the log pounding. Women do the actual weaving, although the master basket maker whittles the handles and loops. A team of five can turn out fifteen dozen potato baskets a week. Strips of shopping baskets usually are dyed gay colours.

Both Micmacs and Maliseets produce fine axe handles, and the latter make loops for lobster traps.

BIG COVE HANDICRAFTS

Today Micmac and Maliseet Indians live on nearly a dozen reservations scattered around the province. Although the Indians have been slow to change, most are facing the world more squarely and thinking about their future more definitely than ever before. And all want to preserve their identity as the "original Canadian."

In 1961 a Micmac chief of the big Cove reservation on the Richibucto river approached Dr. H. Crowell, director of the Handicraft branch of the New Brunswick Department of Finance and Industry. His people had artistic talent, said Anthony Francis, but had forgotten many of their old crafts. Could they be taught new ones to help them earn a living?

When Dr. Crowell investigated he found the Micmacs did indeed possess artistic ability. An original Indian head sculptured in red clay from the bank of the Richibucto river, sparked the interest of both Provincial and Federal authorities on Indian Affairs. Ottawa officials authorized a grant for a one-year project, and on October 1, 1962, Dr. Crowell began an active program of handicraft instruction at the Big Cove reservation.

Construction of a new brick school permitted conversion of the original wooden schoolhouse into a craft centre. There, classes were established in weaving, silk-screen printing, wood turning and pottery, and soon, after an initial timidity, men and women were flocking to classes taught by professionals.

Before long, Dr. Crowell began looking for design talent among the Indians. He found it in Michael Francis, who had been born in Big Cove and educated at the Indian Residential school in Shubenacadie, N.S. Dr. Crowell invited Michael Francis to study at the main school in Fredericton for two weeks. He has been there ever since. Michael Francis has produced remarkable work and his designs lead the Big Cove group in the field of silk screen printing and hasti-notes. All his colourful designs are based upon the legends of his people, stories passed on to him by his Micmac grandfather of "The Little People", tiny Indian figures similar to the leprechauns of Ireland.

Each design Francis turns out bears his signature, a picture of

"Tatler the Loon", the meaning of his Indian name. Many honours have come to him. Five of his paintings were accepted by the National Indian Council for an exhibition of Canadian Indian art in Winnipeg, and in 1966 the entire Indian Art exhibition will go on tour in West Germany.

Michael Francis also made a series of designs for the 1965 national IODE calendar, ten based on his legends. The other two were Eskimo designs. Probably his most outstanding designs are for the tapestry series being hand-woven for Teachers' College, located on the University of New Brunswick campus. Actual weaving of the tapestries is the work of Dr. Crowell who does it as a hobby in his own home. The full colour outline drawing known as a cartoon is enlarged to the full size of the tapestry. The weaver works from the back, in reverse with coloured wool on a warp of strong shoemakers' linen.

Stephen Dedam is another gifted Big Cove artist and designer. With his lively sense of humour he sketched a series of bridge tallies and score pads known as "The Doings of the Little People." His tiny figures smoke the Indian pipe (the flower); play the fiddlehead (greens); feed the pussywillows; ring the Bluebells.

The works of both Dedam and Francis are reproduced by the men and women at the greatly enlarged Micmac Craftsmen Centre in Big Cove, where one entire wing of the building is devoted to silk-screen process. Indian officials from other reserves have since gone to Frederiction to study the program with an eye towards establishing something similar on their reserves.

THE ACADIANS

French exploration of the New Brunswick area dates from the time of Jacques Cartier, who skirted the eastern and northern shores in 1534, and named a great indentation "le Baye de Chaleur", Bay of Heat. However, except for occasional visits by European fishermen, further exploration did not take place until the coming of the geographer, colonizer and writer, Samuel de Champlain. It was he who actively examined the coast and discovered the St. John river on June 24, 1604, the day of St. John the Baptist, and so named it.

The entire Maritime area became known as Acadia, and a number of adventurers and traders sought their fortunes in the fishery, fur trade and in piratical excursions along the coast. Hollanders from

New York and Puritans from Boston took turns claiming possession of the section now known as New Brunswick. But the French continued to predominate and successive international treaties confirmed their hold throughout the seventeenth century, with fur and fish monopolies being established over a wide areas.

Among the early adventurers was Nicholas Denys who operated fishing depots in the Gulf of St. Lawrence and built a fort at Miscou. His most lasting memorials are two books published in Paris in 1672, in which he described the history, geography, customs and crafts of the Indians and his own Acadian settlers.

Rivalry raged among the French seigneurs who followed and later gave way to strife between the French and English. When war broke out between France and England in 1689, the entire area became a place of conflict. This phase ended with the Treaty of Utrecht in 1713, ceding Acadia to Britain.

However, for 40 years, the area that is now New Brunswick remained in dispute bewteen the two nations. After 1763, with the war finally over, the British government and Halifax authorities relented, and many of the expelled Acadians were allowed to begin the long trek back. At Memramcook, Pre d'en Haut, Cocagne, Buctouche and Caraquet, they received grants of land and laid the foundations of the prosperous communities there today. Some who had left the St. John river area were given land they had originally farmed. French Canadians from Quebec used the portages and rivers and fused with the Acadians to form settlements at Madawaska.

As with all the early settlers, the articles used by the Acadians were handmade and with a simplicity of form in the wooden artifacts they produced for their daily use. When St. Joseph's University was established at Memramcook in 1853 by Father LaFrance, an attempt was made to collect and preserve as many old things as possible in a small museum. Local people responded with wooden cradles, spinning wheels, farm utensils, chairs and tables all labouriously fashioned by hand from the trees of the forest, and held together with wooden pegs or blocks. Much later items appeared with hand-forged iron nails.

When St. Joseph's University became the vigorous, bilingual University of Moncton and moved to a new campus in 1965, the small Acadian Museum at Memramcook was transferred to spacious new quarters in the Library and Art Gallery building. There, sparked by the interest of University president, Father Clement Cormier, the collections have been arranged for public display. Two enthusiastic Moncton women, Miss Creola LeBlanc and Miss Alberta Gaudet are in charge of the Museum, and the artistic arrangement of the smaller items has been done by Claude Roussel, resident artist and curator of the Art Gallery.

A large hand-made iron pot dug up at Fort Beausejour is the oldest piece to date in the Museum. Probably buried during the siege, it had contained a clock with all its machinery made of wood. This was thrown away by the youth who found it. The oldest pieces are a small wooden table and several wooden chairs dating around 1800. The chairs are all ladder-backs, with rungs extending through the front legs clearly visible, and fastened together with wooden blocks. Although constructed in a crude manner, early Acadian furniture reflected French ecclesiastical styles, and the lowness of the chairs enabled the women to sit comfortably when performing household chores before the fireplace.

Several antique looms have been set up. There are a number of wooden distaffs and wool winders made from small tree branches, a large wooden compass, wooden flails for threshing wheat or flax, and home-made wooden sabots, from men's large sizes to baby shoes with scuff holes through the soles. If today's farmers want to see how the Acadian rid himself of potato bugs, they should inspect the ingenious home-made wheel barrow arrangement with a moveable centre section to tip the bugs into it.

The Acadian pattern of life revolved around the home and church, with religious festivals taking precedence over all others. No girl could marry until she could weave a piece of cloth, no boy until he could make a pair of wheels.

In another section, the fine handwork done by women of a later period is shown in a hope-chest arrangement with the traditional bride's trousseau. The stitchery, embroidery and crocheted lace shown on petticoat, nightgown and camisole were taught by convent nuns. At one time excellent linen was woven from home-grown flax at the Convent of St. Louis in Kent County.

THE FRENCH

In 1724 Caraquet was home to a group of French people from Normandy. They were followed by a few Acadian refugees. Then in 1784, the Nova Scotia government gave land grants to thirty-four French families. They were followed by English and Scottish settlers, and fishermen from the Island of Jersey. Somewhere along the line there was an infusion of native Indian.

At Caraquet where the village strings out for 10 miles to form the longest main street in Canada, and gray sandstone cliffs dip to the Bay Chaleur, the soil is fair and once produced flax and wool for a grand old lady, Madame Blanchard, one of New Brunswick's earliest and most noted craftswomen. For many years Madame Blanchard dyed her own wool, spun flax threads, wove hundreds of yards of woollen materials and fine linen. She hooked rugs, crocheted and knitted, and encouraged local women to help her. Today, her work is being carried on by Mrs. F. A. Blanchard and the original Blanchard workshop now has become a handicraft centre and Museum. Like Madame Blanchard, Mrs. F. A. Blanchard employs Caraquet women to weave, hook rugs and make quilts.

At the flourishing new centre the accomplished weavers are weaving bed covers, scarves, place mats, stoles, pot-holders, aprons, dress materials and runners. An unusual feature of their work is a distinctive type of Christmas card, a combination silk-screened, hand woven design, mounted on a deckle-edged card. This project had its beginning in 1963, when Mrs. Gerard Dugas, a weaver, and Allan Crimmins, a silk-screen printer, co-operated to turn out a hand crafted card by silk-screening a pattern on warp threads, and later weaving a different coloured thread over the design. On display by the New Brunswick Handicraft branch at the 1965 National Gift Show in Toronto, the unique card attracted the attention of Japanese buyers who placed a substantial order for them.

Caraquet's Acadian Museum opened in 1963 with sixty household articles. By 1966 they had acquired over one thousand items, and the Museum and Handicraft Centre have become the focal points on the Acadian trail, Caraquet's ambitious Centennial project. Mrs. Francois Blanchard and Mrs. Jean Blanchard are the proprietors, and invite visitors to try the four modern looms and weave a piece of cloth. One of the most interesting rooms at the Museum contains a history of the flax industry, from the seed to the flax crusher, to a towel woven on an ancient loom dating back four generations. In 1964 several farmers in Beresford and South Teteagouche planted five or six acres of flax and used a combine to process their crops, but in the down shore areas of Caraquet most flax is grown in small garden patches.

Each summer there is an Acadian festival, beginning at Grand Anse and continuing through to Caraquet, with horse-hauling contests, parades with floats carrying an 1871 hand-pumped fire engine, and an

1890 blacksmith shop. Women and children wear the colourful Acadian costume, light blue dresses with black bands at the hemlines, white aprons, Dutch-style caps and front-laced bodices of black. And always there is the Blessing of the Fleet as the fishermen set out to sea.

UNITED EMPIRE LOYALISTS

The Revolutionary war between Great Britain and her American colonies was primarily responsible for the greatest influx of English speaking settlers into what is now New Brunswick. In April 1783, the first fleet of twenty transports sailed from New York with three thousand persons for the mouth of the St. John river. They disembarked on May 18, and ever since that day has been celebrated as the anniversary of the "Landing of the Loyalists."

Their numbers having swelled tremendously, the Loyalists found themselves at too great a distance from the seat of government at Halifax and asked for a separate province. Their request was granted in 1784, and the land north of the Bay of Fundy became the Province of New Brunswick. The following year, on May 18, Parr Town and Carleton were made into one city by Royal Charter, and renamed the City of Saint John.

Among the New Brunswick Loyalists were men and women from every walk of life: merchants, soldiers, lawyers, farmers, mechanics, clergymen, free negroes and negro slaves. Some had been able to bring their most valued possessions, but the majority had lost everything.

For the next few years many Loyalists were compelled to live in a very primitive fashion in small log houses, scantily furnished with but the barest homemade necessities. All cooking was done at an open fireplace; moose meat was roasted on iron spits; stews and soups were prepared in iron kettles hanging from cranes, and boiled food became so common that spoons were the commonest table utensil, "spoon meat" being served at almost every meal. Bread was cooked in a Dutch oven, or in a bake kettle covered with hot ashes.

In farm homes the dishes were mostly pewter and their number limited. Home-grown Indian corn was used to make cornmeal, and the housewife helped her husband hoe potatoes grown among the burnt stumps around their clearing Later, in all but the wealthiest homes, the kitchen was the common room, sometimes even a bedroom. The hearth corner held trivets, peels and skillets; above the clavel

78

Stone carving at Povungnituk; *De-partment of Northern Affairs and National Resources.*

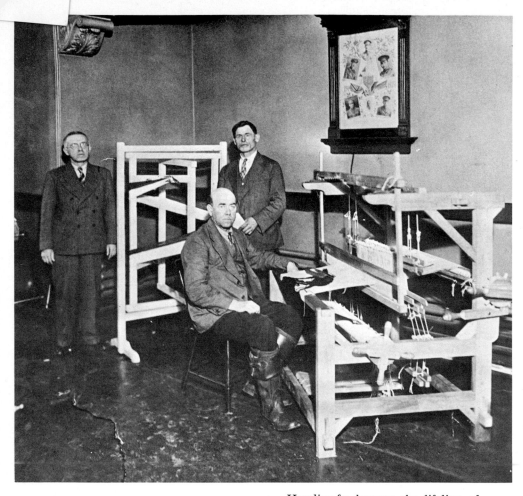

Handicrafts became the lifeline of existence for thousands of Newfoundland families during the lean years of the 1930's. Here is a typical scene as rubber-booted fishermen learn to operate looms as a means of improving their livelihood.

Hundreds of hand-crafted items are displayed in the attractive gift shop operated at St. John's by the Newfoundland Outport Nursing and Industrial Association (NONIA). Included in selection are examples of hand-woven ladies' wear and the popular carved miniatures of fishermen and dories.

During its early years as the leading sponsor of handicrafts in Newfoundland, Jubilee Guilds promoted its work by exhibiting at provincial exhibitions. Scene shows a room completely furnished with articles made by Guilds handicrafters. Jubilee Guilds is now a unit of the Federated Women's Institutes of Canada and Associated Countrywomen of the World.

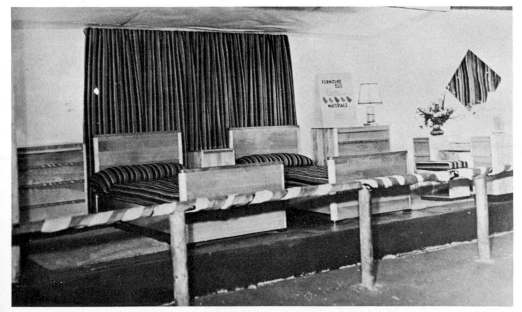

Prince Edward Island

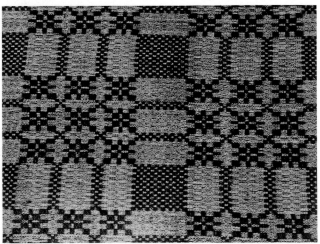

The picture of this early Canadian spinner from Prince Edward Island was taken in 1847 and copied in 1967; *photo by Gordon R. White.*

Handwoven linen bedspread over 100 years old, woven from homegrown flax, owned by the MacGowans's of Kilmuir, P.E.I.

An example of the Log Cabin Quilt from Prince Edward Island. It is one of the oldest traditional designs used by the pioneers; *photo by Edith Robinson*.

Nova Scotia

A display of original ceramics by
Nova Scotian artists; *Nova Scotia
Information Service, Halifax, N.S.*

Wood carving; *Nova Scotia Information Service, Halifax, N.S.*

Wood sculpture by Nova Scotian carvers; *Nova Scotia Information Service, Halifax, N.S.*

New Brunswick

Stoneware and pottery designed and created by Erica and the late Kjeld Deichmann of Moss Glen and Sussex, N.B. Deichmann pottery is internationally renowned.

Place mats and serviettes on heavy white Scarlett fabric, silk-screened by hand with an original design of a provincial flower. They were designed by Lil F. Robertson of Studio Arts, Lancaster, N.B.; *The National Film Board of Canada.*

Handmade, painted cork disks with dowel set in were created as coasters by Roger S. Wright of Canadian Cork Craft, Riverview, N.B.; *The National Film Board of Canada.*

Child's rag doll in Eskimo design covered in cotton or calico and filled with foam rubber, created by Anthony and Eleanor Paine of Saint John, N.B.; *The National Film Board of Canada.*

A display of hooked rugs from the School of Handicraft, Quebec; *Province of Quebec Film Bureau.*

17th century French-Canadian furniture: Pine cupboard and Salamander chair.

French-Canadian furniture: Chair, handwoven tray, table, and carved head.

Examples of hand-screened place mats of original Canadian design created by Nina Lepage of the Silk Screen Studio, Ste. Marthe-Sur-Le-Lac, Quebec; *The National Film Board of Canada.*

Handmade Quebec snowshoes; *Photo by Gerry Lemay, Sherbrooke, Quebec.*

Wood carving by M. Bourgault, Saint-Jean-Port-Joli, Quebec; *Gerry Lemay.*

Pottery tea set by Tess Kidick, Jordan, Ontario.

Leathercraft by Jean Agnew; *Canada Pictures Ltd., Toronto.*

George Couchi, an Indian, with some of his wood carvings of wild life.

Carved and painted linoleum mural "Ontario Wild Life" designed by Thor Hansen, executed by Art Thorn; *B.A. Oil Photo.*

Manitoba

This loon, handcarved in Manitoba birch, oil stained and waxed finish, was created by W. C. Friesen of Winnipeg, Manitoba; *The National Film Board of Canada.*

Northern Manitoba's The Pas, although now a modern community, has never lost the frontier atmosphere and many links with its storied past are still preserved. Visitors "North of 53" find The Pas a good spot to shop for the colourful beadwork and buckskin items made by the Cree Indians in the area; *Department of Industry and Commerce, Manitoba.*

Pottery candle holders created by Studio Pottery, Winnipeg, Manitoba.

Pottery lidded containers created by Studio Pottery, Winnipeg, Manitoba; *photos by Department of Industry and Commerce, Manitoba.*

Pottery coffee set created by Studio Pottery, Winnipeg, Manitoba.

Mocassins made
by Saskatchewan
Indians.

Hooked mat made by Mrs. Cecil Copeman,
Regina; *University of Saskatchewan Extension
Division, Saskatoon, Sask.*

Enlargement of Indian beadwork Medallion, Saskatchewan; *University of
Saskatchewan, Extension Division, Saskatoon, Sask.*

◀ Original sampler, telling story of the life of Johanne Larsen, Wauchope,
Saskatchewan; *University of Saskatchewan Extension Division, Saskatoon,
Sask.*

Alberta

A handmade stoneware ceramic lidded container created by Ed Drahanchuk
of Calgary, Alberta; *The National Film Board of Canada*.

These unique hanging planters, handmade with a high-fired stoneware body and glazed tops, were produced by Ed Drahanchuk Design Associates, Calgary, Alberta; *The National Film Board of Canada*.

Bag and trinket box made from wheat straw by Mrs. Stagg, Okotoks, Alberta, during the 1930's; *Photo by G. Garon, High River, Alberta.*

Ukrainian Handicraft; *Ukrainian Women's Association of Canada, Edmonton Branch.*

Ukrainian embroideries, Mundare Museum; *Alberta Government Photograph.*

British Columbia

Mrs. Louie Phillips of British Columbia shows how her "modern" Indian work compares with ancient man's handicrafts.

Pottery in glazed stoneware created by the Dexter Studio Pottery, Okanagan Mission, B.C.; *The National Film Board of Canada.*

Place mats, tote bags, wall hangings, and hasti-notes in Haida Indian or Eskimo design. All items are made in homespun or burlap, in assorted colours, and silk-screened. They were created by Okanagan Cabin Crafts Limited, Vernon, B.C.; *The National Film Board of Canada.*

These mukluks and this replica of an old fishing hook were made by the Great Bear Cooperative, Fort Franklin, N.W.T.: *The National Film Board of Canada.*

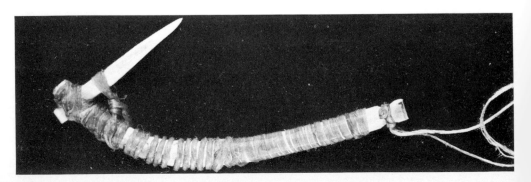

piece hung festoons of dried apples and corn. The housewife made marmalades from wild fruits, mint water, cordials, apple mose and apple crowdy. In her frost-proof cellar she stored salt pork and ham, hogsheads of corned beef, tonnekins of salted shad and gaspereaux, dried codfish, kilderkins of lard and firkins of butter.

THE PENNSYLVANIA GERMANS (DEUTSCH)

After some years of breaking the soil in Pennsylvania, a group originally from the Rhine Valley learned of free tracts of land in Britain's northern colonies. Nine families decided to emigrate again. These people have become known as the Pennsylvania Dutch, and as Deutsch was corrupted, so were their names over the years. Stief now has become Steeves, Lutz Lutes; Treitz now is Trites; Johnnes is Jones; Schmidt, Smith; Reicker, Ricker and so on.

To them goes the honour of establishing the first permanent settlements at present day Moncton, then known as "The Bend." They hacked out their homes from the forest, building first log cabins, then frame houses, and finally a few brick ones with bricks handmade from the clay along the banks of the river. They favoured the type of building they had known in their homeland, and in Moncton's Free Meeting House, built in 1821 and occupied by every denomination worshipping in the city, traces of German architecture still can be seen in the roof supports.

Their first crafts were simple, suited to their immediate needs. The men hollowed out pine logs to make large troughs. These were filled with river water which was allowed to stand until the mud settled. Then the water was poured off into iron pots and boiled down for salt needed to preserve their fish and game.

They learned how to make maple sugar and syrup from a friendly Acadian, and constructed birch bark containers, wooden spiles, wooden shoulder yokes to carry wooden sap buckets to log fires. Wives and daughters helped their men hold maple and ash strips in steam above boiling water, until the wood became supple enough to carve into snowshoes. The men liked caribou hide for lacings, and often used the Bear Paw snowshoe shape to wear travelling in snowy bush country to their trap lines.

When they had succeeded in growing flax, these early settlers spun thread for sewing and linen on handmade looms. Many housewives made straw hats for their daughters out of wheat straw.

Making soap was another household chore. The women added water to a barrel of hardwood ashes and leeched it off to obtain lye to add to the fat they had saved. It took one woman one whole day to make a barrel of soft soap which would pour into small dishes.

SCOTTISH, IRISH AND SWEDISH

During the long wars with Napoleon, Britain made a great effort to open up the forests in the New World for pine masts and lumber to supply her navy. New Brunswick, with its untouched stands, received special attention. About 1800 a number of Scottish merchants established agencies in Saint John, and soon New Brunswick-built ships, loaded to the gunwales, were pitching and tossing their way across the Atlantic. Frequently they returned with immigrants, English, Scottish and Irish, who wanted to pioneer in the province.

Many of these newcomers fanned out through the countryside to farm, or to become part of New Brunswick's great era of shipbuilding. On the Miramichi, Alexander Rankin was a Scotsman who became head of Gilmour, Rankin and Co., and feuded with Joseph Cunard, brother of Samuel Cunard, founder of the line of famous merchant steamers, who had established a great timber empire on the south bank of the river. These men joined other Scottish settlers, pre-Loyalists and Irishmen who had been in the British Army, and were already settled in the Miramichi area.

Irish immigration was also heavy during the 1800's, but because many came without capital they were forced to become labourers at Saint John, and on the Miramichi. Some farmed at New Ireland, Mechanic Settlement, St. Martin's and many other places. After the failure of the Irish potato crop in 1847, they arrived in even greater numbers. Thousands died of cholera en route and many were buried in a common grave at the immigration station on Partridge Island, off Saint John harbour, where a memorial stands today.

During the early part of the twentieth century a number of families arrived from Sweden and settled at Nordin. Some families moved to the United States, but there are still a number of Swedish names in the vicinity today. And in 1872 the first large group of Danish settlers arrived to settle in the upper Saint John valley.

New Brunswick boasts the first Danish settlement in Canada, and the largest. The story of New Denmark is one of disappointment, courage and renewed faith. Lured to the province in 1872 by the promises of a glib Land Agent, the Danes expected to find cleared farms and comfortable lodgings. Instead, after leaving their side-wheeler river boat at Grand Falls, they inched over a rutted road to find stump-covered hillsides in the centre of wilderness.

These Danes, and others that followed, toiled from dawn to dusk, wearing homemade wooden sabots when their leather shoes gave out. With grim determination they built log cabins and shoved back the forest. The housewives cooked on drum stoves, square cast iron boxes on legs, chair-high, with ovens shaped like long cylinders several feet above the stove tops. Homemade tallow candles supplied the only light, but each family treasured a loom and spinning wheel.

Though life was hard in the new settlement, often there would be a barn raising or a quilting party. In the fall each farm had a "Folsgilde," a sausage feast, at hog butchering time. At get-togethers, they sang their old country songs and performed gay dances.

On the seventy-fifth anniversary of their arrival, the National Film Board did a documentary film, and although there had been no organized effort to preserve old world traditions or handicrafts, enough Danish costumes came from old trunks to be worn for the outdoor dances to tunes played by a handful of old-time fiddlers. The girls wore snowy aprons over long, dark full skirts, laced bodices over white blouses, and perky caps tied under their chins. The men's double-breasted vests with double rows of brass buttons were topped by handmade stocking caps ornamented with tassels.

A descendant of these Danish settlers has become a noted New Brunswick sculptor. He is Winston Bronnum who had a habit of carving horses with a jacknife on his school desks as a very small boy. During his years on his father's farm, and later, as a high rigger and bridge supervisor in Ontario, Bronnum traded his jacknife for better tools and began turning out remarkably life-like animals.

In the 1950's Bronnum returned to New Brunswick to devote all his time to carving, and he won first prizes at the Pacific National Exhibition in Vancouver and the Canadian National Exhibition in Toronto for his sculptured horses and buffalo. One of his carved plaques now hangs in the Grand Falls High School; a commissioned Beaverbrook Coat of Arms is displayed in the Town Hall, Newcastle, and another of red granite adorns the grounds of Canada Hall of the Hebrew University in Jerusalem.

Bronnum's most impressive work is the recent creation of Animaland, an outdoor exhibit near Sussex. There, sculptures of wild animals are displayed in their natural surroundings, deer, moose, otter, beaver, wild cat and others. Bronnum devised a method to reproduce his sculpture in Portland cement concrete, reinforced with steel to enable it to withstand the elements and the test of time. One area of Animaland is a children's garden where the youngsters are permitted to play and climb all over the sculptured elephants, turtles and swans.

HANDICRAFTS

In 1937 the New Brunswick Department of Education joined a Dominion-Provincial Youth Training Project to train rural young people in long forgotten handicrafts. The courses set up included carpentry, weaving, sewing, crocheting, needlepoint, quilting and rug making. It also included art appreciation, instruction in the preparation of foods, physical and health education, and clubs to study local economic problems. The month long courses were held in sixty-two different communities and over two thousand girls alone attended. Six hundred of them specialized in weaving. Many boys learned to design and make furniture from New Brunswick birch and maple.

The program continued until 1939. That year at the graduation ceremonies of the Carleton County Vocational School, the girls wore tailored skirts of handwoven tweed and lacy wool sweaters they had produced themselves. At Fredericton, Saint John and Moncton, graduates of the project held fashion shows and modelled coats, suits and dresses they had woven from native wool.

The Youth Training Project lapsed with the start of the Second World War, although the skilled knitters continued to supply sweaters, gloves, mitts, socks, helmets and scarves for the Armed Servicemen. After the cessation of hostilities New Brunswick again thought of handicrafts. So, in 1946, the province invited a well known Maritimer, Dr. Ivan H. Crowell of McGill University, to set up a Handicraft branch with headquarters in Fredericton.

Dr. Crowell, known far and near as Bill Crowell, was born in Nova Scotia and educated there. He graduated from Teacher's College and taught a manual training course in Nova Scotia for a few years before taking forestry at the University of New Brunswick. Later, he graduated from Miami University and Harvard University where his speciality was plant pathology. Still later, Dr. Crowell taught at Mexico State College, then McGill University. While at McGill he started a hobby club as a means of helping students earn while learning. That club developed into a full fledged department at the University, and during the war years, Dr. Crowell was in charge of training instructors for hobby camps and Red Cross Hospital assistants.

With the inauguration of the new handicraft program in New Brunswick, Dr. Crowell arranged to have qualified and talented instructors sent out around the province to teach men and women, some in groups in community or church halls, others in their own homes. New Brunswick-made looms were supplied for the weaving courses, available for purchase at a nominal cost at completion if students so desired. Materials were supplied for all courses. Included among the many courses were basketry, corkcraft, jewellery in copper and silver, weaving, woodworking and leathercraft. Hundreds of people took advantage of the opportunity to learn and, later, to earn.

When Fundy National Park in rugged Albert County was opened in 1950, the New Brunswick School of Arts and Crafts was set up under the direction of Dr. Crowell. There, visitors and tourists registered for instruction in a variety of crafts. Some made sheep shearling slippers or a change purse in a day. Others, on a week's vacation, learned to weave scarves, towels, luncheon sets. Men flocked to basic wood turning classes, making lamps and bowls while their wives fashioned lampshades.

Each year the Fundy National Park classes have grown in popularity. Teachers, tourists, even children from all over Canada and the United States often register a year ahead for admittance. Classes run from early July to late August, and the craft program has been expanded to include enamelling, copper work, polished stones from Fundy shores set into metal, handmade sterling silver jewellery, stencilling and fabric painting.

Today, New Brunswick's ambitious and hard-working craftsmen have organized into community groups. Members of these key organizations meet regularly to arrange courses, plain projects such as local exhibitions and discuss problems. Among them are the York County Craftsmen, Hampton Handicrafts, Sussex Crafts, Carleton Arts and Crafts, Woodstock Weavers, Craftsmen of Saint John, Moncton Handicraft Guild, Cottage Craft Limited, and many others. Each worker in the province has the privilege of joining the New Brunswick Craftsmen's Council.

Throughout the summer months a number of local craftsmen display their work at several New Brunswick Tourist Bureaus, and nearly all have work for sale at their own studios, or in various gift shops.

WOOL

The history of sheep raising in New Brunswick goes back to the early Acadian settlements when animals probably were shipped to the farmers from France, along with a few cattle, horses and pigs. There is a record of sheep along the St. John river near St. Anne's (now Fredericton), which were destroyed in 1785 by soldiers under orders from Brigadier Robert Monckton.

The rich intervales along the St. John river produced vegetables and grain of all kinds, including hemp and flax. On the river islands the people raised hogs, heifers, calves and sheep, fattening them on ground nuts and nourishing long grass.

Like the Acadians, the pre-Loyalists settlers gave over one corner of their barns to workbenches, where chairs, tables and shelves were made, as well as equipment for use on the farm, including wool cards and looms. Although some spinning wheels were brought from Massachusetts, many were hand made, the smaller wheel for spinning flax, and the larger one for spinning wool.

During this period, two Scotsmen, William Davidson and John Cort established the first English-speaking settlement on the Miramichi river. Sturdy Yorkshire settlers sailed direct from England and joined a group of New Englanders who already were established on the rich marshlands of the Isthmus of Chignecto.

All these settlers found sheep raising profitable and many had their own sheep marks burned into the ears of their animals. Some are listed in an old Town Book of Sackville, a copy of which is in the Archives at the New Brunswick Museum. As soon as young girls were old enough they were taught to knit, and to spin and weave material for clothing, and coverlets for their beds.

For in spite of all their regular work, the women had to find time to weave and spin. Wool and flax was raised on nearly every farm and each household had both a flax wheel and wool spinning wheel. The spinner sat at the flax wheel, but spinning required the spinner to step swiftly back and forth for a good day's work of six skeins of yarn, in which she would have walked over 20 miles. Nearly every household had a handmade loom and the wives and older daughters

84

produced the ordinary clothing and bedding for all the family. As the settlers became more prosperous, tailors and dressmakers visited the homes and remained until all the sewing had been accomplished.

COVERLETS

The weaving of coverlets, one of the earliest developed home crafts, was thought to be peculiar to the United States. Shortly after he established the Handicraft Department in Fredericton, Dr. Crowell stated that coverlets had been woven in New Brunswick, and set out to prove his statement by visiting old farmhouses by the score. He found the first coverlet near Welsford, and others followed in quick succession. Today he has a large and valuable collection of the craft which reached a high development over two hundred years ago.

The woollen yarn for the coverlets was raised on New Brunswick farms, carded and spun by the women and vegetable dyed. Most were woven in blue woollen yarn on a white cotton background, although many different colour combinations were used. There were three main types: the overshot was the most common with its slightly raised pattern; the summer and winter coverlets were woven on a six or eight harness loom; the third was woven with a double geometric pattern. Some were woven on a fine linen warp with blue yarn. Still others were all pure linen. One of the finest coverlets in Dr. Crowell's collection is a rare blue and white geometric, woven by a man, James Crawford, about 1780. Another valuable one dates from 1790 and is all linen.

Almost at the doors of the farmhouses were the plants used to make the rich vegetable dyes, colours which remain as bright today as when they first were prepared two centuries ago. Some were the same dyes used by the Indian craftsmen before them.

As the settlement grew in prosperity, carding mills appeared on the scene. One of the oldest still doing business on the same site today is Briggs and Little Woollen Mills at York Mills, near Harvey. They were established by George Lister in 1857, as a custom mill doing carding work for the local farmers. Alexander Little took it over in 1901 and his descendants run it today in new quarters, producing hand knitting and rug hooking yarns, partly from pure native wools.

In Moncton the Humphrey Woollen Mills originated "Humphrey Cloth" in 1881, a heavy material for pants and overcoats. By 1965 the mill had become the largest in the Maritime provinces to produce fine quality woollen yard goods. It is owned by the Collie family of Appleton, Ontario, and managed by John D. Collie. Sales director is William A. Humphrey, fourth generation descendant of the founder.

The Copp Woollen Mills at Port Elgin produced fine woollen blankets for many years, both white and coloured, in addition to knitting and weaving yarns. Brown's Woollen Mills at South Nelson used to produce weaving and knitting yarns. St. Stephen Woollen Mills in Charlotte County was another producer, and the Golden Grove Woollen Mills near Rothesay specialized in knitting yarns. It was one of the few mills to card wool in rolls for hand spinning. It also made the well known hand-woven New Brunswick floor rugs.

All the mills prefer using Maritime-raised wool. "It has a finer strand, is softer and easier to weave," they say. "Unfortunately it is getting scarcer all the time. Local farmers just are not raising as many sheep as they could."

WEAVING

Weaving is New Brunswick's favourite handicraft. Craftsmen use both local wheeling woollen yarns, imported worsted yarns and a great variety of cottons, linens, rayons and metallics in twist and speciality threads. The beautiful blended yarns originated by Dr. Mowat are spun into warp and weft yarns, and used for weaving into the two-harness homespun so characteristic of Charlotte County.

Most weavers belong to community groups and exhibit at community shows. Among local groups producing outstanding work are the Woodstock Weavers, who make placemats, towels, scarves, ties and ladies' and children's wear. They also have taken innumerable prizes in open competition on both provincial and national levels and are making a splendid contribution to provincial weaving. There are other groups at Hampton, Sussex, Saint John, Moncton and many lesser centres producing on a smaller scale.

Most of the community groups and individual weavers received their original instruction from the Handicrafts branch under Dr. Ivan H. Crowell. His chief instructor and probably the most outstanding creative weaver in the province today is Mrs. Adele Ilves, who came from Toronto in 1948 at Dr. Crowell's invitation to take over the weaving department. Mrs. Ilves was born in Estonia where she received her first training in handweaving. She studied in England on the student's exchange and came to Canada before the Second World War to continue her studies at the Ontario College of Art.

The practical weaving course Mrs. Ilves introduced to New Brunswickers proved very popular and is still in use. The looms and all weaving equipment that are made in New Brunswick, are sent out on a rental basis, and instruction is given to small groups. If the students decide to carry their weaving further, more advanced lessons are given later. No other province in Canada has such a wide weaving program and it has attracted national attention. Mrs. Ilves was invited to Regina by the Saskatchewan Arts Board in 1957 to introduce her methods of teaching and conduct a weaving course there.

In recent years she has spent much time developing new ideas and experimenting with new threads, colours and patterns to keep up with the ever changing trends and tastes of the buying public. And each summer for two months Mrs. Ilves teaches weaving at Fundy National Park at the Craft Summer School, where she has received international recognition for her work.

Her weaving has received numerous awards at Canadian National exhibitions and her rug, the "Month of May," received one hundred per cent rating at the Women's International Exposition. Other pieces were shown at the National Gallery of Canada, National Fine Crafts exhibitions and numerous other galleries.

COTTAGE CRAFTS

The oldest group of weavers in New Brunswick, and one of the oldest in Canada, is Cottage Craft Limited, at St. Andrews, Charlotte County. It owes its origin to the interest and imagination of the late Dr. Helen Grace Mowat, artist and author, who revived the art of spinning and weaving in her home district about 1914.

Dr. Mowat had a capital of ten dollars when she first established Charlotte County Cottage Craft. An artist who had studied in New York and England, Dr. Mowat interested women all over the county in hunting out old spinning wheels and weaving looms, and producing beautifully blended yarns for skirts, suits or coats in homespun tweeds, with knitting yarns for sweaters to match. She showed them how to make woven shopping bags, rugs, chair seats and blankets, and designed rugs for them to weave and hook, patterns to adorn the bags and chair seats. She taught them to abandon commercial stamped patterns and instead, incorporate local seascapes, farm scenes and events into their work.

The products from the New Brunswick farm homes did so well that Dr. Mowat was paying her workers more than twelve thousand dollars by 1921. The business was operated until after the Second World War when Dr. Mowat passed it to the son of a college friend, Mr. William Ross.

Today, as Cottage Craft Limited, the weavers make a range of twenty shades complemented by heather mixtures and checks. All the distinctive yarns reflecting the colour of New Brunswick continue to be dyed and spun locally. Cottage Craft Limited has maintained steady production and today its weaving products are still more widely known than any other.

Another group of weavers at St. Leonard in Madawaska county have established a wide reputation for the quality and range of their work. The Madawaska Weavers Limited, owned by A. J. Gervais, started out as a family business with family workers, but expanded rapidly until it now has both men and women working in a modern studio producing "tissus Madawaska," for ladies' and children's skirts with wide borders in metallic threads; men's neckties; scarves, stoles, purses and bags, all bearing the approval stamp of the Guild of New Brunswick craftsmen. This seal represents, in conventional form, the "fiddle-head," the curled head of the ostrich fern, one of New Brunswick's greatest spring delicacies. Many other weavers and craftsmen in different fields also carry this mark of quality, and sketches appear on handicraft paper wrappings.

TAPESTRIES

The New Brunswick Handicraft Department artists and craftsmen have produced ten unique tapestries since 1961. These now hang in the ten tourist bureaus in the province and each one portrays a story. Some represent Indian legends, others are historical.

They were designed by a staff member, Mrs. Margery Donaldson, an artist who graduated in Fine Arts from Mount Allison University. Actual weaving of the tapestries was done by Dr. Crowell on an upright tapestry loom. Tourists who watch the Reversing Falls at Saint John also see his fine tapestry telling the Indian legend of the Fall's origin.

At Woodstock they can admire the tapestry depicting Snowshoe Island, one of several oddly shaped islands in the St. John river, believed by Indians to be the footprints of Glooscap. In Moncton there is the tapestry story of how the robin received his red breast and the Indian legend of how the trees turned red in the autumn.

At Gagetown the studio of the well-known Loomcrofters occupies the oldest building on the St. John river. Once a storehouse from which supplies were distributed to the early settlers, the studio proudly displays a handmade grain shovel carved from a single piece of wood. Established about 1949 by Miss Patricia Jenkins and Miss Muriel Lawrence, the Loomcrofters have several dozen women scattered throughout the community, who spend many hours every week weaving in their own homes and doing the fine finishing work. As director for the Loomcrofters, Miss Jenkins was commissioned by the Royal New Brunswick Regiment to weave a motor robe for presentation to its honourary colonel, Lord Beaverbrook. Miss Jenkins also designed a tartan with symbolic significance: forest green for New Brunswick's vast timberlands, light green for its meadows, blue for rivers, lakes and sea, gold for its mineral wealth, red for loyalty to the Crown, and beaver brown to express appreciation to Lord Beaverbrook. When the robe was finished and presented in 1958 to Lord Beaverbrook, it won wide acclaim. The Premier of the province at that time, Hugh John Flemming, liked it so much he announced the New Brunswick government would adopt it for an official tartan. It was officially approved by the Court of the Lord Lyon in Scotland, and registered also in Ottawa and Washington.

This was not the Loomcrofters' first achievement. The Misses Jenkins and Lawrence designed a distinctive tartan during the Second World War for the RCAF Pipe Band to wear on its Canadian tour. This beautiful tartan in azure blue, dark blue, crimson and cream became the official Royal Canadian Air Force tartan, and is the first tartan outside the British Isles to be recorded by Lyon-King-of-Arms in Edinburgh, Scotland.

The quality of the Loomcrofters' weaving has brought them many outstanding commissions, including drapes and rugs for Lady Sheila MacDonald of Scotland, and articles of wearing apparel for Mrs. Eisenhower, Mary Martin and Greer Garson. They wove New Brunswick's gift to Queen Elizabeth in 1951, and to Princess Margaret in 1958. In 1961 the City of Fredericton tartan was designed by them and registered. In 1962 the Lion's Tartan, the official tartan of the Lions Multiple District 41, which includes the flags of three nations, was designed by them and registered. This also is the official tartan of the New Hampshire Lions. In 1963, Miss Jenkins designed and registered still another official tartan for the Highland of Haliburton, Ontario.

The Loomcrofters also weave a wide variety of other things, including luncheon sets, tea aprons, towels, runners, baby shawls, drapes, afghans, suiting tartans and tweeds, and all bear their own hallmark of quality, a hand-loom.

HOOKED RUGS

With little material available to cover floors, pioneer mothers utilized the last fragments of worn out clothing and bedding to draw through pieces of handwoven linen to make mats for earthen or rough board floors. Pioneer fathers surely built the sturdy wooden frames to hold the backing, stretched tightly to the frame, for hooking. During the 1930 depression period, rural families in New Brunswick frequently used potato sacking as bases for their hooked rugs. As a craft, rug hooking seems to flourish more extensively in the Maritime provinces than anywhere else in the world at the present time, and rural areas have been happy hunting grounds for dealers who traded cheap floor coverings for many fine old mats.

True original primitives are hard to find and many modern hookers use ready-made designs and commercial dyes instead of the soft, muted colours obtainable with vegetable dyes of great grandmother's time. Most of the early primitives have flowers, farm animals and household pets in their designs, and are eagerly sought by collectors. Some bear the monogram or initials of the hooker hidden in the pattern but it is almost impossible to find one dated prior to 1880. The New Brunswick Museum owns the oldest New Brunswick hooked rug with a date. In it, the design is a haphazard arrangement of a dove, eagle, vase of flowers, house, and a cow beside a tree. The inscription reads: "Worked by Abigail Smith at New Maryland, 1860." (New Maryland is outside Fredericton). This rug is worked almost completely in wool with a small portion of some coarsely knitted wool fabric in small background areas. The design is very similar to those on samplers which little girls stitched at the beginning of the nineteenth century.

Next in popularity to the primitives are the geometric designs often broken up into tiny squares with larger portions of Hit-and-Miss. There is romance in some of the old pattern names – Irish chain, Sunshine and Shadow, Patty-pan, Thistle, Shamrock and Rose, Steeple, and Whip. Sometimes geometric centres or borders were heavily combined with floral designs, roses being the most popular. Often the flowers were raised up from the background and sometimes clipped. This type of rug was known as a "raised" or "riz" rug.

Modern hookers prefer to use wool instead of woollen materials. Landscapes, nautical and animal designs, conventionalized flowers, all are popular, along with the whimsical half-moon shaped Welcome mats, lying just inside the front door. Nearly every farm woman in New Brunswick can hook a rug; those in the St. John river valley, descendants of the United Empire Loyalists and later Irish and Scottish settlers are especially noted for their dexterity. So too are the Acadian-descended people of the Memramcook valley.

Another type of early hooked rug is the Corn Husk Rug, in which it was necessary to keep the husks steaming hot while working, in order to make them pliable. One such rug worked in the Gagetown area over a hundred years ago is still in existence in almost perfect condition. The attractive maize-yellow of the natural husks predominates, with a simple leaf pattern and border carried out in green-dyed husks; the green still is brilliant and shows no signs of fading.

Rug making is not a prerogative of the women in this province; many men are accomplished hookers, including Charles Keith of Coverdale, while another, Dr. J. W. Dodson of Moncton weaves beautiful woollen rugs on a large floor loom.

CHURCH EMBROIDERY

Embroidery is an handicraft so ancient its origin is lost in the mists of time. In New Brunswick today richly coloured embroidery in original and imaginative designs is being produced by a number of devoted women who are giving new vitality to the art of religious needlework. Mrs. Ronald McNeill of Fredericton is one of several women in the province skilled in this art. She holds regular classes in her home where the needlewomen produce pieces for many churches in the Anglican diocese. They work together or separately, each one helping the other, and have turned out vestments for St. Mary's, four complete sets for the new St. Anne's Church in Fredericton, and work for Trinity Church and Mission Church in Saint John, and churches in Kingsclear, Newcastle, Durham Bridge and many others. These women use original designs indigenous to the province wherever possible.

In a white altar frontal recently made as a memorial and presented to Christ Church Cathedral in Fredericton, Mrs. McNeill combined both history and religion to produce her design, in which a Tudor rose, fleur-de-lis and bean leaves were worked into the superfrontal pattern above a large gold frontal cross. Used since the thirteenth century as a symbol of the Christian faith, the Tudor rose is emblematic of the Loyalists who brought the Anglican faith to New Brunswick when they arrived in 1783. The fleur-de-lis honours Father Biard, a French priest who conducted the first know Christian worship on the St. John river. The bean leaves represent a hidden horde of beans miraculously discovered by starving Loyalists during their first winter at St. Anne's Point, now the city of Fredericton. Mrs. McNeil also created for the Cathedral the green Trinity frontal. The beautiful design is derived from the painted trillium, a New Brunswick wild flower.

The late Mrs. Harry C. Cameron of Moncton was a local pioneer in this type of slow, exacting church needlework, beginning over twenty-five years ago when she made a book marker for the Bible in St. George's Church, Moncton. Today, worshippers in St. George's church, West Saint John, gaze upon her beautiful handiwork on brocades, moires and linens every Sunday. So do parishioners in Campbellton, Salmonhurst, Shediac Cape, Richibucto, Moncton, Andover, Taylor Village, Nashwaaksis and St. Martin's. Mrs. Cameron took eight months to complete antependia for St. James Church in Moncton when it opened in 1958. She made a complete set in red brocade, edged with gold fringe; fashioned white pulpit and lectern hangings, four green hangings, and a four piece purple set emblazoned with gold crosses in silk floss and metallic. Her favourite was one of her own design for the Nashwaaksis church. It was embroidered with grapes in various shades of purple enhanced with blended green leaves.

Another woman who specializes in ecclesiastic embroidery is Mrs. Dorothy E. Burden of Saint John.

In New Brunswick the earliest forms of needlework go back to colonial days when little girls were taught their stitches by working samplers, squares or rectangles of coarse hand-woven linen. Usually there was a border of flowers, the alphabet, and the numerals, a bird or two, a small farm scene, a verse, the name and age of the workers, the date and place.

During the latter part of the nineteenth and the early part of the twentieth century, New Brunswick women turned out very attractive teacloths, tray cloths, tablecloths and napkins, in eyelet embroidery and heavy satin stitch. Some were trimmed with yards of hand-knit lace, produced with fine spool cotton threads on steel needles. This varied in width, from one-half to four inches wide, and the patterns often were handed down from mother to daughter. Some maiden ladies are known to have made their living producing lace-trimmed embroidered luncheon cloths, pillow slips, dinner cloths and napkins, sitting hour by endless hour with their needles and threads.

Mrs. Archie Nixon of St. Andrews attained fame for her embroidery as Mary Helen Gilman, with work of her own design. A tea cloth on which she worked a design representing a Charlotte County fair with a procession of livestock and fair patrons, now is the proud possession of the Royal Ontario Museum. She also worked one for the New Brunswick Museum with original designs representing the four seasons. After the First Great War she worked runners for the British Empire Exhibition which depicted New Brunswick industries and recreations including pie socials, country dances and rural skaters.

Miss Marion Walker and Miss Marguerite Davis turned out an exquisite piece of petitpoint to carpet the chancel and steps of St. Paul's Anglican Church at Hampton. It took them three years to complete the petitpoint carpet, dark wine with a pattern of gold trefoils.

A husband and wife duo, Lt. Col. and Mrs. George Blakney who live near Moncton began needlepoint as a hobby several years ago. Now, Lt. Col. Blakney has taken over the work almost entirely, and his reputation with the needle has gone far afield. Blakney needlepoint and petitpoint pictures have travelled to Ontario, Alabama, New Jersey, Massachusetts, Montreal and Toronto. One of his most dramatic pieces is "Christ in Gethsemane," worked in blues and purples. This huge picture requiring 72,000 stitches and 220 hours of work, hangs now in the auditorium of the Wesley Memorial United Church in Moncton.

Lt. Col. Blakney works from charts mounted on heavy cardboard and hung at eye level on an easel-like stand. His second invention to speed his work was the preparation of two dowel sticks the exact width of the canvas, and fastened so that he can roll up the needlepoint as he works. The selection of colours is frequently his own and he always trams his work so that each stitch has another thread beneath it exactly the same colour. He uses a number 21 needle for needlepoint and a smaller one for petitpoint.

TEXTILES AND SILK-SCREENS

One of New Brunswick's foremost artists, Miss Violet Gillett, ARCA lives in a century old home overlooking the St. John river at Andover. A graduate of the Normal School in Fredericton, she studied at the Ontario College of Art and became an artist in the Department of Medicine and Pathology at the University of Toronto. She obtained her degree at the Royal College of Art in London, England, and later studied on the continent. When the Saint John Vocational School was built, she was invited to establish its new Department of Fine and Applied Arts, a position she held until 1947, when she went to New York to study sculpture. Returning to New Brunswick, she established, with her sister, an Art and Handicraft Studio at Andover, where she turned her talents to producing hand-stencilled fabrics and gift articles that caught the flavour and atmosphere of her native province.

As Miss Gillett saw it, New Brunswick was a distinctively picturesque region: a land of covered bridges, sleigh rides, colourful lumberjacks, stream drivers, country stores, salmon pools, hills and valleys, maple sugar camps, fertile farms, orchards and beautiful wild flowers. It is on such subjects Miss Gillett bases her designs, stencilling drapery fabrics, silk dress materials, scarves, aprons, luncheon sets, shopping bags, caps and children's pinafores, and many other things including pottery and etched glassware. Her unusual silk dress materials on which she pioneered hand-printing in New Brunswick, bear such intriguing titles as Choke Cherry and Cherry Bird, Humming Birds and Columbines, Jack-in-the-Pulpit, and Purple Iris. Her colours are clear and vivid as those produced by nature herself.

94

Two of the newest applied arts to be developed in New Brunswick are silk-screen tapestries and textiles. Contributing to the development are Anthony and Eleanor Paine, who arrived in 1963 from England to teach art in Saint John schools. As independent craftsmen they devote all their spare time to decorative arts, painting, print-making and creating striking designs on brilliantly dyed machine-woven cottons. Their lengths of fabric are fifty inches wide.

They recently had an exhibition of thirty wall hangings at the Confederation Centre Art Gallery in Charlottetown, and the New Brunswick Art Centre at the University in Fredericton. In 1965 they were invited to display their work permanently at the New Brunswick Museum in Saint John.

Several other silk-screen artists in the province are also producing good work. Notably among them is the team of Lil and Syd Robertson in Lancaster. They produce hand-cut stencils with their own original designs, and make table settings in jute and linen, aprons, bridge sets, coasters, and a series of their own hasti-notes and greeting cards. In addition, Mrs. Robertson makes wall hangings in white duck with silk-screen designs suitable for children's rooms. She also turns out small cotton books for children, doing her own illustrations and text.

DOLLS

To the late Dr. Mowat of St. Andrews goes the honour of creating New Brunswick's best known character dolls, many of which are now in private and Museum collections. These are Cottage Craft dolls created in Charlotte County and are the soft, stuffed type, dressed entirely in homespun to be representative of the early settlers. The small men sport whiskers and sideburns of wool, gray and fuzzy. They wear soft homespun trousers, snug red jackets, gray mitts knitted with thumbs in them, black hats with woollen crowns and wide navy brims. The women are dressed in long heather-coloured skirts, with red knit petticoats, blue jackets and yellow mitts to match homespun waists, with white wool ruffs cascading down the fronts. Realistic gray wool hair is parted and drawn back into buns. They wear black bonnets trimmed with clusters of roses and carry muffs hooked and cut in regular rug technique. Dolls representing children frequently have skates on their feet or carry snowshoes.

Modern New Brunswick doll makers turn out stuffed dolls of various types; other women make and dress dolls in Colonial, Loyalist and historical costumes. Some also create home-made wigs for their dolls, while others specialize in handmade doll clothing. Mrs. Harold Betts of Riverview, graduate of a doll making course, created a series of nursery rhyme dolls with all their individual settings. These are on display each summer with a world-wide collection of dolls at International House, on Prince Edward Island.

An art student who turned her talents to doll making, Mrs. E. D. (Nel) Walsh, is renowned throughout New Brunswick as "The Puppeteer." For the past thirty years she has been creating puppets and staging her own original shows in private homes, public auditoriums and on television. She constructs her figures of rockwall, asbestos, flour, salt and water mixed together into a workable substance. She shapes small heads with exaggerated features and bakes them in her kitchen oven. They then receive garish paint jobs with heavily made-up eyes to project down into an audience. The puppet bodies are either the rag doll type, or carved from wood and fitted with mortised joints. Mrs. Walsh prefers the latter type because they are the most agile.

About five years ago Mrs. Walsh began making character dolls for collectors. She spends hours in research on clothing, hair style, jewellery, footwear, and makes numerous sketches and drawings to bring her dolls to life with as much authenticity as possible. Mrs. Walsh works closely with the New Brunswick Handicrafts branch, and her dolls are on display each summer in the Tourist Centre at Saint John's Reversing Falls.

Her one-of-a-kind dolls include The Loyalist Lady of the late seventeen hundreds, with bouffant skirt, lace shawl and mob cap. The Fundy Fisherman wears corduroy trousers tucked into rubber boots, bright skirt, red sweater, oilskins and the Fundy sou'wester. A New Brunswick Indian is togged out in buckskin, leggings, breech-clout, tunic and moccasined feet. Touches of bright beadwork adorns the costume.

Nel Walsh also operates a doll hospital and can re-make and repair any type of doll, however old. Several dolls from Museum collections have reached Mrs. Walsh for expert repairs.

QUILTING

Quilting is still as popular in New Brunswick today as it was several hundred years ago. It is the most ancient of crafts in countries all over the world, and the patchwork quilt as we know it is a merging of two of the oldest forms of decorative handwork – the piecing together, and the actual quilting. The first New Brunswick quilts were square patches joined together in a Hit-and-Miss pattern to make the common quilts for everyday use. Not many have withstood the wear of years. The best quilts treated with special care have survived, and many New Brunswick families treasure them still.

Each girl's dower chest had quilts ready for the frame and finishing, but it was not until there were serious intentions that the bride's real quilt was started. It may have been all white, relying on intricate quilting patterns for its beauty; or, it may have been colourful applique such as the old Rose of Sharon, Wedding Ring, single or double, and the Star patterns. Quilting bees were popular occasions during great grandmother's day when friends from miles around joined forces to finish the quilts with their finest stitches. And it was a good way to catch up on news and local gossip.

Members of Women's Institutes, Church groups and hundreds of individual workers in New Brunswick continue to produce beautiful pieced and appliqued bed covers with superb quilting. This very large group of workers exhibit at all country fairs and provincial exhibitions and some take top honours. Although they are not organized into any one group, their total contribution in the craft field probably equals that of any handicraft group in the province.

POTTERY

Various types of pottery were made in New Brunswick during the last century, but unfortunately most pieces were unmarked. The first potter, Samuel Bullen, lived in Saint John where he took out his freedom papers in 1797. In 1832 James Ellis made pottery at Dipper Harbour; Robert Brittain at Saint John, in 1838; John Thomas at Portland Point in 1849; the Valley Pottery was operated in Portland by a Mr. Thompson in 1849, and the City Pottery by Henry Robertson of Saint John in 1863. He brought out Newcastle-on-Tyne potters to work in his pottery.

In all these the main products were stoneware crocks and jugs, bean pots and large quantities of Rockingham ware.

The most outstanding New Brunswick potter of the past was Francis Clementson. He manufactured large quantities of printed ware and his mark has been found on pieces depicting such old landmarks as The Victoria Hotel, Saint John. He began business in 1859 and was burned out in the Great Fire of 1877.

The Foley Pottery of East Saint John is very well known locally. It started in 1862 as Warwick and Company, and passed to Joseph White upon his arrival from England in 1864. With him were his two sons, James and Fred, and a daughter, Mrs. Charlotte Foley.

The three Whites made teapots, bean pots, cream pans and stone crocks. They later were succeeded by Mrs. Foley's sons, James and Fred Foley, and as the Foley Pottery the business has been carried on continuously ever since. Some years ago it was given the name Canuck Pottery, because a large part of production was in souvenir goods sold to Americans, and looking for a connection, the Foleys chose Canuck, the American slang word for Canadian.

Over the years the old stoneware crocks and bean pots were discontinued, and modern production centered around fancy vases, ash trays, bon bon dishes, etc., sold under the name Evangeline Ware. The new name was chosen because the clay was from the Bay of Fundy shores and many plant operators were descended from early Acadian settlers. The plant burned in 1965 and unfortunately moved its operations to another province.

Some small brick making concerns operated from time to time in various sections of the province, and a few old houses still standing, contain bricks made by the original owners, utilizing clay from nearby river banks.

Many New Brunswickers have experimented with local clays, but none so successfully as Danish-born Kjeld and Erica Deichmann, who became Canada's internationally recognized potters.

Although they began experimentation when Kjeld, trained in art and wood sculpture, discovered clay on the farm he had bought on the Kingston Peninsula, they later obtained their supplies from Middle Musquodoboit, Nova Scotia. When fired it produced hard gray stoneware.

Connoisseurs compare Deichmann stoneware to the golden age of Chinese ceramics of the Sung period, 960-1279 A.D. The Deichmanns produced the same simplicity of form and hardness of glaze the Sung potters achieved, but they also recaptured glaze effects rare since that period. One is the unusual purple patch, a red blush on a light blue or green glaze.

Around 1958 the Deichmanns moved their pottery to an old house in Sussex where thousands of visitors saw their original and exciting work in both handmade stoneware and porcelain. They created bowls, plaques, jugs, pitchers, vases, pendants, plates and many other interesting art forms designed by Erica. They actively experimented with technical problems and produced as many new pieces as when they began. After Kjeld's sudden death, Erica packed away their work and closed the pottery. Today, Canadian Museums and Art Galleries feature displays of the best Deichmann pieces, and private collectors horde their own treasures.

BLACKSMITHS

Without the skill of men who worked in iron, the lot of the pioneers in clearing land and developing the country would have been much harder. Their demand for handmade nails, plough shares, hinges, horse shoes, pokers, rods and many other essentials, kept the local blacksmiths on the job year in and year out. The blacksmith shops usually were low frame buildings with doors wide enough to allow a team of horses to be driven inside. The forge and chimney were a mass of masonry for the red hot fire fanned with heavy leather bellows.

Many local blacksmiths had fine reputations for their winter sleds and bob-sleds, others were famous for the skates they turned out. The Whelpley family on the Long Reach of the St. John river were famous for their skates and later established a skate factory where they standardized the shape, size and equipment. Known as the "Long Reachers", the Whelpley skates had long blades and a screw in the heel to prevent side-slipping.

As the need for blacksmiths lessened in the twentieth century, many turned their talents to other fields. Some continued the work as a hobby and turned out wrought iron candelsticks, door knockers, hinges, garden furniture and so on.

A Saint John man named William Sonier whose Acadian ancestors once had a busy blacksmith business in the Memramcook Valley, is today a well known craftsman in wrought iron work. He specializes in fine furniture, both modern and traditional, interior and exterior railings, lanterns, signs, candelabras and decorative pieces. He hand forges and hammers his work in shop and forge at his East Saint John home. Thousands of hammer marks form intricate patterns on his glass topped tables and dining chairs. Mr. Sonier has won top awards for design and workmanship at the Pacific National Exhibition in Vancouver and several Canadian National Exhibitions in Toronto. During the summer months he and his wife own and operate the Old Lantern Shop at Penobsquis near the road junction to Fundy National Park.

As was customary in the early days, most local cabinet makers also were undertakers. In Saint John, Fredericton and Woodstock, the Loyalist settlers who combined these talents turned out some fine pieces of furniture for the homes that were beginning to replace the first crude dwellings. The pieces extant today have become treasured pieces of Canadiana, some still in private homes, others in Museum collections.

Three styles of chairs have become identified with these New Brunswick craftsmen. The first was the familiar ladder-back; the second, the arrow-back, nearly always painted black; the third type was associated with Saint John cabinet makers and featured sloping backs ending in rabbit ears. The cross splat was wide, and halfway down four upright rungs were set into a narrower splat. The seats were heavy and carved to a sloping front.

The Museum in Saint John has chairs of the latter type marked with the maker's name, Humphrey, and his place of business, Portland, north Saint John.

The firm of Hunter and Ross worked in Fredericton as early as 1788. They made furniture for Judge A. Ward Chipmen of Saint John, shipping it down river by sloop. The business address on all Hunter and Ross letters is the Fredericton gaol where they were imprisoned for debt, and they probably made their furniture there, including Chipman's "small neat chest of drawers."

In 1820 William Kent was working in Fredericton producing household furniture "in the neatest manner," as he advertised in a local newspaper. The Museum at Saint John has a set of three beautiful chairs in the Regency style, with cabriole legs, and a fine boot chest with a divided closet. The chest has small bun feet, probably hand shaped. All are made of white walnut (butternut) polished to a dark golden colour, by Samuel F. Jones who was manufacturing chairs as late as 1842 in Fredericton. Many New Brunswick craftsmen used butternut for their wood and the furniture, therefore, is very distinctive.

In Woodstock in 1858 and 1859, cabinet maker R. B. Davis was producing spinning wheels for twelve shillings six pence and upwards, and tables for ten shillings up. At Emery's today in Saint John, fine craftsmen still are handcrafting beautiful pieces of furniture (footstools, fender benches, TV stools, chairs, etc.) to order, and some amateur workers throughout the province are turning out good individual pieces for their own use.

Other woodworkers in the province specialize in native bird's eye maple to turn out looms, chair frames, stools, benches, tables, desks, lamps, book ends and novelty boxes.

The firm of Lordly, Howe and Company had a long career in Saint John. Albert J. Lordly, who had been born in Chester, N.S., began to make furniture in Saint John in 1854. John D. Howe, a native of Saint John, learned his trade with Lordly, and set up a factory at Moss Glen on the Kennebecasis river with his brother Jonas in 1860. Then they moved back to Saint John and became partners with Lordly in 1869.

After several disastrous fires the Howes dropped out and set up a separate firm, J. and J. D. Howe in 1886. They became quite well known for their children's Boston Rockers. These chairs were 22½ inches high, and the originals had stencilled and painted ornamentation.

Foster, Fowler and Company made kitchen chairs near Upham for some years, and Thomas Nisbet was another cabinet maker who produced mahogany secretaries with fall fronts in the 1820-30 period near Rothesay.

Between 1785 and 1800 the pioneer settlers along the St. John river and its tributaries were making their own furniture for the first log cabins and later frame houses. One of the most unusual pieces the pioneer craftsmen turned out was the curious Washademoak table-bench, named after the lake near where it first was built. No record exists of the first maker but a few table-benches have remained to this day – we saw one in a summer camp near Gondola Point.

It was a wonderful piece of furniture and had many uses. Made of many different kinds of native woods, knotty pine, birch, bird's eye maple or basswood, the Washademoak table-bench frequently was left in its natural wood finish. Sometimes it was oiled and rubbed smooth. Infrequently, it was painted.

Basically it was a wooden chair with a deep drawer across the front.

The arms were flat pieces of wood in one with the sides. These supported the round back made of planks, which, when lowered over them, formed a round flat table. Used as a table at mealtimes, the owner needed only to remove a wooden pin, or unfasten a hook, tilt the top up, and move it against the wall, and presto, it became a chair.

The Washademoak table-bench went out of style about 1849.

WOODWORK

Woodworking is done differently in New Brunswick from anywhere else in Canada. Every step has been changed and improved including the method of preparing wood for turning and the way in which wood is dried. New kinds of chisels are used, new ways of sharpening them and different techniques in using them; the sanding, polishing and the finishing are also all new and different.

These major developments were evolved at the Provincial Handicraft Department in Fredericton by Alfred Pringle, head instructor with the department, and are the first material changes in hundreds of years. His new method of drying wood resulted in a new industry for Stanley, N.B. Mr. Pringle teaches the subject to hundreds of people, including many industrial arts teachers from Canada and the United States, who come to him each summer to learn his special methods, and see the famed "Pringle touch," at the School of Arts and Crafts at Fundy National Park.

Today more New Brunswick men than women do woodturning. Mr. William Bruce of Kingston turns bowls, mortars, lamps and candy dishes from native woods in his own original designs. Harold Clarkson of Cross Creek specializes in rough-turned kiln dried bowls, sandwich plates, candlesticks, salts and peppers which he will either finish for a purchaser, or allow them to finish. Lloyd Cove of Moncton turns TV stools, sandwich trays inlaid with Lodge emblems, needlepoint frames and salad bowls from native bird's eye maple. He also uses imported woods, teak and ebony to make coat buttons and earrings. Mr. C. C. Parker of St. Andrews holds seven awards from the Canadian National Exhibition for his skillful turnings. He uses mainly native hardwoods and his original designs for salad tossers and herb mullers are his best items. Several woodcarvers in Saint John and on the Fundy Islands, Grand Manan and Deer, carve graceful seagulls and mount them on pieces of polished driftwood. Mr. and Mrs. Pen Starr of Rothesay produce hand carved pins, pendants and earrings as well as wood turned pieces.

Much of the finest woodcarving in North America was done by local craftsmen in Saint John, when New Brunswick and Nova Scotia-built ships sailed the seven seas in the nineteenth century. Edward Charters was an early Saint John woodcarver who had a very famous pupil named John Rogerson, his nephew, who arrived from Scotland in 1849, at twelve years of age, to learn the trade. Rogerson became the best of the local carvers, creating many of the splendid figureheads that graced New Brunswick's speedy sailing ships. His most common was the full length female figure, larger than life size, and always of pine to withstand the weather and salt water.

Rogerson was both an artist and a craftsman. The figureheads of several pieces of wood dowelled together gave the suggestion of flying forward, and the flowing drapery a sense of speed, so that silhouette and contour were more important than detail. Examples of his work are in the Kendall Whaling Museum, the Bourne Museum and the New Brunswick Museum, while private collectors cherish pieces of his work.

Rogerson also carved pulpits, pillars and capitals for many of Saint John's churches: the Young Memorial in King Square, and the President's Chair for the St. Andrews Society for which he collected wood from seven different countries. Some authorities claim the intricately carved chair his best work; others feel The Pine Lady was his masterpiece. He completed The Pine Lady in 1877, after working all winter with mallet and chisel in a loft studio over a grocery store, while his daughter Helen patiently modelled the draperies.

The Pine Lady was painted and trimmed with gold leaf and placed in a box, packed with shavings, and shipped to the Rexton shipyard of J. & T. Jardine on the Richibucto river. There she became the figurehead for the ship *Wacissa*, and sailed the Atlantic sixty times. Her twin sister made for *Ticoma*, also a Jardine built ship, now is the property of the New Brunswick Museum.

A carved wooden lion over a doorway on a house opposite the Roman Catholic Cathedral, Waterloo Street in Saint John, is also Rogerson's work and can be seen today.

Another well known carver was John Howe, the furniture maker. He did the beautiful carving for the altar in Trinity Anglican Church, Saint John.

Carvers, gilders and painters made a very good living a century ago by making advertising trade signs and carved wooden figures to stand outside particular shops. Carved boots were trade signs of a shoe store or repair shop. Livery stables had wooden carriages and horses on hanging signs; there were golden teeth, golden fish, big cigars and carved wooden Indians for tobacconists.

SILVERSMITHS

A French soldier by the name of Pidart seems to have been the first recorded silversmith in the Maritime provinces. In 1703 he was using a furnace, bench and iron moulds in the establishment of M. de Brouillan at Port Royal, to convert French silver coins into silver plate. In fact, he used so much silver that he caused an acute shortage of coins, and greatly embarrassed the French officers who needed the money for legal tender.

The arrival of the United Empire Loyalists in 1783 marked a turning point in the history of the silver craft in the provinces. John Booth worked in gold and silver around 1796 in Saint John, producing silver teaspoons and gold rings. John Rule, who dated his work, made silver plate in 1798. Examples of his work are in the Museum in Saint John. Jeremiah Brundage, a Loyalist from New York, worked first in Saint John in 1785 as a blacksmith. In 1794 he took out his freeman papers as a silversmith and set up shop. A quantity of spoons bearing his initial JB, and a little sunflower punch, are seen today in various parts of New Brunswick. The New Brunswick Museum owns a helmet-shaped cream pitcher with a small bright-cut border around the rim bearing his hallmarks.

Another Saint John silversmith who worked from 1795 to 1828 was Alexander Munro. He had a son, John, who became very well known as a silversmith, working from 1813 to 1864 at that trade. There is probably more silver in the province bearing the initials of John Munro than that of any other craftsman. He devoted the latter part of his life, from 1864 to 1875, to the production of Victorian jewellery, another branch of the trade. He used designs from gothic to rococo to North African, which he worked into the very popular hair jewellery. The lockets he made often showed a tomb or an urn, with locks of hair set under glass on the reverse. One of them contained the hair of sixteen persons arranged in a sheaf of wheat bound with gold and small diamonds.

Possibly one of the first pieces of silver made by a Loyalist is a silver bowl now on display in the New Brunswick Museum. Four circles stamped just below the rim contains the initials WB, with the weight of the silver engraved on the bottom. This bowl was the work of William Brothers, who was supposed to have melted all his available silver into bars before leaving his American home, and carried it to Saint John where he was able to begin work as a silversmith soon after his arrival in 1783.

The most outstanding silversmiths in the province today are a husband and wife team, Mr. and Mrs. Barth Wttewaall of Sussex. Their silvercraft is the outcome of a course given by the Handicraft department under Dr. I. H. Crowell. Lucie, the former Baroness van der Feltz, and Barth Wttewaal arrived in Canada from Holland in 1938 to open a greenhouse in Sussex; they now create beautiful silver work as a hobby, using their family crest for their hallmark.

When a silver necklace set with gemstones took first prize and full points at the Canadian National Exhibition in 1954, no one was more surprised than Lucie Wttewaall because she had designed and made it only seven and a half months after completing her basic course. Other handwrought silver pieces took first and second prizes the following year, and again in 1956 and '57. Since then the Wttewaalls have continued to win top awards at both national and international shows. Now they create brooches, pins, bracelets, forks, spoons, cuff links and tie pins, and often spend an entire evening to achieve the right tapering for a spoon.

Another husband and wife jewellery team of note are the Mittons of Moncton, Kenneth and Mona, who work strictly on a hobby basis to produce beautiful and unusual bracelets, earrings, pendants, pins, rings, tie-tacks, bars and cuff links. An amateur prospector, Kenneth Mitton, has been cutting stones since 1954, specializing in agate, bloodstone, jasper and chard from Nova Scotia, and carnelian, jasper and epidote from New Brunswick.

Mona Mitton has been doing silverwork since 1958 over a basic course with the Handicraft department, and two other advanced courses. She does the original designs and the silverwork for her husband's stones, and recently won third prize at the Canadian National Exhibition for creative work. The piece was completely handmade and boasted the biggest agate ever cut and polished by her husband. The Mittons have a registered hallmark.

The first record of glass making in New Brunswick was in 1857, when the first Saint John business directory to be printed carried an advertisement by G. F. Thompson & Co., which called itself "Stained Glass Manufactury, the only one of its kind in British America."

The Thompson company, after building a factory for glass making, manufactured church windows, hall windows, dome lights, side lights, fan lights and stained glass. They were in business until 1868 when they retired to manufacture only lead paint.

The New Brunswick Crystal Glass Company followed with incorporation in 1874, and the shareholders were all prominent Saint John business men. Their factory was located at Crouchville, and workers made window glass and bottles with blow-pipes. The glass was used in greenhouses, and the bottles mainly for aereated water.

The Maritime Art Glass works followed in 1900 and produced a large number of stained glass windows for Saint John residences and churches. Stephen Cusack, who worked at stained glass windows in this firm, identified The Guardian Angel in the Church of the Assumption in West Saint John, as a Maritime Art Glass piece and said it had been designed by a Saint John artist, the late Percy Woodley.

Moncton also had a Glass works — the Humphrey Glass Company, dating from the 1915 to 1920. The Humphreys began in Trenton, N.S., with bottles of every description: fruit jars, glass rolling pins, patent medicine bottles, flasks, lamp chimneys, globes and fly traps. As production increased the Humphreys brought in additional glass blowers from Belgium, Bohemia and the United States, and moved to a better location in 1901. From then until 1915 they made tumblers in twenty-one different styles, salts and peppers and vinegar cruets. They turned out some fancy designs in pressed glass where objects were held against revolving stones, using sand and oil. Their Victoria pressed glass plates and comports of that period can be seen in the Nova Scotia Provincial Museum at Citadel Hill in Halifax, and the Royal Ontario Museum in Toronto.

Attracted by natural gas in Moncton, the Humphrey brothers decided to move their business to that city in 1915, and take advantage of the cheaper cost of production. Their output, however, was limited to lamp chimneys and globes, and when natural gas rates went up in 1920, the firm ceased operations.

In the early part of the century it was the custom of itinerant glass blowers to set up booths at regional exhibitions, blowing fanciful novelties such as birds of paradise and little boats. William Quinn was a Saint John boy who used to help the glass blowers when they set up at Saint John exhibitions. Consequently he became an expert at blowing whimsies.

Moncton today has only one glass blower who blows strictly as a hobby. Donald Boudreau produces swans, deer, vases, Christmas tree ornaments and birds. He works in a basement workshop in his home and blows from tubes of coloured glass.

5 ❧

Quebec

CARTIER WAS THE FIRST FRENCHMAN to be chosen as leader of a serious effort to plant a colony in Quebec. It is recorded by some that he had been to Brazil and perhaps to northern waters, so besides his daring and skill, he knew something of an Atlantic crossing. He and his sixty sailors, blessed in the Cathedral at St. Malo, sailed on April 20, 1534, in one little ship. Their crossing was prosperous and in three weeks, they reached the mouth of the St. Lawrence river at the Strait of Belle Isle. As he sailed westward, he noted how barren the shore was. At one haven, he met a French fishing vessel from La Rochelle. Then he turned south reaching what is now Prince Edward Island; again changing his course, he coasted New Brunswick and reached Gaspé. Here he was welcomed by natives, who seemed very poor. The French gave them beads and trinkets, and the Indians offered furs. It was at Gaspé that Cartier raised a thirty foot cross with the shield bearing the fleur-de-lis and the carved scroll "Vive le Roi de France."

Thus begins the story of what is now Quebec, the oldest of Canada's ten provinces. And while it might at first appear that the history of Quebec crafts cannot begin before 1608 and Champlain's first permanent settlement at Quebec city, we must remember that this land was by no means unpopulated when the white man came, and that the peoples he found here were skilled in unique and important crafts of their own. Hence no survey of Quebec's handiwork could hope to be complete without a study of our first citizens.

THE ESKIMOS

The Eskimos, of Mongolian origin, are not tall people, but are sturdily built and well muscled. They are strong and resourceful, else they could not survive the long winters and big storms of the Northland. The short summer lasts about two months beginning in July. The sun is high and does not set for several weeks. The flowers and birds are everywhere, so also the mosquito. The winter is much longer, and the days short. The sun disappears for several weeks, when a few hours of twilight each day are the only relief from darkness.

This is the background for Eskimo life. Their clothing has to suit the climate, so they use the skins of caribou and seal, principally; though polar bear, fox, and other furs are useful. Eskimo women tailor the hides, making the garment fit the person who will wear it. They are skilful with a fine needle or awl and use caribou sinew mostly for thread, sewing with fine, even stitches and taking pride in well fitted garments, carefully mended, if necessary, to keep out the cold. Boots of sealskin with tight double seams keep the feet dry in all weather, and mittens are fashioned to suit the season.

However, as the Information Division of Department of Northern Affairs states in the Canada Year Book 1957-58 edition, "Greater penetration into the Arctic from the south, and the unstable precarious fur market, a decreasing game supply, and an increasing population, have combined to alter the long established patterns of Arctic life very rapidly."

But nothing indicates the reality of this change so dramatically as the tremendous success of the modern Eskimo's stone work. Eskimo soapstone carvings are world famous. The demand for soapstone has in fact been so great, that further supplies of it, some quarried in Brome County, have been shipped to centres where the Eskimos work. They are very modest about this art, keeping their best carvings carefully wrapped up, and they show them reluctantly.

These carvings are now purchased through the trading posts of the Hudson's Bay Company, and marketed by the Company and the Canadian Handicraft Guild. Calculated steps have been taken to protect this native art and to give as high a return as possible to the Eskimo artist. Their ivory and soapstone carvings, although lacking intricate design, are indisputably distinctive works of art.

Fame has come to an Eskimo woman, Mrs. Jeannie Snowball, who fashioned a bug-eyed owl which became a hit over-night. The owl was made of sealskin, but because of the high cost of sealskin and the great demand from children around the world, supplies are now getting low. Ookpik, the name given to the toy, is now being manufactured by machines, as the Eskimos were unable to keep up with the demand. The Fort Chimo co-operative handles them as well as sealskin rugs, kayaks and soapstone carvings produced in the area.

INDIANS

Quebec has over 25,000 Indians now, most of whom still live on Reserves.

From a list furnished in December 1961 by the Indian Affairs Branch of Quebec's Department of Citizenship, we note the following craft specialties done on the several Reservations. At Maliotenan and Seven Islands, wonderful bead work is done on moose and buffalo skins. Mocassins and embroidered and beaded leather coats are produced. At Schefferville, Montagnais and Nascopie Indians do attractive crocheted wool work as well as leather work. At Romaine, Ningan and Natashquan lovely bead work is done, but unfortunately they lack a market. One notes the work of Charles Courtois, artist wood carver at Pointe Bleue. He depicts typical scenes of Indian life. At Maria, the Indians specialize in making baskets in over thirty designs from sweet grass. Beautiful leather, beaded coats, belts, purses, canoes, snowshoes and moccasins are all manufactured at Loretteville (Village Huron). At Odanak, baskets of ash, sweet grass and some synthetic materials are made, while at Maniwaki Indian dolls are to be noted as well as the leather work.

Fifty years ago the Indians appeared to be dying out due to disease, indifference of the white people and neglect, but now they are increasing at the rate of about three per cent a year. The Director of Quebec Indian Homemakers Clubs journeys among these groups, encourages them and hopes these skills will become a real factor in the economic advance of the Indians.

Nowhere were crafts so numerous and so varied as in the homes of our forefathers, whether French or English. The first homes were built of logs. Notching these logs to fit together was a craft in itself. Moss was gathered and used to fill small uneven places, and later mud was applied. In time, lime became available, and the chinks were plastered. All log cabins had peaked roofs with two slants. In the beginning, fireplaces and bake ovens were built of stone at one end of the log structure. A few of these may still be seen, but most were replaced many generations ago. The iron cookstove, using wood for fuel, has passed through many fashions and today is losing favour as gas and electricity become increasingly popular.

When Jean Talon was Intendant in 1660, the typical settler's home had one large room with a loft above. In the room the family lived and prepared all the food. As in the old country, some smoked meat and dried herbs hung from the rafters, but our climate in summer prevented storing fresh meat this way.

SPINNING AND WEAVING IN QUEBEC

In the earliest days of the French colonies on the St. Lawrence, little attention was paid to the skills of spinning and weaving. The many wild animals furnished furs and skins for garments. The traders, coming from France, brought woollen cloth and wool yarn for knitting. Indeed, those in charge did not encourage home industries of this kind, for it would have lessened the ship's cargo from France. Domestic animals were introduced, a few at a time, and increased in numbers as the years passed, so that a few decades later the wool from the sheep became the means of establishing a delightful home industry which is still important in French Quebec.

Talon visited the farms, encouraged the men to clear the land, and aided them to get seeds to produce grains and vegetables. In the homes, he insisted that the women learn to spin and weave. He introduced and encouraged the cultivation of hemp and flax in Canada. In 1669, linen, drugget and serge were woven on a scale large enough to meet the needs of the population and a surplus of 44,200 pounds was sold to Louisiana and the Antilles. In November 1671 Talon wrote his King: *J'ai des productions du Canada, avec la laine des moutons, de quoi me vèter du pied à la tête.*

For a long period the housewife had to work with natural wool and unbleached linen, but the desire for self-expression, anchored deep in her soul, sent her searching for bark, leaves, grasses, berries and nuts that field and wood provided. Vegetable dyeing is as old as civilization, and the happy housewife, through her experiments and her creative instinct, brightened her home with the colours she longed for.

The introduction of English textiles to dress the new British subjects in Canada caused a gradual decrease in the home industries. In 1830 however, 13,500 looms were functioning in Lower Canada, and importations were increasing, either as raw material or partly processed. So came the period when home industry gave way to mills.

In the Archives at Ottawa is an old print of a Woollen Mill owned by the British American Land Company in Sherbrooke, which along with the Paton Woollen Mills in Sherbrooke was the first in Canada where the entire process of making cloth was carried on. This wool craft has continued in Quebec for three hundred years. In the annals of Megantic County we read of a wool mill at St. Patricks, where the sheared wool was cleaned and processed to make cloth.

Then came an era of larger woollen mills, with machines. Itinerant men, with wool gathering carts, scoured the countryside, buying the raw wool by weight, and selling yard goods and blankets to the farmers. These woollens were always very durable, and the plaids and stripes were artistic as well.

The difficulty of reaching the only markets at Montreal, Three Rivers and Quebec was a great drawback. From ten to twenty days was needed for an ox team to make the trip to and from these places. Sometimes they went by boat down the St. Francis, the Chaudière or the Richelieu, taking along pearl pot ashes. These were among the first marketable products of the early inhabitants of the southern part of Quebec.

Mr. Jesse Penoyer tells of his efforts to secure Government aid to develop the hemp industry in the Eastern Townships. This ended in failure and hemp growing was finally forbidden by law as it contained marijuana.

FARM UTENSILS

During the summer days the men were always busy on the land, but the winter forced them to spend some time indoors where they directed their industrious bent to the making of household necessities. There are still wooden dust pans cherished as souvenirs, and the old mortar and pestle was a homemade tool, used to grind corn, peas and wheat ready for food. The butter bowls and trays, the butter print and its flower or acorn print were other items which took many hours to make. In the barn, all the troughs were made with tools wielded by skilled axemen. Pumplogs too were prepared by hand axe and gouge. It is only in this century that these craftsman have been really replaced.

At first water was carried, as it still is today in some eastern countries, by fitting a wooden yoke about the shoulders and hanging a bucket at each end. Buckets were made of staves of wood coopered by a craftsman. The same kind of bucket was used in our sugar bushes for over a hundred years, and not many years ago they could still be seen in some districts.

The next advance from carrying water in buckets was the laying of pump-logs and fashioning pumps of wood. This was not easy, but again skill won. Wells were dug nearer the houses and sides walled up with field stones, carefully placed.

THE RENAISSANCE OF HANDICRAFT

IN QUEBEC FROM 1930

An article in *Canadian Geographic Journal* states:
"There were always a few older women who continued to weave on their ancient looms, but there was a time when rural art in the Province of Quebec almost became a thing of the past. Fortunately, in the County of Charlevoix, around Murray Bay, and on the South Shore, at L'Islet, Kamouraska and Temiscouata, the old patterns were cherished and were handed down to modern weavers. Different agencies contributed to the revival of crafts. The Canadian Steamship Line, the Canadian Handicraft Guild, the railroads, the Cercles de Fermières, the Ecoles Ménagères, all helped, and in 1929 the Quebec Government ordered an investigation into the condition of home industries. It was found that in almost every part of the province, the old technique had been lost and the old looms had fallen into decay.

"The women were eager to learn everything pertaining to these neglected crafts, but the facilities were lacking. Hence the decision of the Department of Agriculture to create an organization for the revival of handicrafts and rural industries in this province. Observers visited other countries and collected specimens of rural art, particularly weaving and spinning. Hon. J. L. Perron, at that time Quebec's Minister of Agriculture, introduced to the Legislative Assembly the programme for reviving the handicrafts, which was formally begun on June 10, 1930.

"Today, the outlook is most promising for handicrafts in Quebec and the credit for the revival of these handicrafts should go to the Department of Agriculture. The extension service of Home Economics and Handicrafts sends its travelling staff of technicians to answer the requests of Cercle de Fermières, Women's Institutes, Junior Agricultural clubs and 4-H Clubs the year round. Mr. Oscar Beriau, Director-General of Handicrafts in Quebec Province for many years, was one of those most interested in this renaissance.

"An out-growth of this revival was the formation of a new group of weavers in the Eastern Townships known as the Valley Weavers Guild of Quebec. It was organized in 1961 and is the first weaving group in the province to be registered with the Guild of Canadian Weavers. But many weavers and various groups work throughout the province and all testify to the satisfaction and pride of being able to weave cloth for any home requirement.

"A visit was made to the workroom of one real craftswoman, Mrs. L. Galvin, near Stanstead. She had just completed the spinning of dog hair from combings. Samoyeds gave creamy white yarn while poodles gave brown and black. Her looms were set up; one for place mats, one for rugs; and she displayed beautiful dress materials, all handwoven, as well as smaller articles. Rugs and stair carpeting are woven of coarser yarn or evenly cut rags and the stripes are very colourful. Catalan, woven in forty inch wide stripes can be fashioned into an entire floor covering.

"Miss Emily LeBaron, of North Hatley, using her ingenuity, wove a beautiful set of place mats, using linen and asbestos from Quebec's mines, to accompany a wooden salad set that the Quebec Women's Institute sent as a wedding gift to Princess Elizabeth in 1947."

RUGS

Excerpts from a paper prepared by Madame T. C. LeBeau of the Department of Agriculture, Quebec, state:

"At the beginning *catalogne* appears to have been made and used by French settlers both as bed and floor coverings. Supplies were practically non-existent and means were very limited in earlier days, so *catalogne* was made up of every bit of scrap material procurable.

"Early writers think that the idea of *hooked* rugs came to Canada by English settlers. Some authorities claim that this fascinating floor covering antedated the American Revolution, and some place the time before 1700.

"Born of necessity, the hooked rug was to become an object of rare beauty. French women still remembered the sumptuousness of Aubusson, and many early rugs reflected the elegance of the masterpieces, thus giving French-Canadian rugs the reputation of beauty.

"Environment was a main source of inspiration. Some designs were crude, others well balanced. Picturesque representations of life around the home, the animals, sheep, horses, cats and dogs adorned more than one hearth. Patterns of flowers, leaves and ferns were also often used. Sometimes these were combined in a nosegay, wreath or border. The reproduction of the house was popular too.

"Sometimes these rugs were so precious they were kept face down till a visitor came. With the *catalogne*, upon which they were often displayed, they were quite in harmony with the rustic French-Canadian furniture and all the surroundings."

WOOD

One of the great beauties of Quebec is her forests, and from these forests come some of our chief exports: timber, and pulp and paper products. The wondrous beauty of our maples in Autumn and the maple products of the spring should make all of us in Quebec conscious of the need for conservation of this precious heritage. To the Quebec country dweller, wood has always had a special importance. The early settlers built and furnished their homes and burned acres of beautiful woodland to get potash and perlash, the only product they had that could be sold for cash. But there were much better uses for wood as the settlements grew.

Examples of some early utensils hewn out by pioneers can still be seen today. No place in Quebec has preserved relics of the past more carefully than have the Sisters of the Congregation of Notre Dame at their stone farmhouse opposite Nuns' Island on the edge of Montreal. This stone building was begun in 1681 and has changed little with time. Here may be found many relics; the stone sink hewn out of a single block of stone; the high-posted curtained beds, reminding one of the bleakness of the winters; and in the attic, now a museum, the altar of Mother Bourgeoys, made of white pine and ornamented with faded, painted flowers. Spectacular too are the pine coffers with huge hand-forged hinges brought from France.

About 1690, many homes in Quebec City, Montreal, and at the Manor houses along the rivers, showed furniture advanced from the primitive and beginning the French-Canadian design. The former Sulpician Seigneury at St. Scholastique, now owned by Mr. Roger Burger, is one of the finest examples of the work of Quebec craftsmen.

The work done by hand or with pioneer tools shows plain lines. Maple and birch have long been favourites with wood crafters but nothing is as good as pine if the surface is to be scrubbed often.

Beautiful pieces of carved furniture came from France and later from England to add to the dignity of Quebec homes, then the village shops began to appear and these soon turned out excellent beds, chests and cupboards. In our own commercial, mechanized time, the designs of these early workmen are still often copied.

WOOD CARVING

Wood sculpture in Canada originated about 1675 when Mgr. de Laval, Bishop of Quebec, founded a school of arts at Cap Tourmente, on the St. Lawrence. The purpose of the early carving was decoration of the church, so for about one hundred and fifty years it was mainly religious.

The oldest carvings done by jack-knife were thus of religious subjects, but there were also hand carved spoons and smaller objects such as butter moulds and maple sugar moulds representing flowers, acorns, birds and animals. The sugar moulds were made as covered dishes, so the top could be removed, the sugar poured in, then the top adjusted. When cold, a perfect duck, hen, or even a maple sugar cow appeared.

The tourist in French Canada today will find wood artists who carve from our native wood. Also, among the Indians there is an occasional craftsman who does scenes from Indian life and woodland birds and animals from wood. The crafts division of our rehabilitation centres after the wars introduced woodcraft, and we find technical schools offering such courses.

In *Vocation Artisanale du Québec*, published recently by the Quebec

Government, mention is made of the school of Saint Jean Port-Joli on the St. Lawrence where wood carving is taught, and as early as the nineteenth century the carving of figures of Saints and biblical characters showed the imagination and skill of the workman. Topics varied: the Eugene Leclerc family of St. Jean Port-Joli won a handicraft Grand Prix for their hand-carved schooners. A local subject by Midard Bourgault of "The Day after Election" won a provincial Grand Prix d'Artisant. Other carvings of interest show the animals, community ovens, and farm operations seen in rural Quebec. There is an almost endless variety of subjects to attract the visitor, and the wood sculptors who make Saint Jean Port-Joli their capital, are perhaps the most widely known handicrafters in all Canada.

Special mention should also be made of a fine wooden salad set of bowls, six salad plates and a pair of salt and pepper shakers, that Mr. Frank Libby of Huntingville, crafted for the Quebec Women's Institutes as part of their wedding gift to Princess Elizabeth, now Queen Elizabeth II. It is interesting to know that the black cherry used in the set came from Megantic County where the Duke of Hamilton settled some of his crofters in the early days of this province's colonization.

NEEDLECRAFT

As the humble jack-knife was the tool which created wood carving, so the common-place needle and thread were and are the tools used in all needlecraft. When you examine lists of pioneers who crossed the Atlantic, you always find some listed as tailors, seamstresses and shoemakers.

In early colonial days, the christening dress was always of the finest white lawn or muslin available, and each stitch in the tiny tucks and inserts spoke of endless patience and mother-love as well as skill. So many hours work went into one garment that it was generally worn by each baby of the family, possibly for several generations.

The samplers often done by young girls were used to teach budding damsels perseverance and perfection. Some of these samplers are very beautiful.

Then there was the hemstitching and drawn work. Again, patience and a true eye helped to complete a piece of table linen or bed linen, making it a thing of beauty. Counterpanes were worked in very interesting designs. Petit point and needle paintings which are also stitched are two crafts which adapt old skills to modern needs. One needle painting of a realistic winter scene by Anne Marie Matte won a Quebec Handicraft Award recently.

QUILTING

Quilting was one of the ancient arts developed in the East. When the Crusaders of the eleventh and twelfth centuries returned from Palestine they brought robes of rich materials, quilted, which had been used by day or night in the Turkish and Saracen palaces. Alice Morse Earle, authoress of *Home Life in Colonial Days* or *Early Days in North American Homes*, writes, "The feminine love of colour, the longing for decoration, as well as pride in the skill of needlecraft, found riotous expansion in quilt piecing."

Since cotton grew in the southern States, the idea of cotton patchwork quilts grew very popular in America. The materials woven then were of high quality, a piece of "chaney patch" or "copper-plate," a hundred years old, will be as fresh and bright today as when woven. There was no analine dyeing and no composition or filling used in those cottons of the early American Era.

The early French women in Quebec were taught spinning and weaving, and have always continued this as a home craft. The bed covers were woven of wool or of cotton rags, and a cotton warp was used as it is stronger. Generally the rags are woven in stripes about a yard wide and carefully sewed together to make a covering for a double bed. This type of cover, referred to as Catalan, is often very beautiful. In appropriate colours, it is used also as carpeting on floors or stairs.

When people began to come into Quebec from the English colonies on the Atlantic seaboard, quilts were among their prized possessions. Tiny bits of cloth were used. One quilt pattern, Charm Quilt, had no two pieces alike, so it must have entailed considerable trading among neighbour women to get enough pieces. The Log Cabin, The Rising Sun and The Ox-bow were often used patterns. Square or oblong blocks were also arranged to form designs.

Appliqued quilts, such as Dresden Plate, Flower Basket, Fan and Nursery characters are just as popular in this generation. Sometimes a sash of a dainty petal shade separates the blocks and enhances the beauty.

118

The Crazy Quilt has long been a favourite. Bits of any shape could be used. Pieces of treasured gowns in silk and velvet were preserved thus, and feather stitch and cross stitch, often beautifully done, outlined the many divisions. The Album Quilt became popular as groups of women wanted to raise money for schools or churches. The names of everyone who paid ten cents appeared on the quilt, and we can get quite a picture of a neighbourhood at a given date by examining such autographs.

The filling for the quilt was of wool in the early days, for warmth in those first homes. So, whatever the outside, the filling was placed carefully on the lining, which was firmly sewed to the quilting frames. When the top was in place, the quilting began. Very fine, even stitches were made. This was called a pressed quilt. The quilting itself was done in intricate patterns, circles, tiny squares or leaf and scroll designs.

The Quilting Bee has almost disappeared now. Since it took so long to do this fine sewing, the idea of *tacking* grew in popularity until intricate patterns appeared and the chenille bedspreads came to the fore. Some of these are heirlooms. The idea has been commercialized and now the machine product merely reminds us of grandmother's handwork.

The Federated Women's Institutes of Canada, wishing to revive the old craft, placed grandmother's quilt blocks in the Handicraft Division of the Tweedsmuir Competition in 1957-59. Many of the branch Institutes took part, and samples of the lovely old patchwork and newer and original designs were made. Quebec did not win a prize in the final judging but several of our blocks were taken for the National display, which has been filmed.

Mrs. Richard Brown of Lennoxville, with her Lone Star design in red and white, has been entered in competition in Quebec, winning first place. It, along with first place winners in the other provinces, was on display at the Canadian National Exhibition in Toronto as well as all the large stores across Canada. Another artistic beauty, called the Broken Star, was a first place winner in Quebec competition.

DOLLS

Indian children loved the dolls given them by the traders in Canada's early years. These were of many types. The humble little corncob doll, with its silken hair and a dress of corn husk, and the rag dolls dressed in soft skins or bits of cloth were real treasures. The lovely bisque dolls, or china-headed dolls, were prized by the first English children. Others were made of papier-maché and painted.

It was, and still is, a craft to dress dolls. In many of our museums we can see the dolls of a hundred years ago. One in the Brome County Historical Museum has a china head, golden curls and blue eyes, and the hands and feet are fashioned of kid. She was given to a little girl in 1790 and dressed with great care in clothes of that period. Here too are doll carriages, beds, rocking chairs and bureaus that are perfect in detail and exact miniature copies of similar articles found in Canadian homes, years ago.

The dancing dolls, made of well polished wood with movable joints, entertained pioneer children. One, made out of wood (thought to have been a discarded gun stock), was given to a little boy in 1828, and is still treasured by his descendants.

History is often understood better if we see the character dolls of different periods. The collection of dolls at Ottawa's House of Parliament, assembled by the Parliamentary Wives' Association, shows dolls from each province. Quebec's exhibit includes: Helen de Boulle, wife of Samuel, Sieur de Champlain, 1620; Jeanne Mance, who founded Montreal's first hospital, 1642; Marguerite Bourgeoys, Montreal's first school teacher, 1645; Paul Chomedy, Sieur de Maisonneuve, founder of Ville Marie, 1642; a Lady of Fashion (dressed from a portrait of Sir Hugh Allen's wife); Sister of Nursing and Teaching Orders, 1635-1653; a snowshoer of Montreal's Amateur Athletic Association, 1840.

GEMS

Cutting, polishing and setting semi-precious stones is a craft that is attracting attention nowadays. These stones come from all parts of the world, but Quebec seems to have more than her share. Jasper, amazonite from the Gatineau region, agate in the Gaspé area and serpentine, as well as crystal, are all found in our province.

The craft is an old one, and is carried on in many centres. Men and women who have undergone severe injuries or crippling diseases are among those who find interesting work in this line. The Gem Shop on Ottawa St., Montreal, employs some of these people in an unsheltered workshop where a livelihood may be learned and earned.

Agate is found along the east coast in Gaspé as well as in Nova Scotia. Not too long ago it lay unnoticed on the beaches, but now it is sought so eagerly by those who like to work with stones that it is no longer easy to find.

The process of turning a piece of agate into a beautiful gem takes time and patience. Saws of all sizes and grinders are used. Agate is polished with silicon and put in a bucket-like machine run by electricity, where, in water with abrasives added, the stones tumble about for a month. The reds, browns and silvery greys become more distinct by this process.

Now the stone is ready to be used in rings, pins and other jewellery. Sterling silver is the choice of many experts as a setting for these gems, though cheaper metal settings are used where an article must be sold at a lower price. An exchange of stones from other lands adds variety to the collection. Amber (petrified resin), labradorite from Newfoundland, dolmite from New York State, and to the real collector, stones from Africa, Scotland and Austria prove attractive by their colouring and beauty.

METAL WORK

The earliest deposits of iron were found in La Mauricie, as the French called the valley of the St. Maurice River. Early settlers used the metal for necessities such as horse shoes, kettles, frying pans and other home and farm tools. Next there was a great demand for iron in shipbuilding. Since expert iron workers were hard to find, the French sought them in France and in the American colonies.

When Haldimand became Governor of Canada in 1778, he became much interested in the development of the iron mines. Des Forges is the birthplace of Canada's heavy industries, her iron and steel manufacturing. In this century, the opening of iron mines further north and northeast, which yield fifty per cent or more iron ore, have added greatly to Quebec's wealth.

The demand for fancy trimmings and railings, for metal chandeliers and many small articles have led craftsmen to work again with iron. "Metal work exists in a world whose borders are still undefined," writes Jean-Paul Morisset. The fine examples of the distinct past show Spanish grills and irons of the Renaissance periods, and bronzes of

China. And all point to the use of metals both for useful and ornamental purposes. The present wrought iron railings cannot be compared in design or workmanship with these earlier examples, yet we do see imagination and originality in many of them.

The copper weather-vane or steeple cock, not often seen on newer buildings, is cherished as an example of early craft in many of our museum collections. One of the finest of these is in the collection of Paul Lacroix at Quebec.

Silver is also a metal which craftsmen love to fashion into modern vessels. In the workroom of Marc Beaudin of North Hatley, a Swiss who learned his trade in Montreal, a real craftsman may be seen hammering and raising his precious metal into desired forms. Religious chalices, basins, and medallions are designed here. The latter are enamelled on silver in three colours and are known as *cloisonné* and *plique à jour-types*. The enamel is dried in a kiln.

The beautiful and imaginative work of the late Royce Gale of Waterville also showed a great love of craft. The delicate lines of a poised bird, the simplicity of form in the silver tea service and the wall sconce for candles in iron, illustrated the breadth of his vision as well as the skill of his veteran's hands.

New Canadians have added their knowledge of the metals and the Provincial Winners of the Awards for Silver Chalices in 1962 bears this out. Hans Gehrig and Walter Schluep are names from across the sea and Canada welcomes such craftsmen.

DISHES: MODERN CERAMICS

In the 1800's, ironstone china was made in Saint-Jean, Quebec. The English ironstone was mostly a dull white in wheat and corn patterns, and in lustre tea leaf. Pieces of this old ware generally bear a trade mark featuring a lion.

Dishes were needed for all homes and this, at an early date, led to making pottery. At Massawippi, jars and jugs with soft curves were made. They were brown in colour, glazed inside and with smooth, unglazed outside surfaces. We often see this in old bean pots. Later the same kind of pottery was made on a commercial scale. So the one you have now may or may not be genuine handmade pottery.

At Cap Rouge, long ago, they made platters and plates. They were brown, spotted or stippled with white. About 1850, the Port Neuf potters began introducing borders on their bowls and platters. Some had borders of bow-knots, roosters or strawberries or other motifs in red or blue on a dull white background. Many other simple designs appeared on these dishes. There were also a pottery at Saint-Jean, Quebec, noted for the lion design they turned out. Henry Ford later purchased the Farrar Pottery at Saint-Jean and moved the whole concern to the United States, shrewdly realizing the value of such a possession.

Near the end of the last century, came a period when people had more dishes. Many were imported from England. Ironstone, bone china, porcelain and expensive pieces such as Wedgewood, Royal Doulton, Royal Worcester and many others. Also from the United States and Japan came pretty designs. So our own manufacturing of tableware soon vanished. Now pottery, or ceramics, has been revived as a hobby.

Today one can buy Beauce pottery, highly glazed a royal blue, with simple designs. At North Hatley, Gaeton Beaudin's summer students learn by doing. They use clay, some imported and some from Oka, and the glaze materials are local, the quartzite coming from Capleton. This stoneware is very durable, and the colours vary from brown to green, blue and yellow.

The story of glass making is a long one. The Egyptians made glass by moulding two thousands years B.C. They also knew how to stain it. Later came transparent glass, which was very valuable. In Venice, they specialized in glass for church windows. There are records of it being sent to Britain in the thirteenth and fourteenth centuries. About 1700 A.D. glass became more common. To meet the needs of the present day, the old blowpipe and rod have given way to modern, commercial methods, but pieces of valuable Canadiana were made by these processes.

Where the Ottawa River joins the St. Lawrence, on the northwest, we find Hudson, Hudson heights and the parish of Vaudreuil. Across the Ottawa River is the Indian Reserve and Oka. The beach at Oka is beautiful white sand and on the west shore are small sandy coves. On this west shore, the first Quebec glass was made about 1847. Both clear and coloured glass was made, and among the articles listed are window panes, chimneys, bottles, containers, and, by 1866, insulators of aqua-marine colour.

Known first as the Ottawa Glass Works, then as Canada Glass Co. Ltd., from 1875 on, the glass house declined and by 1891 had fallen in ruins. At about the same time, a glass factory, where lamps were made, was operated at Como in the same vicinity. The clay used was often imported and in 1867 the materials included soda ash, saltpetre, borax and red lead. Other chemicals were added for colouring.

John Spence was the best known pioneer of the art of glass staining in Quebec, though there may have been an earlier one. He produced articles of many colors – honey amber, blue, green and brown. The first glass factory built at Montreal was called the British American Glass Works, later came the Montreal Glass, St. Lawrence Glass and others. Saint John also had an early Glass House, owned by Foster Bros. about 1857. They made covered bottles to carry vinegar, kerosene, and oil in bulk, for which protective woven covers were made. These men had a plantation of willows, and from these came the twigs from which the covers were woven. Here, too, were found plain flint glass goblets made by moulding a non-lead glass.

The variety of the articles made increased. Special pieces called vigil lamps and stained glass for church windows, goblets and other items of tableware, and interesting ball-shaped paper-weights appeared in 1897-1940.

In 1855, at the Universal Exhibition, Paris, listed by Mr. Spence, Montreal, Lower Canada, was a work-table of glass, painted and gilded. This entry aroused great interest and was bought and sent to Sydenham Palace in England, as a nucleus for a permanent Canadian exhibit.

Mr. Harry Norton, Ayer's Cliff, was a collector of fine glass. Some pieces in his collection (163 of Ancient Glass) dates back to 1500 B.C., as well as including Canadian glass. This collection, the finest in Canada, was given by Mr. Norton to the Montreal Museum of Fine Arts. His sister, Miss Helen Norton, gave her collection to the Royal Ontario Museum in Toronto.

REVIVAL OF OLD CRAFTS

This is an age when hobbies are playing an ever increasing part in our way of life; as the work week becomes shorter, many feel the need for something creative to fill their free hours.

Working with driftwood has proved an interesting hobby to many. Where lakes or rivers have flooded driftwood is found. These pieces drift about and finally lodge along the shore. There is great variety in size and shape; some are suitable for making lawn and veranda decorations, and the smaller ones may be used as desk pieces, vases or other ornaments. With imagination, one can see resemblances to birds, animals, fish or other forms.

It is better to choose smaller pieces and clean them thoroughly. Ordinary tools serve – a stiff brush, a gouge or knife and steel wool are all useful. They may be polished with an old toothbrush in any shade obtainable. Paste floor wax or shoe polish also make a lovely natural finish. Pieces may be fastened together to give a support or base. Flowers or candles look well on these homemade decorations. A number of people have found these articles attract buyers, but it is not likely this hobby will grow into a big commercial venture.

A hobby of the nineteenth century, but not seen often now, was the skilful fashioning of figures inside glass bottles. Beautiful sailing ships made piece by piece, and slipped inside the bottle into position with a wire, were exact replicas of ships seen on the seas. Quebecers who live along the St. Lawrence have always had a weakness for this interesting kind of work.

Another hobby which is being developed into home industries is the reconditioning of old furniture. The earliest chairs made in Canada of birch wood were from the Island of Orleans and dated about 1790. Others were built in a straight, plain style with seats woven with rawhide at Chambly and La Prairie. Cane, rush and sea-grass were also used for chair bottoms. These early chairs are now much admired by collectors.

6 🎋

Ontario

IN ONTARIO AS IN OTHER PARTS OF THE WORLD, traditional handicrafts have been handed down from parent to child through generations. In more recent years there has been a movement to foster an interest in these crafts as well as to introduce new crafts, to provide training in craft skills and through handicraft to encourage self expression and creativity.

The Community Programmes Branch of the Department of Education, through its staff of specialists and district representatives distributed over the province, conducts training schools for local leaders in a very comprehensive range of crafts.

Quetico Training Centre at Atikokan in Thunder Bay District, in a federal, provincial and municipal program to retain people for vocations, gives courses in handicraft with the primary purpose of developing people. Instruction is especially directed towards stimulating the students' imagination, originality and pride in the work of their hands.

Hockley Valley School near Orangeville in Dufferin county has a program for the whole family in a wide range of creative arts including spinning, weaving, ceramics and wood carving.

The Home Economics Extension Service of the Department of Agriculture working with Women's Institutes and other women's groups offers courses and leaders' training schools in rugmaking, block printing, copper tooling, leathercraft, and needlework.

And to preserve an interest in the crafts of the pioneers we have replicas of century-old communities at Upper Canada Village near Morrisburg in Dundas county and Pioneer Village near Woodbridge in York. Here visitors can see demonstrations of carding and spinning, weaving linsey-woolsey and plain brown linen, dyeing with natural dyes, pioneers' original old looms in operation, and the still popular arts of quilt and rug making.

The years since the Second World War have shown a steady development in crafts as a commercial enterprise. Some of this grew out of the skills developed as crafts were practiced for the craftsman's personal satisfaction in creative work and to provide articles for practical use in the home or the community. Immigration following the war brought some highly skilled craftsmen or professional artists from Europe, who had no difficulty in finding a market for their work in Ontario. A number of these are serving as instructors in schools or studios and are thereby raising the standard of work of our amateur craftsmen.

INDIAN HANDICRAFTS

Traditional Indian handicrafts are carried on to varying degrees in different communities and by different individuals; and a number of Indians are also showing definite ability and interest in crafts that are not traditionally Indian, such as pottery and printing. In Ontario there is now a general trend among Indian leaders and on the part of handicraft specialists who work with them to concentrate on those handicrafts which have an Indian background, and to have designs reflect the Indian culture, traditions, legends and history.

Mr. Sunahara of Community Programmes (the Provincial Adult Education Branch) says "Teach Indian students basic techniques but encourage them to develop their own designs and to resist being pressed into turning out souvenirs en masse for the tourist trade." The results of his teaching are evident in many places where Indian handicraft is offered for sale.

As children of the forest Indians naturally learned to work with wood, and their craftsmen make everything from axe-handles, canoes and paddles, snowshoes, lacrosse sticks and hickory canes to the finest of wood carvings such as totem poles and replicas of wild life. Nathan Monture of the Six Nations Reserve is internationally known for his wood carvings of heads, some of which are valued at around one thousand dollars. George Couchi also does beautiful carvings of wildlife subjects. Snowsnakes, used in a traditional winter game, are popular with young people wherever they are known.

Some of the early Indian women were expert weavers. They made handsome and durable bags of nettle and basswood fibres, forerunners of the present popular birch bark and sweet grass baskets. They still make boxes and wall plaques of porcupine quill work and floor mats after the style of the old woven rush mats.

Leatherwork is another traditional Indian craft. They specialize in moccasins, usually decorated with beadwork, and in jackets which are generally fringed and sometimes beaded. These are made entirely by hand, frequently from doeskin, and the dealer who takes them to New York is likely to receive an exorbitant price for them. Small leather articles such as belts, wallets, and book covers are also made for the tourist market. Indian beaded jewellery is woven, and such pieces as headbands are fastened to strips of leather to give firmness. Indian corn with its very deep yellow colour is grown especially to make Indian corn bead necklaces.

For souvenirs, Indian handicrafts include rattles carved from cows' horns after the style of the rattles used in some ceremonial dances; Indian drums – tom-toms and kettle drums; boards and pouches for carrying a papoose; masks used in ceremonial dances; corn husk dolls; even Indian clubs – now thought of as a piece of physical exercise equipment rather than a weapon of war.

Another thriving Indian handicraft centre is in operation on Curve Lake Reserve near Peterborough, under the direction of Harry Whetung. Here members of the band from teenagers to old people are earning a steady income producing wood carvings, feathered headdresses, totem poles, moccasins, dolls, leather jackets, gloves and handbags, birch bark and quill work and a variety of novelties. These Ojibwa handicrafts are sold in thirty retail stores across Canada; they are also exported to the United States, England and West Germany.

SPINNING AND WEAVING

Spinning and weaving are two of the oldest crafts practised in Ontario. They were introduced largely by settlers from Scotland, first in 1784 by the Highlanders from British regiments disbanded in New York State following the revolutionary war, later in the early 1800's, by a goodly number driven to the New World by the hard times in Scotland. Most of these Scots settled in Glengarry and farther west along the St. Lawrence. Others came later to Colonel Talbot's settlements in Elgin and Middlesex counties, and through the Canada Land Company to the areas around Galt, Guelph and Goderich. Wool, almost the only textile available to the pioneers, was especially suitable for blankets and winter clothing for our cold winters; and most farmers tried to raise a few sheep, even though the wolves in many districts made this difficult. Most of the work connected with the wool industry was done by women. Late in the spring men would wash the sheep in a creek; the women would then help with the shearing and did practically all of the carding (combing the wool on carding boards), spinning, dyeing and weaving of the wool. In the early 1800's carding mills in most districts took over most of that part of the work, returning the carded wool to the farmer for spinning.

"The wheel used for spinning woollen yarn was a large one, so the operator stood as she worked," writes Edwin Guillet in *Pioneer Arts and Crafts*. "The wool was placed on the point of the spindle and the wheel worked with the right hand while the left held the spindle. As the wheel whirled around, the operator walked three steps back and forward, and the wool twisted and the yarn wound on the spindle. In a day she might walk twenty miles while spinning half a dozen skeins of yarn."

Natural dyes were used to dye wool after spinning or sometimes after it was woven. The "hodden gray" flannel worn by men was not dyed but made from a mixture of the wool from black and white sheep. Some women were experts in getting the colours they wanted for dyeing from native plants, bark and lichens. White maple boiled and set with alum gave a good brown gray. Purslane weed and logwood set with alum gave a bright blue, though indigo plants were usually grown for this colour. Madder produced a bright red; and onion skins, horseradish leaves, smartweed and goldenrod were used for yellow. The lye of wood ashes with a little copperas made an orange dye. Logwood chips boiled in an iron pot with cider or vinegar gave a good black. Yarn was sometimes clouded various shades of blue by braiding the skeins before dipping them in the indigo vat. And our ancestors also knew something about "tie-dyeing." To make yarn dark and light alternatively, tight bands of cotton were wound around the skein at equal intervals before dipping in the dye.

Weaving was done on two types of looms, a hand loom for small work and a large loom for heavy cloth. One historian tells us that "in the month of October, great webs of this homespun could be found in the house of almost every settler." Sometimes the homespun cloth was sent to a factory for "fulling," a process to make it shorter, thicker and stronger. Sometimes this was done at a fulling bee. This usually took the form of a neighborhood frolic. The web of cloth, well soaked and soaped, was spread on a long table and the guests seated at intervals along the table pulled and twisted the part before them, keeping it moving around the circle to the steady rhythm of a song. When the cloth had been thoroughly worked over, it was smoothed out flat on the tables and left to dry. The fulling bee usually ended with supper and a square dance.

The spinning and weaving crafts have had a rather marked revival in Ontario in the last few years. Miss Ileen Muff of Community Programmes reports that there are now over four thousand men and women members of Weavers' Guilds throughout the province; and they weave not only in wool but in cotton, rayon and metallic and combinations of these. A recent Weavers's Fashion Show included a tweed afternoon dress; a beige coat and suit ensemble; an aqua blue suit for general wear; a "gold dress" woven from honey-toned silk, a cotton thread and gold metallic. Many weavers are weaving upholstery and drapery materials, and of course such small articles as ties, scarfs and ski-belts.

The old hand woven coverlets, many of them brought in by United Empire Loyalists, are highly prized in Ontario. There is now a revival of this sort of weaving and the Ontario Spinners and Weavers own a few ninety-inch looms which weavers can borrow. The original coverlets were made of wool, usually white interwoven with red or blue. Cotton, rayon or chenille are mostly used now and the colours are usually chosen to be in keeping with the decorations of the room.

Some French-Canadian groups in eastern Ontario and Polish Canadians in the north weave rag rugs. A woman may do custom weaving, the customers bringing their rags cut into srtips, just as our grandmothers did years ago to have a rag carpet woven.

Mrs. Edna Blackburn, who has taught and demonstrated spinning and dyeing for many years, lives on a farm in Peel county. Along with their purebred cattle, she and her husband have flocks of Corriedale and Southdown sheep and a herd of Toggenburg goats. The sheep and goats provide beautiful material for spinning.

Dorothy and Harold Burnham are known for their ecclesiastical weaving, done mostly in silk and mercerized linen and always in consultation with the minister, priest or rabbi of the place of worship concerned. An outstanding piece of work was a Lenten array for St. John's Church in Jordan, Ontario, the decoration being symbolic of the stations of the Cross.

A rather typical Ontario Spinners' and Weavers' Guild has its headquarters in Glebe Road United Church in Toronto, and draws its one hundred members from both the city and the surrounding district. One of the moving spirits in the group is Mrs. Harry J. Kirk who, as a young school teacher, learned to spin and weave and took special courses whenever she had an opportunity. After she was married she took more training through the Women's Art Association and she is now well equipped to teach others in the Guild.

The Kirks have twenty spinning wheels: a walking wheel for spinning wool and a smaller one for flax, both types used in most Ontario pioneer homes; and a little wheel brought from the Orkney Islands by Mrs. Kirk's family over one hundred years ago. These wheels were made small to take up little space in the cottages. They have a modern wheel made by an Ontario school teacher who makes a few wheels every year as a hobby; a Quebec wheel over a century old with two treadles for fast work and a very compact little wheel in a box ten by fifteen inches, the style promoted by Gandhi for the women of India to use in their homes. Mrs. Kirk also has a spindle for hand spinning, cards for carding wool, and of course she has a loom. She weaves everything: place mats, runners, scarfs, stoles, tablecloths, draperies and material for suits and dresses. Tweeds are a speciality and they may be made from wool that has been home-dyed in a wide range of lovely colours, or occasionally from the undyed wool of black, white and gray sheep. Mrs. Kirk is also one of our Ontario weavers who uses natural dyes and who teaches this art to a number of classes every year.

Ontario weavers get their raw materials from various sources. Sometimes a raw wool fleece is bought direct from the farm and the weavers do the complete processing – washing, carding, spinning and weaving. Or the wool may come from the Co-operative Wool Growers' or the Wool Brokers, all ready for spinning. A few Ontario crafters are spinning goats' or Angora rabbits' wool or dogs' hair-combings from sheep dogs, the chow, Afghan hound, the samoyed, or the collie. At least one goat breeder, Mrs. Dorothy Maier of Moffat, clips Angora goats, the fleece of which provides mohair.

Two outstanding tapestry weavers in Ontario are Lithuanian-born, Anastasia Tamosaitiane and her husband (Mr. and Mrs. Tamosaitis).

After graduating from the Institute of Applied Arts in her own country and having studied further in Austria and Sweden, Mrs. Tamosaitiane taught weaving in Germany. The couple came to Canada and in 1950 they set up a studio near Kingston, Ontario, remodelling an old cheese factory into a charming home.

Mrs. Tamosaitiane is also a painter and the painter's approach can be found in her tapestries and in all her designing. She weaves a great many native costumes, skirts, blouses, head-dresses, even trousers for men. For one of her recent projects, a couple flew up from Washington to commission her to weave the material for costumes to be worn at an event in the White House. The couple has orders for work to keep them busy for five years, along with a number of engagements to teach at special courses and to demonstrate at art and crafts exhibitions.

The Lithuanian Canadians living in northwestern Ontario do beautiful weaving as anyone can testify who has visited the Lakehead Exhibition. Their craft displays always include hand woven rug-type wall hangings in rich, warm colours with soft browns, greens and golds often predominating and the Lithuanian national flower, the tulip, usually in evidence.

RUG MAKING

Our home craft of rug-making probably came to Ontario with settlers from the British Isles, where the parlour carpet had followed the floor covering of rushes in the middle class home.

The first rugs used by our early pioneers were door mats made of braided straw, an appropriate material for an earthen floor. Stalks of grain were usually cut before they were quite ripe and not too brittle; rye straw and the straw of wild rice were among the most pliable. The straw was first braided into strands and these were sewn together to make a flat round or oval mat. (The strands were also shaped into hats and baskets which were usually bleached by sulphur fumes in a covered box or barrel.)

The first rag rugs were used on rough pine floors to bring a touch of warmth and colour and comfort to the settler's cabin. They expressed the pioneer woman's thrift as well as her ingenuity in trying to make her home attractive; for they made use of the last good scraps in worn-out clothing. The material was cut into srtips which were then stitched together, end to end, and wound into balls for the convenience of the rug maker. The strips were sometimes braided into strands and the strands sewn together as in the making of straw mats, giving the attractive braided rug featured in many of Nutting's pictures of home interiors. Sometimes, but not always, the rags were dyed before braiding.

Then there was the woven rug which was just a strip of rag carpet. This had to be woven on a large loom so the rags were usually sent to a weaver in the district who did such weaving as custom work. The hooked rug was made by hooking strips of rags through canvas, using a tool much like a large crochet hook.

In rug making, as in all handicraft, more and more attention is being given to originality and creativity in design. The pioneer woman was certainly original in designing a rug; she had to be, for there were no commercial patterns or other guides to help her. As a result she contrived some interesting patterns from things at hand such as geometric designs, using a knife or a broom handle for straight lines and plates and cups and saucers to trace circles. A beautiful shell pattern developed from tracing a line around the heel of a man's boot and repeating the line in smaller and smaller dimensions to make a shell. Later our rug makers came to depend largely on commercial patterns, but in the last few years there has been a strong trend to original designs.

Two of our best known rug makers in Ontario today are Ted and Margaret Rowan of the Rittermere Studios at Vineland. As with many another handicraft, their enterprise began with a girl learning a craft from her mother. Margaret Rowan was Margaret Rittenhouse before she was married. The Rittenhouse family came from Pennsylvania in 1798 and settled on the land where the studio now stands, in the century old, seventeen-room brick house that replaced the original log cabin and the frame house that followed it. Mrs. Rittenhouse, Margaret's mother, made rugs because it was a family custom. Sometimes she made them for foot wipers at the door; sometimes she made nicer ones for a bedroom or even the parlour. A young woman who was a neighbour saw them and asked Mrs. Rittenhouse if she would teach her and some of her friends how to hook a rug. Friends continued to congregate until Mrs. Rittenhouse found herself conducting something of a school.

Margaret, a school girl interested in art, started making designs for rugs. Mrs. Rittenhouse specialized in dyeing rags, and Mr. Rittenhouse helped in printing designs on the burlap rug foundations. Now over half of the ground floor of the big house is given to the craft of rugmaking, with rooms for teaching, for storing supplies, displaying samples and a work-room for designing ,printing and dyeing.

Doing war work in England, Margaret met and married a young English officer, Ted Rowan, a graduate of art schools in Britain and Europe. Now he gives all his time to the rugmaking craft and the administration of the Rittenmere Studios. He works mostly in modern, abstract and geometric designs. Margaret's rugs are more traditional. One named Vineland has a centre featuring the fruits of the area and a grapevine border. Others have floral designs of Queen Anne's lace and goldenrod, of the magnolia and dogwood found in the locality.

The Rowans are popular instructors for the Department of Education's rug making courses but they do not charge for the hours of instruction given to those who come to the studio at all hours of the day for help in planning designs or colours or in the actual work of rug hooking. They now have more than three thousand students scattered over Canada. The studio's business is selling all kinds of rug making materials – burlap especially woven in Scotland, fabrics from textile mills, cut into strips ready for hooking and a wide range of commercial dyes. Being true artists, when the Rowans give instruction in design their purpose is to teach principles but to give the student leeway to make his design his own. For example a woman who had come from Russia followed a traditional Canadian design, but used her own colour sense, and her rug has a distinctive colour combination after the style of the traditional Ukrainian colouring of an Easter egg.

QUILTS

The quilting craft was brought to Ontario not only by settlers from the British Isles but from many parts of Europe. The art of quilting stitchery was practised in England in Elizabethan times, but the sewing together of layers of cloth to make a bed covering grew out of necessity in most parts of Europe in the severe winter known as "the year of the great freeze" in the fourteenth century.

The Ontario pioneer woman's quilts, like her rugs, were things of utility. Winter nights were cold in the log cabins and the provident homemaker was probably more concerned about keeping her family warm than about creating a masterpiece of beauty in a quilt. Worn clothing and every available scrap from cuttings of new material were saved and worked into either a quilt top or a lining. Most of these quilts were not quilted but were "tied" – yarn in a darning needle was drawn through top and lining at intervals of six to twelve inches and tied to hold the two layers of material together.

After a few years when the settlers were more prosperous, women began to take a pride in making beautiful quilts. They bought quilt patterns from travelling peddlers or newspapers; they exchanged patterns; the quilting bee was a popular social event; and quilts became a special attraction at country fairs. As a girl grew up she started piecing quilt tops for her trousseau, and after her engagement her friends were invited in to stitch or quilt these to the lining and filling of cotton batting. Sometimes the quilting or stitching design was as decorative as the pieced top. A bride's chest was supposed to contain a baker's dozen of quilts.

Many of the pieced quilts made from these early days up to the present followed the authentic traditional designs, as popular today as they were one hundred years ago: The Irish Chain, Double Irish Chain, Log Cabin, Dresden Plate, Saw Tooth, Star of Bethlehem and an endless variety of other star patterns.

During the past few years, quilt making in Ontario has made some notable progress both in the choice of good conventional designs and in the creation of original designs. We have an illustration of this in the work of the handicraft group in Simcoe county who organized the annual Simcoe County Quilt and Rug Fair. The purpose of the project is not only to revive community interest in the native crafts and to improve workmanship in quilt and rug making, but to develop the talent for creative designs. The exhibits show conventional designs and there are some antiques in the displays, but several of the group are producing most imaginative and beautiful designs of their own.

Design and colour as they appeared and developed in the needle-craft of the province had their beginning in the ethnic backgrounds of the people, but they show the influence of the environment in which these people found themselves in a new country. For example, the designs of crewel work which began in the east, found their way to England and were brought by the English to Canada, have changed subtly through the years. The influence of our wide open spaces is shown in a more open, less compact design; and our bright sunshine and white snow have led to the use of more brilliant colours.

Crochet work came to Ontario mostly with British and Flemish settlers. Around the turn of the century, crocheted lace was used rather lavishly to decorate all sorts of household linens and lingerie. Later there was a revival of the crocheted bedspread and tablecloth. Embroidery was a conventional decoration for both household linens and clothing; Beautiful specimens of embroidery, crochet work and fine drawn thread work on christening robes are now treasured heirlooms in many families.

Mrs. Elsie Shelepiuk of Fort William, a Canadian of Ukrainian descent, speaking at a convention of the Ontario Agricultural Societies said: "Embroidery has long been among the most popular and highly developed arts in the Ukraine. It has been carried to a high degree of perfection in its two great branches: folk and ecclesiastic. Folk embroidery includes articles of domestic use such as towels and scarfs as well as clothing. Traditions are strictly followed by the peasant women. Design and arrangement of embroidery vary both with the locality and the age of the women. For instance, open work on blouse sleeves would be considered inappropriate for the older woman. They use geometric plant stylization with leaves and branches. The pattern also indicates the region from whence it came."

On this point, Miss Evelyn Halliday, also of Fort William, who has made a study of the handicrafts of the different ethnic groups in the area, says: "The embroidery from the West Ukraine is solid and usually in straight rows – horizontal, vertical or diagonal, and the colours are black and white on red, red and white on black, or black and red on white. This is an agricultural district and the embroidery is supposed to represent the furrows of a field. As you travel farther south you will find additional colours creeping into the designs. Also the designs gradually become less solid, more airy. . . . Music seems to follow the same pattern as the designs – heavier in the northwestern area, becoming lighter and gayer as you travel south."

Miss Halliday adds that the Ukrainians, the oldest of the Southern European settlers around the Lakehead, have made a great contribution to the district; and that to keep their culture alive, they have special classes for their young people. "So we now find traditional embroidery designs turning up in different colours, the colour preferences of the young woman learning the old stitches."

A present trend among our skilled Ontario workers in needlecraft of any kind is not only to develop good workmanship but to raise the standard of design and colour; not to lose the traditional but to develop creativity and originality.

The use of applied design in linoleum printing, block printing and silk screening, is an old art that has been revived in the last century. Block printing, which had its origin in the Orient, found its way to England in the middle ages and was applied to the printing of words. The printing press in its most primitive form was simply a means of applying block printing to paper. Now we have come to think of applied design almost entirely in the field of art and handicraft.

Ontario's best known craftsman in applied design is Thor Hansen, a Danish Canadian who has lived and worked in Ontario for the past thirty-five years. Mr. Hansen has made a name for himself in industrial design; and we have carved linoleum wall panels, plaques, murals, tiles, draperies and other interior decorations of his designing in several of our new industrial buildings and church halls and in the Hall of Provinces in Casa Loma, Toronto. He makes effective use of Canadian themes and motifs, especially featuring wild life – the trillium, the wild goose, the moose and deer, the kingfisher and other native birds and flowers. Mr. Hansen's illustrated lectures, and his personal counselling of local groups, have had an effective influence on the designs adopted, or more often *created*, by many of our non-professional craftsmen.

Walter Sunahara, born in Vancouver of Japanese Canadian parents, moved with his family to London, Ontario, during the Second World War. He graduated from secondary school in London and went to the Ontario College of Art, won a scholarship that gave him further study in Japan, Southeast Asia, India and Ceylon, and returned to Ontario. Batik, in which he excells, is an art native to Japan and Indonesia; there is no doubt that his work has been influenced by the East, but he reminds us that Canada's art, like her people, comes from many national origins. He may bring Eastern techniques to apply to Canadian subject matter but he has no desire to design in bamboo. Now on the Department of Education staff doing extension work with adults, Mr. Sunahara is making a valuable contribution to the advance of Ontario handicraft, particularly with the work he is doing with Indian students in the Quetico Training Centre in Thunder Bay district.

In block printing and silk screen work, Elizabeth Hooey of Elm Tree Farm near Georgetown uses such motifs as maple leaves, ferns and pines to decorate luncheon cloths, tea-towels, drapery material and stationery. She is known for her designs of butter moulds used on Ontario farms nearly one hundred years ago. These have been printed on both textiles and paper correspondence cards.

There is a trend in Ontario as elsewhere, for instructors in handicraft to encourage their pupils to be original and creative in the designs and colours they use. Where the Home Economics Extension Service of the Department of Agriculture has given block printing courses in tourist areas, many women are featuring local interests in the souvenirs they offer for sale. Luncheon sets, tea towels and aprons are decorated with patterns of leaves or flowers found in the locality. In a neighborhood where visitors come to see the fish hatchery, a woman decorates her souvenirs with an attractive and cleverly coloured fish design.

POTTERY

The craft of the potter is one of the oldest known to civilization, and was probably inspired by the ancient custom of cooking food in a covering of clay. It was the potter who shaped and moulded the water jugs and other household vessels of Biblical and earlier times, and the changes throughout the ages of ware and form, firing and ornament, provide a thread by which the modern scholar can retrace his steps back through history. Today the mass-produced products of the factory can supply any need of utilitarian pottery. There is no longer any practical reason to make a pot by hand, but the craft still provides the man or woman who takes time to master it, with an opportunity to express an aesthetic experience. In pottery the artist speaks to us through the language of shape, colour, texture and ornamentation. From humble materials he creates objects of beauty for our pleasure and use.

It is unlikely that the early settlers of Ontario were much concerned with the ornamental qualities of the pottery they used – baking dishes and crocks for butter and cream and pickles. Here and there over a district a potter who had learned his trade in an older country would set up a kiln and wheel, and settlers would come from miles away to buy the things they needed. Sometimes a potter trained apprentices to his trade; but it is only within the last fifty years or so that anyone in Ontario thought of turning to pottery as an artist turns to painting.

In 1936 a small group of Ontario potters formed the Canadian Potters' Guild with the purpose of "raising and maintaining a high standard in Canadian ceramic art and craftsmanship." The Guild now has members all across Canada. It has established a gallery in Toronto as an outlet for members to exhibit and sell their work, a centre where pots and sculpture can be juried for exhibitions and where students and others can see what is being produced by our ceramists. Workshops and exhibitions are held annually to improve the potter's skill and the public's appreciation of the craft.

A view of one of these exhibitions gives some idea of how the craft of ceramics, in pottery, sculpture and enamel has advanced in the last few years. In the 1965 exhibition, work by Ontario potters and sculptors included vases, floor vases, bottles, bowls, tea sets, punch sets, platters and other dishes in stoneware with varied glazes and colours; a porcelain punch set with cobalt decoration; such ceramic sculpture as a candle holder, an owl, a racoon, a mother and child piece.

Perhaps pottery as an Ontario handicraft can be described best by a brief reference to the work of an individual potter. Miss Tess Kidick, a public school art teacher, took a course at the Ontario College of Art, discovered that she wanted to spend the rest of her life making pottery and set up an establishment in the village of Jordan. She specializes in stoneware, using a mixture of different clays and making mostly things for the house — dishes, lamps, vases, plaques ovenware (her casserole dishes are very well known).

Much of Miss Kidick's work is sculptural, its decorative design taken from things in nature suggestive of movement: leaves or grass blowing in the wind, the flight of a bird. Or she may create a textural surface such as the bark of a tree.

Miss Kidick says that Ontario has a rather high proportion of her people doing handicraft. She believes this may be due to the public interest created by the number of art galleries distributed over the province and the art and craft exhibitions held at various centres; also to the fact that there is a comparatively good market for handicraft in Ontario whether it is produced by craftsmen in Ontario or those in other provinces.

Perhaps pottery is not generally considered a traditional handicraft of the Indians but in the *Indian News* published by the Department of Citizenship and Immigration we read: "The famous old pottery craft of the Iroquois people is being revived on the Six Nations Reserve in Southern Ontario where a half dozen or so Indians are using local clay to make pottery based on traditional designs. The pottery is made for sale and it is reported that their products are sold almost as quickly as they can produce them."

Miss Kidick, who also teaches pottery classes for the Department of Education, is enthusiastic about a class on the Six Nations Reserve. She says that they not only show originality and a capacity for sustained effort; but if they make a pot that is not up to standard they are ready to have it broken rather than to put it on the market and so cheapen the reputation of Indian work.

Mr. and Mrs. Oliver Smith of the Reserve are leaders of the group. Mrs. Smith and her husband, after taking instruction in making pottery themselves, set up a kiln with modern equipment at their home. Clays from different parts of the Reserve produce pottery of different colours and surfaces, and shale found in the clay gives an unglazed effect very much like the smoky appearance of the ancient Indian pottery. Usually the pottery now made on the Reserve is decorated with a carved-in traditional design.

LEATHERCRAFT

In *Pioneer Arts and Crafts,* Edwin C. Guillet writes of the use of leather by the early settlers of Upper Canada: "The reminiscences of Loyalist settlers suggest that the use of skins to make clothing was widespread. . . Buckskin breeches and jackets, skirts and petticoats, gloves and mittens, and coonskin caps and bonnets were sometimes an important part of the family wardrobe. There were deerskin saddles and bed covers, and buckskin moccasins provided the first footwear."

Some of the pioneers had their first lessons in tanning skins from the Indians. A little later settlers from the old world brought this skill with them and in the early 1800's tanneries were set up at many points across the province. Usually they had a thriving local trade, for leather was necessary to make shoes for the men, women and children of the district as well as harness, saddles and other leather equipment used on the farm.

Many of the earliest settlers made their families' boots themselves, and sometimes a man who was particularly skilful at the work would become an itinerant shoemaker, travelling from house to house, boarding with the family, and making a year's supply of shoes at one visit. As the settlements developed, each had its shoemaker's shop, usually a harness shop and sometimes a saddler's.

It was years later, after factory-made leather goods had been available for sometime, that craftsmen began to see the possibilities of creating something distinctive in hand-worked leather. Now we have leather hand-bags, wallets, belts, book covers, book ends, plaques, trays, desk sets, jewellery, originally designed for both use and beauty, the material and workmanship fine and durable, the decoration done with an artist's imagination and discernment. A few craftsmen have done interesting work in moulded leather, in which the leather is soaked, shaped and baked until very hard. Some of the products are puttees, trunk corners, and moulded trays.

Mrs. Robert Muma of Toronto, president of the Canadian Society of Creative Leathercraft, reports active leathercraft guilds at Barrie, London, Hamilton, Belleville and Toronto, and plans are underway for organization in other centres.

Jean Agnew teaches leathercraft in the Home Economics Extension Service of the provincial Department of Agriculture; and the Department of Education engages a number of instructors in leathercraft for its program. Thus the craft is being taken directly to the people. Others teach leathercraft as therapy in hospitals and sanitoria.

One of Ontario's outstanding craftsmen in leather is Robert Muma. Mr. Muma specializes in book binding, book covers and restoring valuable books, mostly for a library in the United States. He has done exquisite work on plaques for universities and colleges, and the colour inlays in his book binding might be the pictures of a master painter. He has conducted summer courses for teachers in the United States and the western provinces as well as in Ontario. He is the author of several books including: *Colour in Leathercraft, Colour, Decoration and Finish of Leather*, and a set of four volumes *Mumart Tooling and Carving Designs for Colour in Leathercraft*.

WOODWORK

"The Ontario pioneer lived in an age of wood," writes Edwin Guillet in *Pioneer Arts and Crafts*. "Many complicated machines and contrivances consisted entirely of wood; and most of the equipment of the pioneer home was hand made and of wood. When a door took the place of a blanket or some makeshift covering of the entrance to the log house, its hinges, lock and latch were often of wood. . . . Many a pioneer house was floored with half logs roughly formed by adze or broad-axe, for smooth boards were available only at saw-mills, but saw-mills were at first as scarce as grist-mills. . . . As the years passed, the saw-mill was often the nucleus of a settlement."

For the first few years the furnishings of a log shanty were usually limited to a bed, a table, a few benches, and stools made from sections of tree trunks, the bare essentials in cooking and table equipment, tubs and water vessels. A child's trundle-bed was a sort of bunk that could be pushed under the parents' bed out of the way during the day. Sap-troughs were often used for cradles at first, but it was not long before almost every home had a proper cradle, made by the head of the house or some other man in the settlement with a flair for such work.

Quoting Edwin Guillet again: "Chairs and sofas of pine stuffed with wool were also made by handy settlers during their spare time in winter. The first rough table of boards often gave way to fine drop-leaf tables of walnut or cherry, while hardwood pegs driven into the wall or ceiling to hold various implements and stores, were eventually replaced by cupboards and chests of various types. . . . A curious rock-ing-chair-cradle was constructed by William Hunter of Cavan township, so that his wife might sew and rock her baby at the same time. It was made of basswood, the seat of the chair and the base of the cradle being in one piece, fifty-two inches long with a rocker at each end. It was still in use over a century later."

Probably the first wood carving done in rural Ontario was the decoration some devoted father whittled in the headboard of his baby's cradle, or the design a man hollowed out in his wife's wooden butter mould. We have specimens of these hand-decorated butter moulds in some of our rural museums. Some communities were so fortunate as to have among their immigrants a cabinent maker from England or Germany or some other part of Europe; and pieces of furniture made by these men are still treasured in many Ontario homes. In these days when most of our furniture is factory-made, some manufacturers keep skilled craftsmen on their staff to do hand carving as it is required on high quality furniture.

We have several highly skilled and creative wood carvers in Ontario, most of whom, like Nathan Monture and George Couchi, take their subjects from nature. Mr. Johnson of Chatham features wild life in his work. Ron Campbell of Toronto does stylized carvings of birds. Tom Hunter of Flesherton carves native birds and paints them authen-tic colours. Wilmer Nadjawan does carvings of birds and other animals such as very spirited greyhounds. He is also known for his naturally crooked canes made from swamp willow. Richard Tompkins of Cooks-town used butternut wood and specializes in birds. Sometimes he shows a whimsical humour in his work — for example a set of butternut wood cheese tray and knife includes a little wooden mouse.

Sam Raeburn of Caledon took up cello playing, sculpture and wood carving after retiring from his work as a mechanical engineer eleven years ago. He is now eighty-three and producing a steady output of very fine work. The heads shaping an array of briar pipe bowls are carved in the likenesses of friends. The carved head of a greyhound straining at the leash makes the curved handle of a walking-cane. Characters from myths are among his favourite carving subjects.

Wood turning is interesting an increasing number of Ontario folk who enjoy working with tools; and there is a steady market for wooden bowls and trays such as those turned out by Ted Ingram. Several cabinet makers and others are taking up wood inlay or parquetry.

METAL ARTS

The first skilled craftsman in metal work in the early Ontario settlements was the blacksmith — with the possible exception of the travelling tinker who went about the country stopping at settlers' homes to solder holes in leaking utensils or do other simple repair jobs. As agriculture and the trades progressed, the itinerant tinker gave up his precarious way of making a living, while the blacksmith's work increased as farming developed. Indeed the industry could not have operated without him.

Every village had its blacksmith shop where horses and oxen were shod, ploughshares made and sharpened, and farm implements repaired. The blacksmith was adept at making the spare parts that today come from the factory. He was clever at making hand tools too, from a crowbar to a rug hook. He produced the hardware (nails, hinges and door latches) used in building the early barns and houses, following the era when the pioneer, himself, whittled these out of wood.

The blacksmith shop was something of a social centre for farmers, too, rivalling the hot stove forum in the village store. In busy seasons, work-horses were usually shod in the evenings so farmers had time to loiter and talk; there was no law limiting the blacksmith's working hours. Andrew Fussell, today a very fine craftsman in metal work, recalls that as a young man at these sessions he liked to join the blacksmith at the forge, both swinging their sledge-hammers in alternating blows to speed the work while the iron was hot.

As some of the blacksmith's work was taken over by factories, and as automobiles and tractors replaced horses, it was not uncommon for a blacksmith to turn his skill with metal to the wrought iron craft, making such things as stair rails, fire place accessories, bird baths, candle holders, lamp stands and door knockers.

Another highly skilled worker with metal who opened his shop in most Ontario towns almost as soon as the town was established, was the watch-maker. Many of them came from Britain and later from Switzerland and other parts of Europe. They sold and repaired clocks and watches and most of them became the towns' jewellers, though perhaps very few of them ever did make jewellery. This is one of our highly specialized crafts in Ontario, and the man or woman who works with expensive metals and precious stones requires a skill and an artistry worthy of the materials used. Silver-smithing and enamelling are enjoying a growing popularity with both craftsmen and their customers in Ontario, and many of our metal craftsmen are working with our native copper.

Andrew Fussell does a wide variety of metal work in addition to giving special courses in summer schools and other schools for teachers. He makes aluminum trays, sometimes hammered and usually anodized to harden the surface so it won't need polishing and won't rub off to mark a white linen cloth. Some of his copper is hammered, some silver plated. And Mr. Fussell does a wide variety of jewellery, mostly in silver; but his great love is in ecclesiastical work, such as the alms basin he made for Trinity College Chapel. He says: "There's a great satisfaction in making something that you know is going to live long after you have gone."

Harold Stacey is another Ontario silversmith who is hard-pressed to fill his orders for ecclesiastical silver from churches all over the country. Another silver craftsman is Douglas Boyd who was recently commissioned to supply all the altar silver for Beverly Memorial Chapel in Toronto. Mr. Boyd does domestic pieces too, and some jewellery. Incidentally he made the cigarette case presented to our present queen on her last visit to Canada as Princess Elizabeth. He works only in silver, gold and platinum, believing that good workmanship deserves a medium that will last. Another of his philosophies is that design in handcraft should be, first of all, functional. The craftsman, as distinguished from the artist, makes an article for use — after that he works for beauty; and beauty may come, in no small measure, from the article's fitness for its purpose.

Jarko Zavi, a graduate of the School of Fine Arts in Prague, now a resident of Ontario, makes jewellery of a combination of precious metals, gold, platinum or others and ceramics in a wide range of colours — browns, orange, turquois, lilac. M. Kortt does jewellery and his wife works in enamel. Mrs. Kortt does beautiful jewellery in a stained glass window effect. Nora O'Day makes pewter costume jewellery and her fine designs feature such native subjects as the maple-leaf, the trillium, the Canada goose. George Dancy works with sterling silver and native stones in jewellery and spoons but is perhaps best known for his fused silver jewellery.

STONE POLISHING

The craft or hobby of stone gathering, cutting and polishing is steadily growing in Ontario. Many communities have their groups of "rock hounds," taking field trips, sometimes to abandoned mines or stone quarries, hunting for native semi-precious stones — the amethyst in Thunder Bay, the blue soladite, Ontario's provincial stone found in quantities around Bancroft, the jasper, moonstone, sunstone, peristerite, all types of feldspar that are used to cut cabochons — that is, a jewellery stone cut in convex form but not faceted.

The amateur lapidary (one who cuts, polishes or engraves precious stones) either tumble polishes his stones or cuts and grinds them. Many who find and cut or polish stones take them to a jeweller to have them set in jewellery. Others, skilled in metal work such as George Palliser, make their own settings. Steve Boyko does this, working in a wheel chair. Many Ontario people are only now becoming aware of the beautiful semi-precious stones to be found in the province; and there is a new and growing interest in the hobby of stone hunting.

7 🦚

Manitoba

AS IN EVERY PROVINCE OF CANADA, handicrafts in Manitoba began with its first citizens, its Indian people. They decorated shirts, moccasins, pouches, belts and other articles important to their culture with superlative bead-work of original design. Some of them produced beautiful baskets: quill baskets incorporating motifs symbolic of particular aspects of their culture, and of course, the more familiar birch bark and willow ones.

Then the tide of settlement began. The Red River settlers arrived at the forks of the Red and Assiniboine Rivers in 1811-12. From then on the trickle slowly swelled into a flood that swept across the prairies. As Canada moved into the twentieth century, Anglo-Saxons, Europeans and people from the Scandinavian countries carved homes for themselves out of lands that until a few years earlier had known only the Indians and the men of the Hudson's Bay and North-West Companies. With settlement came men, women, children — whole families. And the women looked for ideas to help them meet the challenges of that strange new environment.

Ontario organized its first Women's Institute in 1897. The Institute idea moved into Manitoba in 1910 in the form of home economics societies, the first ones in the Morris district in the south-central part of the province and at Valley River in the northwest. Other societies followed. So did World War I.

In those early days the Department of Agriculture and Immigration made the Institute movement a responsibility of the Manitoba Agricultural College. Later, with the passage of the Women's Institute Act, it became the responsibility of the Minister of Agriculture and the Director of Extension Service within that department.

World War I was not without one blessing. It did bring money from the Federal Government into the provinces, Manitoba among them, for an enlarged program of rural education. The Women's Institutes were an ideal outlet for some of the programs that were evolved. Those in which the women were most interested included short courses in dressmaking and millinery, demonstrations in cookery and canning, and short courses in woodwork and sewing for members of boys and girls clubs. Specialists in these subjects would spend a week in a centre instructing the women.

The extension program developed so rapidly that the Extension Service found it necessary to hire Miss Helen MacDougall, a graduate in household science from Nova Scotia, to supervise the societies. Under her guidance they made still more remarkable progress. In 1920 they adopted a new name, Women's Institutes.

Four years later Miss Esther Thompson became head of women's work for the Extension Department. A Norwegian by birth, she brought her enthusiasm for arts and crafts to her new position. *A Story of the Women's Institutes of Manitoba* records that "coming herself into Canada from outside, she was quick to appreciate the heroic struggles of those who try to make the best of a new and foreign country. . . . (She) was impressed by their intense desire to preserve their native arts . . . deeply touched by their dramatic and musical talent, their handicrafts, their sense of colour, their dancing and folk songs — priceless contributions to Canada. . . ." It was inevitable that some of this enthusiasm would rub off on the women's programs designed under her leadership.

Just about this time John Murray Gibbon, publicity director for the Canadian Pacific Railway, discovered the value of publicity in arts, crafts, folk dances and folk songs. He had already organized a successful French arts and crafts exhibit in Quebec City; he was convinced the next festival should be held in Western Canada, preferably in Winnipeg. Montreal already had a handicraft guild, and he arranged for three of its members to travel to Winnipeg to talk with women's groups, among them representatives of the Women's Institutes. The result: a Manitoba Branch of the Canadian Handicraft Guild was set up, its first task that of organizing and arranging the handicraft section of the proposed arts and crafts festival that would include all ethnic groups. The festival, held in June, 1928, was a huge success.

These were the objects of the Guild:

1. To encourage, retain, revive and develop Canadian handicrafts and arts industries throughout the Dominion.
2. To prevent the loss, extinction and deterioration of the same.
3. To encourage and preserve any crafts and industries possessed by new settlers.
4. To aid people skilled in any such crafts and industries by providing markets for their products in Canada and abroad.
5. To encourage industry in homes of the people by making it profitable and honourable.
6. To carry on and take part in exhibitions of home arts, industries and crafts.
7. To provide instruction in, and proper directions for such arts, industries and crafts.
8. To educate the public to the value of such arts, industries and crafts and of good handwork.
9. To keep records of the same in order to prevent their extinction.

The guild also set up a committee to work on new, original Manitoba designs. It produced the first wheat design which featured the fishbone stitch for the wheat head. It wasn't long until the committee developed another new design, this one in cross stitch, featuring the wild goose in flight.

The aims and objectives of the Manitoba Handicraft Guild obviously influenced the handicrafts program of the Women's Institute for an item in the May, 1929 issue of the *Institute News*, reported that "one district is gathering handicrafts to be exhibited at the district convention. This may eventually give the Institutes in the district contact with the foreign people living about them, who have beautiful handwork, as well as the knowledge of how it is made. The handicrafts movement has great possibilities!"

The late 1920's ushered in a depression. Extension programs were curtailed, lecturing staff reduced. However, an amazing volume of local talent in arts, crafts, drama and music emerged. Both the Handicraft Guild and the Little Theatre moved in to help and, as a result, handicraft displays, festival and dramatic performances became the absorbing interest of the day, according to the booklet telling the Women's

Institute story in Manitoba. Centre competed against centre in friendly contest, it says, and enthusiasm rose high as a wave of artistic development swept over the land. Institute members were obviously very much involved.

In October of 1929 Mrs. Evelyn Ames joined the Extension Service to work with rural groups on clothing programs. In November of that year she began the "Clothing the Family" program, working through local leader groups. The program included a little needlework, some basic embroidery and may well have marked the introduction of handicrafts as such into the Institute program. The Extension Service, of course, looked to Institute members to help in the development of the local leadership classes.

Interest in handicrafts continued unabated, for, according to the January 1930 issue of the *Institute News,* conventions at McCreary and Emerson presented handicraft exhibits. The Emerson exhibit included a number of fine pieces of handwork by "New Canadian" women.

The Women's Branch of the Extension Service arranged still another program of lectures which were available to any group that might wish it. The Institutes, of course, were quick to take advantage of the new series. It was made up of six-month courses given by specialists. Achievement days at the end of the six months brought the program to a close. The Extension Service provided still another service by arranging for Guild workers to make rug and quilt samplers to show how these crafts should be done. The Department felt it was easier to maintain good standards by adopting Guild standards which were already recognized as being of high quality. These samplers were found to be particularly useful and indicate the close relationship between the Guild and the Institutes. They were also most useful when the Federated Women's Institutes of Canada conducted a competition in hooked rugs.

In June 1933, the FWIC met in Winnipeg in conjunction with the annual convention of the Manitoba Women's Institutes. The big feature of the meeting was a display of handicrafts in the gymnasium of the Agricultural College. There was French lace; a Polish handicrafter embroidering handwoven linen; a Canadian weaving homespun yarn into scarves and suiting; a Norwegian demonstrator showing how she carded, dyed, spun and wove wool into designs of her own creation for wall hangings. Manitoba's other ethnic groups were represented by Czechoslovakian embroideries, Ukrainian and Polish cross stitch designs; Hungarian cutwork, German lace, Swedish weaving and Hardanger embroidery, the black and red cross stitch of Rumania,

149

the petit point of France. Manitoba handicrafters exhibited beautiful rugs, some made from jute yarns, others of unspun wool and rags. They also showed wool quilts and comforters.

However, by 1933, the country was deep in depression. Every scrap of material was precious; yet farmers who had wool could hardly give it away. At that point the Extension Service handicraft program was enlarged. Quilts, rugs and knitting were added to the home management course. The enlarged handicrafts program was so well received that, in the fall of 1934 and 1935, a new Homecrafts course was set up.

The January 1935 issue of *Institute News* reports that the handicrafts course was most popular. Spectacular results from the courses were reported in various editions of *Institute News*. The McCreary Yarnspinners is an example. This group held a wool fair at which twenty-three exhibitors made a total of sixty entries in nine classes. These exhibits included skeins of yarn, mitts, socks, sweaters and rugs, all of them of a very high standard. Commercial wool was allowed in only one class. McCreary's enthusiasm for wool began when the local Institute bought two spinning wheels and two sets of cards and made them available on loan to anyone who wished to use them. A brief item in May of 1936 reported on the McCreary project this way:

> They are a very live organization and are certainly doing a lot of good here. They own two spinning wheels, two hand carders and a machine carder. These are out among the people all the time. As a result people who couldn't afford a spinning wheel are able to make their own yarn. The Institute will also supply the wool where the people cannot afford to buy it. They are having a wool fair in March and giving prizes for the best homespun yarn and also prizes for articles knit from the homespun yarn.

It is significant that the carders are still available to any one who wishes to use them.

For its 1935 district convention the Winnipeg district executive reported "contests in knitting to promote interest in the knitting exhibit to be held in connection with the rug and quilt contest. Rug and quilt conveners have been appointed." The executive was "looking forward to seeing entries from Institutes that have never before entered the contest."

In May 1936, *Institute News* carried an item about glove making, offering directions for glove making, patterns and personal fittings. Western cattlemen are still very partial to the Manitoba-made "roping gloves" which are generally handsewn and of our native "jumper deer."

Some areas arranged their own handicrafts courses. In Oakburn, five groups were organized, ten leaders appointed and knitting courses extending over a five month period worked out, ending with a display. Clearwater organized four groups with lessons covering such crafts as knitting, quilt and rug making. It, too, ended its project with a display.

LADY TWEEDSMUIR LOAN COLLECTION

Arising out of her preoccupation with the welfare of rural homemakers, Lady Tweedsmuir, wife of the Governor-General, had suggested to the Women's Institutes that they might find it useful to build up a collection of handicrafts. "I think a loan collection of good things to be circulated in country districts might help," she suggested, "and we might have the first one in Manitoba as an experiment."

The idea was discussed by the 1937 convention in Winnipeg. Delegates who were thought to be especially interested in handicrafts were invited to meet for a "little conference." The "little conference" brought out more women than could be comfortably accommodated. Mrs. George E. Simmie presided; Mrs. C. T. Lount, of the Handicrafts Guild and Mrs. Ames, of the Extension Service, led the discussion. Mrs. Lount showed a collection of items made by guild members. After discussing ways and means of helping handicrafters to improve the quality of their work, delegates to the meeting agreed that the Institutes should build up a loan collection.

The next step was to prepare a recommendation to be presented to the 1937 provincial convention. They did so. Their recommendation was endorsed by the convention and then went to the Advisory Board for further consideration.

The following July Lady Tweedsmuir travelled to Winnipeg. Representatives from the Institutes, the Handicrafts Guild and Extension Service met with her to discuss handicrafts in general, and a loan collection in particular. She repeated her earlier hope – that Manitoba would set up a loan collection. She promised to contribute to it.

In October the advisory board voted one hundred dollars to start the collection and appointed a committee to assemble the articles. It was agreed that the collection should consist of knitted articles, small quilts, small rugs, a simple loom and some woven articles, embroideries characteristic of different countries, hand-made gloves, articles carved from wood. The Institutes were to provide funds to add other items.

Early in February, 1938, Lady Tweedsmuir wrote promising gifts for the collection. They eventually arrived, and included a large runner with cross stitch embroidery, a small article embroidered in cross stitch, three patchwork pincushions, a knitted doll outfit, a white toy rabbit, a pair of men's socks and a dress protector. Later that month she sent copies of a book published by the London School of Needlework with the promise of other handicraft books to come.

The following articles, together with those received from Lady Tweedsmuir, made up the collection:

Embroideries:	Table runner	Cross stitch
	Lunch cloth	Italian stitch
	Towel	Needle weaving
	Blouse	Chain stitch
	Handkerchief, serviette	Initialling

Quilting: Quilting in fancy designs, an applique and a quilted quilt.

Rugmaking: Picture, floral and straight line designs worked in with spun yarn, rags, unspun wool and jute.

Knitting: Knitted mitts, single and double as well as plain and fancy patterns.

Weaving: Simple loom and card weaving of scarfs and belts.

Other Articles: Wood turning (picture frame); button-making using fruit stones; leather work (gloves and belt).

In January, 1956, the collection was divided into four small units to increase its usefulness. These units are:

1. Rug making.
2. Quilt making.
3. Embroideries.
4. Knitting and weaving.

Each of these units includes, besides the display pieces, a commentary explaining each piece, study material relating to the making of each article and samples in the making to illustrate the method of making. Institutes requesting the collection pay the cost of shipping it both ways. Already many Institutes who have entered the Tweedsmuir handicraft competitions have found the collection an extremely valuable source of information.

THE WAR YEARS

Handicrafts were not forgotten by the Institutes during the war years from 1939 to 1945. Rather, they were put to a much more practical use in the form of quilts and coverlets for overseas and for local hospitals, in knitted articles for service men and women. An astronomical number of quilts, for example, was made by Institute members; the Birtle district, for one, provided a total of 292 quilts. Other districts made similarly impressive service records.

QUILTS

As in most parts of Canada, quilts represent a traditional craft. Manitoba's Women's Institutes have worked diligently to maintain it as such. During the war years, the quilts were, for the most part, practical; those made and exhibited by Institute and Institute members in more recent years have been a pleasing combination of traditional and original design.

Among the latter was the winning quilt submitted by the Warren Institute in the provincial quilt competition in 1965. It featured a central cluster of flowers. In this cluster were to be found the floral emblems of each of the ten provinces to make a centennial bouquet. This centennial bouquet was edged with green squares on which had been appliqued a map of one of the provinces. Below the map appeared the floral emblem and the date on which that province had joined confederation. The second prize quilt, made by Rivers Women's Institute, featured airplanes of various types.

Nineteen quilts were entered in the competition. They were judged on the originality of design, colour scheme, workmanship, suitability of design and finishing. The needlework was described as "exceptionally good."

Rug making has always been an important part of the Institute's handicraft program. In July 1931, for example, the Winnipeg District reported that rug making was one of the most popular programs. At that point the District had already conducted one rug making competition. It drew fifty entries, twenty-eight of them made by individuals, the remainder by Institutes. With that success behind them the District decided on another such competition. However, it was agreed that while any rug submitted would be considered for exhibit, only those made by Institute members would be judged. There were other stipulations: rugs must have been completed within the past twelve months; and they might be hooked, knitted, scalloped, braided or crocheted.

The Gimli Institute won five first prize for hooked rugs; Norwood W.I. second prize, while individual winners captured the honours in the remaining classes: Mrs. Burt Irwin, Inwood, braided rugs; Mrs. D. Neil, Winnipeg, knitted rugs; and a Norwood woman first prize in the crocheted rug section.

This rug exhibit attracted much attention when it was shown at the Brandon Fair. The rugs themselves were made from a variety of material including old sacks that had been washed and dyed. Rugs from the Gimli Institute, for example, had been made from old sacks, washed and dyed, and hooked in simple, suitable designs in pleasing colours. The material in one rug cost thirty cents; in another, twenty cents. Small wonder that the president of the Winnipeg District expressed the hope that the Institutes in the district would continue to make rugs of such high quality.

While the Institutes do not have a rug making project underway at the moment, interesting things are going on at the Manitoba Branch of the Canadian Handicrafts Guild. There a group of rug hookers, fifteen of them, have produced a rug of modern design. Now they have another underway, this one featuring Manitoba's autumn leaves.

WEAVING

Weaving, as a craft, has never drawn the interest of Women's Institutes in Manitoba to the extent that rugs and quilts have done. Members showed only a mild interest in the box loom weaving that formed part of the Extension Service program in 1932-33. Seemingly they found the big looms too expensive and too complicated, even too large. Still, a lot of good weaving has come from rural Manitoba.

For example, *Institute News* reported considerable interest in the Roblin district. One weaver spun and dyed the yarn for the rugs she produced from a large home-made loom. She also wove heavy blankets and other bed coverings, cushions and tapestries. Other women in the district successfully used small box looms (which had been brought into the district by youth training leaders) for scarves, knitting bags, cushions.

One of the most interesting developments in this ancient craft in western Canada was the weaving department introduced by the Searle Grain Company for farm women on the prairies. It was patterned after the successful weaving tradition in Quebec.

The Searle classes started in 1942. Four travelling teachers taught classes that ran for six weeks, five days a week, with twelve to fourteen members to a class. At the end of the six week period, pupils were quite competent weavers and could produce many of the things needed in farm homes: clothing for men, women and children, bedspreads, curtains, tablecloths, towels and other household articles. Farm women and girls received the courses free of charge; the materials used during the instruction period were also supplied by the Company. At the end of the six week instruction period, pupils were asked to form a "weaving circle." The only requirement made of them was that they, in turn, teach weaving without charge to any farm women or girls who wished to learn. The Searle Company also arranged for forty-five inch six-treadle four-harness looms at cost and supplied cotton and linen thread and wool yarns at wholesale. Over two thousand women scattered over the three prairie provinces learned to weave in the three years (1942 to 1945) during which the classes operated. Even when the classes were dicontinued, Mrs. Dorothy Rankine, who had been in charge of looms and weaving equipment, remained as weaving consultant until the weaving department was discontinued in 1964.

MANITOBA TARTAN

Another important development in weaving in Manitoba was the development of the Manitoba Tartan. This Tartan received Royal assent in May 1962 and is fully authorized and registered with the permission of Sir James Ferguson, Keeper of the Records of Scotland at Her Majesty's General Register House in Edinburgh, Scotland.

The Manitoba Tartan was designed by Hugh Kirkwood Rankine, of Winnipeg. It combines the two distinguishing colours of the Hamilton and Douglas families of Scotland from which Lord Selkirk, founder of the Red River Settlement, was descended. Lord Selkirk's father was a Hamilton by blood; he assumed the Douglas name when he succeeded to the Earldom of Selkirk in 1744 and so combined the two houses.

The Hamilton Tartan is distinguished by three bands of blue, the Douglas Tartan by lines of azure blue. To these two distinguishing colours of Lord Selkirk's ancestry, Mr. Rankine added dark red to symbolize the Selkirk Settlement on the banks of the Red River, white squares for the vast stretches of snow on the prairies, yellow lines to symbolize the golden crops and green lines to indicate the stretches of green fields and forests.

CERAMICS

Interest in ceramics has been slow to develop in rural Manitoba and most of it is centred in Winnipeg. However, a few years ago a group of W.I. members from the Baldur district travelled some sixty miles to Brandon to study ceramics. They returned to teach others in their community and they have also exhibited some excellent work at the annual exhibitions arranged by the Baldur Hobbycraft Guild. There are other potters at Carman, Marquette, Morris and Neepawa. In 1963 the Brandon, Manitoba, Agricultural Extension Centre offered a series of classes in ceramics.

Probably the most well-known of Manitoba ceramists is Leo Mol. Mr. Mol spent his first winter in Manitoba on a farm. After a successful career as a painter of religious subjects, he built a kiln and, with Manitoba clays, he produced a series of small figures that helped to make him famous.

An even more recent development was the effort of a Winnipeg ceramist to create a Manitoba crocus design. She was successful and this design is now available on a variety of articles – trays, coffee mugs, cream and sugar sets – from the Handicraft Guild's Winnipeg shop.

WORKING WITH WOOD

Institute members have not been drawn to wood as a medium in which to work. And yet, at a Hobby Show presented by Fairlight Women's Institute, a driftwood display by a non-member drew extravagant praise. She became interested in working with wood, she explained, when she began to pick up unusual and interesting pieces of ground cedar in the sandhill country adjacent to Manitoba's Assiniboine River, and driftwood from Manitoba lakes. She started out with a jack-knife but later graduated to a set of proper carving tools.

Wood carving in Manitoba is limited to a few, perhaps because it represents such an extremely specialized craft. It is a manly craft, left almost exclusively to such people as Helgi Olsen, who specializes in animals and birds. Many of the others who carved out of wood – the Criddles and the Beedles – have been lost to Manitoba.

HANDICRAFTS IN COMMUNITIES

From the achievement days of the early nineteen thirties, the handicraft exhibits to be found in rural Manitoba have become increasingly sophisticated. In September, 1939, for example, the Hamiota-Rossburn Women's Institute district presented seven hundred exhibits in ten classes, all of them described as of especially good quality. There were beautiful quilts, skilfully done; a large rug exhibit which included crocheted, braided and hooked rugs made from rags, yarn and unspun wool; excellent embroidery and a display of fretwork and wood carving. The Hamiota-Rossburn district fostered these handicrafts through exhibitions that first began in 1934. Originally to have been an annual affair, it later became a biennial exhibit to give workers more time in which to prepare exhibits. While the district structure has changed in the intervening years, the exhibit is still an important aspect of W.I. activity in the area.

The Baldur Hobbycraft Guild had its beginnings back in 1951 when the Baldur Women's Institute decided to sponsor classes in leathercraft and sewing. The classes proved so successful and the articles so interesting that a modest display of the finished work was arranged. That was the Hobbycraft Guild's modest beginning. In 1962 the Guild had seventy-five members, many of them members of the local Institute. The Guild tries to introduce a new craft each year. For example, five members travelled the many miles to Brandon each week to learn ceramics from an instructor there. Once they had learned something of method and material, they gave classes for those in their own community who wanted to learn a new skill.

The Guild has also offered classes in embroidery, crocheting and smocking. Guild members are particularly fortunate because they do have, in their own community, a core of skilled craftsmen and women who can (and will) teach such skills as Hardanger embroidery to the women and woodworking to the men.

Another outstanding development in handicrafts in Manitoba was the decision in 1942, of Manitoba Pool Elevators, a grain handling co-operative, to develop a Rural Art and Handicraft Exhibit.

In the initial planning it was decided that the Exhibit should be non-competitive. There would be no prizes; the work would be appraised by qualified judges and their appraisals would be sent to the exhibitors. The main purpose of the exhibition is to draw attention to the work being done in rural Manitoba and, through the appraisal notes, assist and encourage rural artists and crafters in their creative pursuits.

The first exhibit in 1948 had thirty-nine exhibitors and one hundred and nine exhibits. No restrictions were placed on the number of entries any one exhibitor could submit. However, as time went on, the number of exhibitors so greatly increased that restrictions had to be placed on the number of individual entries. The success of the project is due to the assistance of many groups and individuals, not the least of which are the Women's Institutes.

What has been achieved in the promotion of the Rural Art and Handicraft Exhibit? In general terms, there has been an awakening and stimulation of interest in rural Manitoba in better art and craft. Artists have found satisfaction in the rewarding experience of original work. Crafters, likewise, have been inspired to create articles, both functional and ornamental, very often from so-called waste materials.

The list of exhibits is impressive and it represents a collection representative of every part of the province. It is also indicative of the wealth of talent to be found in rural Manitoba.

There have been woodworking items, among them furniture, lamps, inlays, miniature and standard-sized violins, mahogany-mounted miniature tools, completely operational; carvings and polished driftwood. There have been the traditional handicrafts: quilts of traditional and original design, hooked rugs, basket weaving using wheat straw, seed pictures, crocheting, tatting, cut-work, crewel work, needlepoint, petit point, European lace, weaving, ceramics, copper and leather tooling, aluminum etching, and more recently, Indian beadwork.

But the heart of the W.I. handicraft program is the competition at the provincial and national levels. Then workmanship, originality and suitability of design become increasingly important.

Manitoba Women's Institutes have competed nationally. Basswood W.I. won second prize in the 1949-51 hooked rug competition. They entered forty-two quilts in the 1951-53 competition, thirty-five entries in the later Grandmother's Quilt Blocks competition. Souris W.I. was mentioned in the chair seat competition in 1958-61.

W.I. LEADERSHIP SCHOOLS

Once each year, every fall, Institute members go back to Leadership Schools, as they are called. And that is what they are, for at their Leadership Schools, members, under the direction of specialists in particular fields, learn the how and why of a wide range of handicrafts.

For example, there are the conventional crafts, or variations of them: rug hooking, knitting, weaving, embroidery, glove making. But there are twentieth century crafts too: aluminum and glass etching, copper tooling, winter bouquets made from dried weeds, seeds and grasses, glove making, and many others. When the course is completed, they return home to share their new-found skills as leaders.

In conclusion, it must be admitted that the Institute program of encouraging fine hand work, of sharing in and arranging exhibits of the best in handicrafts, of providing instruction in such crafts, may, in the beginning, have had its origin in the activities of the Manitoba Branch of the Canadian Handicrafts Guild. Still in the years following the first home economics societies, Manitoba's Women's Institutes have developed a handicrafts program in the best tradition of home and country.

8 ❧

Saskatchewan

INDIANS

In dealing with the various groups comprising the Saskatchewan mosaic, one must first consider our own Indians. The crafts of the Plains Indians, because of their way of life, were different from those of the Indians of other parts of Canada. By the middle of the eighteenth century the Assiniboines had embraced all the prairies of Canada as their hunting-ground. The Stones settled in the northern part of the province and had close contact with the Crees and Blackfoot. Their clothing was made from the skins of animals, as was the tipi, their home. The furs used depended on the local fauna — deer, moose, beaver, muskrat, squirrel, or rabbit. Buffalo, being heavy, was used mainly for blankets and bedding. The squaws invariably dressed the hides: sometimes the fur was left on, depending on the garment. There were no patterns; the hides were cut and trimmed and sewn according to the amount of material and their own designs, following methods and styles which they had learned as children. The sewing outfit was primitive, consisting of a knife or stone to cut the material, a bodkin to punch holes, a bone needle, and thread which consisted of sinew from the back or leg of some animal.

The everyday costume of the Plains Indian was usually unadorned.

When embroidery was used it was done with dyed or undyed porcupine quills, goose quills and moose hair. Robes, depicting real scenes from the life of the wearer, war exploits, or dreams were peculiar to the Plains Indians. The costume of the warrior or brave was perhaps the most colourful. His jacket was of six-ply leather in its natural colour and fully embroidered. Shields were of painted buffalo hide. The scene depicted showed an exploit in battle or a vision of a supernatural blessing bestowed upon the wearer. The war shirt and tent were also painted in like fashion. The moccasins were of two styles fashioned of beaver with the fur retained. One style had a single piece of skin with a soft sole, the others being two-piece styles with an added sole of tough rawhide. It has been said one could tell what tribe an Indian belonged to by the shape of his track in the sand.

On the plains the realistic paintings on robes and tents were pictorial records, rather than expressions of an artistic impulse, just as the totem poles of the Coast Indians are family records. Geometrical figures on raw hide of white, red, yellow and black showed considerable skill in line drawing and often produced pleasing effects, but their unceasing repetition of straight lines, zigzags, triangles and rectangles had a taint of monotony. With the coming of the white man, bead work took the place of quill embroidery and still exists among Indian tribes. They still maintain their old geometric designs. Present at nearly every fair or exhibition are representatives of the various tribes, resplendent in their colourful costumes. They perform their war dances and add much to the picture of the western fair. Every souvenir and craft shop has large displays of Indian crafts, and these are much sought after by tourists.

OUR ANCESTORS AND THEIR CRAFTS

In Saskatchewan at the turn of the century, a vast area, in fact a virtual empire, was thrown open to settlement. Moreover the political and economic climate of Europe was favourable to emigration and exploration. Canada was the only place on earth where good land could be had for the asking. Settlers came by the tens of thousands from 1892 to 1912. They came from the Ukraine, Poland, Germany, Scandinavia, Britain, the United States and Eastern Canada. The whole prairie region was clamorous with building, ploughing, sowing, the making of new homes in a strange land, the changing from old ways to new, facing danger, hardship and privation, that one's children might know a better world. And so a type of mosaic developed wherein ethnic groups tended to keep in touch with one another and retain their own Old World traditions. All of them, Dane, Doukhobor, Englishman, Swede, Ukrainian, Yankee, Scot were faced with problems of survival which dictated working together. Out of the lessons of survival grew a tolerance and respect for one's neighbours.

ROUMANIANS

Roumanians formed settlements in Saskatchewan in the early years of the present century, the largest of which were located at Kysart, Macnutt, Canora, Regina, Assiniboia, Flintoft and Cavell. Most were induced to immigrate to western Canada by the CNR and CPR railways, to provide labour for the construction of branch lines. They were mainly of peasant origin and lovers of the soil. As soon as sufficient money was saved most of them settled on homesteads, forming small homogenous communities. Many of their native customs have been preserved. In the old land everything was of necessity made by hand — furniture clothing, tools, spoons, dishes and many other articles. In Saskatchewan they found all things could be bought so that many of the old crafts were no longer needed. For many years just breaking the prairie sod and wresting a living from it took all their time. There were no leisure hours to do elaborate embroidery or wood carving.

With the gradual acquisition of labour-saving devices, women came to have more time that allowed the old crafts to be revived. Roumanian influence may be seen in the delicate crochet and knitted lace of very fine thread, and battenburg, netting, fillet and pillow lace. Georgeous head scarves of real gold thread were woven on a background of real silver thread. Curtains were of spun silk. Wool dyed with vegetable dyes was used for patterns on hand woven linen. The cross, tulip, acorn and carnation were often repeated in the patterns.

Textiles are a main branch of Roumanian folk art and the use of carpets for interior decorating survived for many years among the settlers. They were used for decorating walls, beds and wooden benches, where the rich colours and artistic designs of the rug lent a warm, cosy atmosphere to the cabins of the homesteaders. Lambs' wool was used for weaving.

Roumanian women deserve to be ranked among the world's best

cooks, as those who have partaken of their hospitality can testify. Braided bread, in addition to its dietetic function, plays an important part in the symbolism which pervades so many aspects of Roumanian life. The dough for the bread is rolled and braided, after which it is baked in the form of rings, resembling giant doughnuts, and varying in size from that of a saucer to a dinner plate.

Wood carving and pottery have been revived on a small scale. Elaborate carving was used on wooden scoops, dowry chests and razor cases. Pottery containers for water, milk, cheese, cottage rolls and other foods, could hold enough for two hundred people. Miniature copies of typical ceramic jugs were made and sold at the Roumanian Orthodox festival in Regina in 1965.

GERMANS

While most of the settlers from Germany settled individually, there were two Roman Catholic German settlements: St. Peter's colony, northeast of Saskatoon, and St. Joseph's colony, west of Saskatoon. The Saskatchewan settlers were fairly evenly divided between Lutherans and Roman Catholics. Good music in our province owes much to German influence. German societies have kept alive the interest in native crafts.

At arts festivals there usually is a very large and beautiful display of crochet, wool embroidery on heavy linen, cut-work, hand weaving, knitting, large netted table cloths, wood-carving of elaborate design on plates, carved figures of wood, hand-decorated boxes, handmade boots and clocks. Pottery-making is one of their most interesting and well developed crafts. The hairpin lace done with a hairpin and crochet hook in very fine thread, produces the finest doilies.

POLES

Although Polish refugees from the political upheavals in Europe came to Canada between 1776 and 1825, it was not until much later, from 1890-1914, that they settled on the prairies. They were chiefly peasant farmers, and in spite of many bitter experiences with the peoples already on the prairies, settled on the land and established homes. Fellow countrymen followed these pioneers after the close of World War I. They have taken great care to preserve the traditions and crafts of their native land. When they appear at Folk Dancing festivals, the women wear beautiful white satin costumes trimmed in ermine. Men's costumes are also very colourful. They brought with them from the homeland gowns embroidered in gold thread, in original floral design, in colours of rose, green and blue. Battenberg lace of very fine thread is another of their outstanding crafts.

CZECHOSLOVAKIANS

Most of the Czechs and Slovaks came directly to Saskatchewan from Crechoslovakia, though some came from the United States, where they had settled two or three decades earlier. They usually came in small groups and settled around Esterhazy, Marriott, Glenside and Yarbo.

Czech women display their artistic taste in the decoration of their homes and in the beautiful hand embroidery which is indeed one of the chief arts of the Slovak. In the diary of Mrs. Graves Simcoe we find this tribute to a Moravian neighbour: "A Moravian woman, married to a farmer near here, brought me a loaf of bread, so peculiarly good that I could not but inquire about it. She said it was made with rennet and whey without yeast or water and baked in wicker or straw baskets, which is the method taught at a Moravian school in the United States."

Speaking of their hand crafts we find the Czech and Slovak characteristics in punchwork cushion tops done predominantly in pink with multi-coloured roses. Round tablecloths and doilies hand knit of very fine thread had a lacy appearance. Then there are square multi-coloured table cloths having drawn-thread work in blue, gold, bronze and red. Still another type of tablecloth is done in filigree. No doubt the different styles were designated for use on different occasions. Tablecloths for display in their homes seem to have been a favourite kind of hand work for there is still another — a blue tablecloth with cut-work on white, the floral pattern done in satin stitch. A common article of bedding was the feather quilt, or feather tick, as it was called. The feathers of ducks and geese were stripped at family gatherings or parties. Sometimes several evenings were required to complete the job. These quilts are very, very warm and light. A genuine stripped feather quilt today is a luxury.

HUNGARIANS

In 1885 a Hungarian nobleman, Count Esterhazy, established a Hungarian colony at what is now Easterhazy. Many settlers were brought out from the motherland. They were all lovers of the soil. At the same time two other settlements were started at Whitehead and Stockholm. These people have preserved their knowledge of the Magyar language and a large number still subscribe to at least one Magyar periodical. The language has tended to keep the Hungarians together. It is a language of entirely different origin from that of Slav, Romance or Teuton, and so difficult to learn that only a few of the other nationalities have attempted to learn it. The Magyar culture is one of the oldest and produest of all European cultures, and its favourite proverb is "Not by might but by the spirit shall we conquer."

That they have a love of the beautiful may be seen in the following paragraph "The Hungarian nurse tells her charge, that his cot must be of rosewood and his swaddling clothes of rainbow thread spun by angels. The evening breeze is to rock him; the falling star to awaken him. She would have the breath of the lily to touch him gently, and the butterflies fan him with their brilliant wings."

Their crafts have been preserved in their hand-woven, heavily embroidered shawls. Patterns for embroidery are original flower and geometrical designs. Cross-stitch and satin-stitch are much in evidence. In their embroidery work, almost the entire surface is covered. The colours are very bright reds, blues and greens. Wall covers are often done in felt applique. Silk weaving and woven mats are often seen in their handicraft displays.

THE UKRAINIANS

One of our largest and most active ethnic groups is the Ukrainian. If culture can be defined as the way of life of a people, then the Ukrainian arts and crafts are a very vital part of their total culture.

The destruction of war and the absorption into the USSR have not destroyed Ukrainian culture. True, we could never rebuild or reproduce in Canada any of the irreplaceable historical collections and valuable archives, nor those still in the museums of the Ukraine. But through the Ukrainian Academies of Science, their educational institutions, lay and church organizations, they are rebuilding their cultural sanctuaries in America.

Upon arriving in Canada, far-sighted young women saw that concerted action in any project could best be achieved by organizing women's groups locally, at first. The Saskatoon local branch was formed in 1923. In 1926, The Ukrainian Women's Association of Canada (UWAC) was formed and their first convention was held at the P. Mohyla Institute in Saskatoon, Saskatchewan. The Association rallied Ukrainian women throughout Canada for the purpose of implementing their education to cultural and national consciousness so that its members would become better prepared to participate in Canadian life. Part of the program was aimed at preserving and developing Ukrainian arts and crafts. The major crafts were embroideries, weaving and Easter eggs. Because Saskatoon is near many Ukrainian communities, most of the pilot projects originated there.

The Association promoted and directed exhibitions, workshops, Ukrainian costumes, modelling for conventions of the national, provincial, and regional levels, as well as for festive occasions in Saskatoon and throughout the province. Courses and workshops in these fine crafts are supervised by qualified instructresses.

Interest grew and invitations for displays came from the students at the University, the National Council of Women's Convention, held in Saskatoon, and from various English groups. The UWAC responded to requests for exhibits from other cities of Canada and the United States. Up to about 1941 the articles loaned were mostly privately owned.

Instructions on reproducing embroidery and weaving designs and Easter egg decoration, were sent out to all branches. The women's page of *Ukrainian Voice* assisted with instructions until 1960 when the monthly journal *Promin* took over the arts and crafts section. As interest grew rapidly, it was necessary to find a repository for the collection assembled. This was found in the P. Mohyla Institute and it was here in December, 1941, that the main Arts and Crafts Museum of the Ukrainian Women of Canada was officially opened. A volunteer group from the Saskatoon Association formed the Main Arts and Crafts Museum Committee. The work consisted of educating, collecting, researching, identifying, renovating, classifying, cataloguing and preserving articles both for exhibition and for student study. During World War II, Ukrainian embroidered articles were sold in Toronto, Montreal and Winnipeg in aid of the Red Cross.

Because of limited space it is not possible to list all the articles to be found at the Ukrainian Saskatchewan Museum, but here are a number: twenty-five hundred embroidered samplers, some representative of the different regions of the Ukraine; finished embroidered linens; albums of printed embroidery and weaving designs; complete costumes and parts of costumes; displays of Easter eggs; woven tapestries of homespun and home dyed wool; small library on Ukrainian Arts and Crafts; a typical Ukrainian peasant home in miniature; ceramics from the Ukraine; woodcuts, woodwork and pamphlets on various crafts. The Museum hopes to add a Music Library, Ukraine musical instruments, and complete men's regional costumes.

Other Ukrainian groups in the province contributing to the handicrafts are the Ukrainian Catholic and Ukrainian Orthodox churches. Their contributions included: hand-carved chests, altars, crosses, decorated church pews, church lecterns, and carved picture frames. The beautifully embroidered church linens, church banners, priests' vestments, all evoke feelings of admiration and pride in one's heritage.

Pottery clay was discovered around Preeceville and at least one man fashioned vessels of it. There was a short-lived business in the line of plaster of paris moulding in Saskatoon. Hand-moulded miniature busts of historical personages such as Shevchenko and Franko were produced and sold. During the coronation year of George VI and Queen Mother Elizabeth, their miniature replicas were moulded and sold as souvenirs. Blacksmiths were skilled in metal work. Such things as crosses for churches and cemeteries, ornamental iron gates, ornamental fences, sleigh runners, hinges, keys and locks were made in the blacksmith shop and served their purpose adequately.

The Ukrainian Arts and Crafts Museum, Saskatoon, is a member of the Canadian Museums' Association, and is listed with 4,956 other museums in the United States, Canada and other countries. Guests have registered from all over the world. The present address is: 1240 Temperance Street, Saskatoon, Saskatchewan, Canada.

MENNONITES

Mennonites are members of a Protestant sect which originated in Switzerland in 1525. They, like the Doukhobors, refuse to bear arms or to take oaths. In 1878 about a third of the Mennonite population of the Ukraine came to Canada and the United States. Accustomed to life in the open steppes, they built comfortable huts surrounded by shelter belts. They lived in villages surrounded by tillable land.

The Saskatchewan Mennonites came either from Manitoba, where they had settled earlier, or directly from Russia. In Saskatchewan they settled around Duck Lake, Rosthern, Hague, Warman, Drake, Dalmeny, Hepburn, Waldheim, Laird and Swift Current. Their style of dress distinguishes them from other ethnic groups. The women wear long black dresses, black cotton stockings, stiff black shoes and a long black scarf wound tightly around their heads. For them, there are none of the bright colours loved by so many other ethnic groups. For church going, they wear white prayer caps. They sewed and tailored many articles of clothing. Workmanship is of the highest quality. An article bearing the Mennonite trade mark assures one of the best in material and craftsmanship.

Quilts, always one of their specialties, are made mostly from wool taken in the raw state, washed, pulled and carded. In the early days the carding was all done by hand. Now they use a drum carder operated by a crank. Quilts were finished by placing two or three layers of wool between factory cotton and tying or stitching. A separate washable cover was placed over all. Some covers are pieced of scraps of silk or cotton, joined by feather stitching, which add strength and beauty. Hooked and braided rugs are found in every home. Much embroidery of almost every known stitch was done. Bedspreads and curtains were embroidered to match and sometimes matching work was done on bolster covers for the head of the bed. Doilies were crocheted, knitted or tatted.

DOUKHOBORS

These people who came from Russia were mostly dissenters from the Orthodox Russian Church. They refuse to bear arms, believing that the taking of human life is contrary to the teaching of Christ. They first came to Saskatchewan in 1899, settling mainly at Blaine Lake, Yorkton, Lanigan, Cowan and between Saskatoon and Prince Albert. All colonies excepting the last named were communal. They suffered great hardships in the early days. Money was needed and the men went to work on the railways leaving all the heavy tasks of making a home in the new land to the women who were not used to performing these tasks. When the North Saskatchewan River colony settled between Prince Albert and Saskatoon, poor families dug holes in the river banks until homes of log or sod could be built. This group, although living in a colony, did not favour communal ownership.

Their dress was Russian style; men wore goatskin coats and caps, beshmets and high boots. The women wore bright red and blue skirts, heavy black jackets and coloured head shawls. Their diet was strictly vegetarian. They are famous for their bread baked in large home-made ovens and their borsch soup. The women made their own clothing and stitched blue jeans for the men. They still spin and weave, and these handicrafts find a ready market. Their table linens are considered equal to the finest from Ireland. Their knitting is described as being as fine as the famous Shetland shawls and of the same gossamer quality. The staple colours of the woven fabrics seem to be browns, fawns and greys, but in wearing apparel brilliant colouring is general. They are always singing at their work, for to them music is the breath of life.

HEBREWS

Lithuanian Jews came to Saskatchewan around the year 1906. Their main settlement was in the bush country of the Carrot River Valley. The land was a wilderness, but by 1936, in spite of drought, seven thousand acres were under crop. Other settlements were at Somerfeld, west of Estevan and Wapella. Many of these people had been trained at the Agricultural School of the Jewish colonization school in Galicia.

The Hebrews had a natural instinct for designing and were expert tailors and shoemakers. They made outstanding contributions in music, the arts and business but few of these people stayed on the land.

At the Festival of Arts their display was mostly of a religious character; beautiful silver dishes, candelabra for their festival of lights, prayer shawls, books bound in leather and set with stones.

THE GREEKS

Though the Greek people are a small minority in the province, and generally found in the cities as restaurant owners, they have handed down their crafts from generation to generation. The key theme is used on Greek vases and embroidered in gold and silver on blue costumes. Cross-stitch and satin-stitch are their favourite embroidery skills. Drawn thread-work is used on tablecloths and bedding, sheets, pillow slips and doilies. Lace is done in fillet with heroic Greek figures woven into the patterns. Wall plaques of lovely designs are used in many homes. Shopping bags in very colorful hand-woven tapestry were on display at the handicraft festival of 1965.

FINNS

Among the smaller ethnic groups to pioneer in our province were those who migrated from Finland in 1887 and settled south of the lower Qu'Appelle valley. When the Finns became established they named their colony *Uusi Sicomi*, meaning New Finland. In later years colonies were formed in the Dunblane, Macrorie, Dinsmore, Lucky Lake, Birsay, Glenside and Shaunavon areas.

Finnish men were skilled axe-men and handy with carpenter tools. In their native land they built the cabin and made the furniture. The first school built by them in Saskatchewan in 1896 now serves as a tool shop. It is still in excellent condition — a testimonial to the craftsmanship of the Finnish pioneer.

One of the first things these people did was build their sauna or steam bath. Wherever possible it was built near water but even on farms out of sight of lake or stream there was a sauna. In the pioneer days on the bald prairie the cabin part was often built of sod. In one corner stood a layer of field stones beneath which was an iron fire place. The stones became hot, and cold water was thrown over them to produce steam for the bath. The Finns claim that one emerges revitalized, relaxed and purified.

The Finnish women brought the art of weaving on looms from the old land. Now the looms are mainly used for making rag rugs. Tapestries and rugs were used on floors, walls and beds in Finland for centuries. What gave the rugs their significance was their beauty and their reflection of the life of the people. They were made by rich and poor alike. "The Tree of Life" was the favourite design in church tapestries and samplers. The pioneer Finnish woman in Saskatchewan wove hats, mats and baskets from wheat and oat straw. The straw was soaked to make it pliable, then braided, and finally sewn into the desired shapes.

Other crafts of Finnish women included knitting, crocheting, embroidery and sewing.

There are three Icelandic settlements in Saskatchewan. The first homestead was established in 1885 in a district which came to be called Thingvalla near Yorkton. In 1890, settlers moved in north and east of the Thingvalla district reaching as far north as the present town of Calder. This district was called Logberg. In due time the two merged forming the Churchbridge-Calder district. The third Icelandic settlement was established in the Foam Lake and Fishing Lake areas and is said to be the largest of the three.

Christmas has always been a very religious occasion. Even in the very first years there were Icelandic pastries for Christmas. The delicacy in meat was and still is smoked mutton. One of their national festivities and a day of rejoicing was the celebration of the first day of summer, namely the Thursday between April 18 and 27. Icelandic celebrations consist, in part, of speeches, singing and athletic events including the Gilma, a type of wrestling exclusively Icelandic. Mid-winter concerts for many years drew people from every part of the Lake's Settlement. A band and choir were organized.

In pioneer days, footwear was made of sheep or pigskin and resembled a slipper or a low moccasin. Every home had a spinning wheel, some of which were brought from Iceland. Sheep were sheared; the wool washed, dried, teased, combed, and then spun into yarn for knitting. In most homes both boys and girls were taught to knit. They claim that the Icelandic method of knitting is faster than the one common in Canada. In this style the operation of passing the yarn over the needle is omitted.

Handicrafts distinctly Icelandic in origin include grey wool blankets with floral patterns in two shades of grey. No dyes were used in their knitted sweaters, which were of brown, grey and white wool. Their cross-stitch cushions were done in shades of rose, yellow and green. Some of their table utensils were made of wood. At the Festival of Arts there was a hand-made spinning wheel seventy years old and still in use.

DANES, SWEDES AND NORWEGIANS

The Danes and the Swedes came to Saskatchewan along with other settlers from the United States where their fore-fathers had settled earlier. Thus they knew something about preparing virgin soil for seeding, how to build their own homes and in many cases how to make the furniture.

The Dane brought with him his traditional genius for improving soil and animals — a genius which frequently earns him the title of "The World's Best Farmer." The Dane has also a high regard for education. Of those coming to the prairies, about one-third had taken a course in Folk High School in the old land. This included training in the crafts of the native land and better methods of farming. They were among the world's first people to understand the value of cooperative marketing. And from their homeland they brought this knowledge, thus giving leadership to cooperative enterprises in the land of their adoption. Canada built its cooperative organizations largely after the Danish pattern.

The women are skilled in embroidery and rug making of original design. Crocheting and knitting are also favourite types of hand work. Danish men do excellent woodcarving and landscaping.

The first Swedish settlement was at Stockholm, Saskatchewan, in the eighties. Later ones were established at Norquay.

Women are experts in crocheting, quilting and knitting, in both plain and decorative work. In all Scandinavian homes you will find an abundance of different types of embroidery – hardanger, hedebo work, crewel and cutwork. They excel as cooks, and are noted for their steamed rye bread, coffee ring and brittle bread. Their colourful and heavily embroidered native costumes add brilliance to folk song and dance.

Wherever there is a Swedish settlement of any size there is a gymnasium. Swedes are ardent skiers and have done much to encourage this sport in Western Canada. Most Swedish farmers are skilled as blacksmiths and generally do their own blacksmith work.

In Saskatchewan there are Norwegian settlements in Glen Mary and Outlook. A religious people, interested in education, they founded the Outlook Lutheran College in 1916. Although most Norwegians have intermarried, they have perserved their native crafts. Their homes contain such handcrafts as wood carving, upholstery, crocheting, quilting, knitting, embroidery such as crewel, hardanger, and hedebo work. The landscaping surrounding their homes bespeaks their love of beauty.

THE FRENCH

French Counts settled at Whitewood, in what was then known as the

Northwest Territory of Assiniboia. There was something fascinating about the idea of Frenchmen of the aristocracy living among the other pioneers. They tried various enterprises: growing sugar beets, sheep ranching, cattle ranching and growing chicory, but none of these were suited to the prairie conditions of that time. They invested vast sums in their endeavours, all of which failed, and most of them returned to France, disillusioned.

The social life of these French settlers was most impressive. At the balls, claw hammer coats, white shirts, and low necked dresses were common attire. The Counts were courteous and generous hosts. Moreover, they were fine musicians and gave an air of romance to our early pioneer life.

Other French settlers in Saskatchewan are rather scattered. Among these are some who settled around Cutknife in 1903-04. The early homes, though constructed of sod or logs, were always enriched by the spirit of family life. Parties were often held and a new-comer was always welcome. Their love of the beautiful was shown in the lovely flower beds outside the home and the plants inside the homes. Their crafts were many for they knit and sewed to make their families comfortable. Every home had its share of embroidered and crocheted articles. Mats, braided or hooked, were always in evidence. Their love of homes encouraged them to build fine, new houses as soon as possible. Saskatchewan French have mixed with other nationalities but few descendants of the pioneer families speak French although there are villages settled by French-speaking families from Quebec, where French is still the everyday language.

THE ENGLISH

Toward the end of the nineteenth century, over-population in England and agricultural distress resulted in a heavy emigration to Canada. Two thousand English, at their own expense, emigrated and took up a block of 378 homesteads in Saskatchewan. Most of the English migration became scattered all over the prairies. There was one notable exception: the Barr Colonists, who established a colony of British subjects from all parts of the world near the present site of Lloydminster, in 1903. The first official name of the colony was Britannia.

English influence permeates all aspects of Canadian life — church, professional, Universities, schools, industry, mining, and farms. The

Rhodes Scholarship Fund provides an intellectual link between Canadian and English life. It gives Canadians an opportunity to study in English Universities.

The early English settler in the west was sometimes referred to as the "Green Englishman." He had not had the experience in farming on prairies that most of his neighbours had, but as it has been said, he may have been green but he was far from dumb, and he knew how to adapt.

Their early homes were sod or tar-paper shacks and they brought little but their love of music with them. Both men and women enjoyed singing and playing instruments. Wherever possible, they organized bands. Among the women, the making of patchwork quilts, hooked and braided rugs, crocheting, embroidering, and knitting were favourite crafts. Pioneer English women learned to bake their own bread, make soap, cure hams and bacon, and churn butter. Midwifery was another of their accomplishments.

A warm welcome was always accorded the visitor — one must always stop for a cup of tea. The knitted, embroidered, crocheted or quilted tea cosy was slipped over the tea pot to keep the tea hot, while neighbours caught up on the news.

SCOTS

No one has added more colour to Saskatchewan than the Scots with their beautiful tartans and the sound of the bagpipes. No fair or celebration is complete without the band of Scottish pipers in their colourful kilts playing their stirring airs. Although the Scots did not settle in groups and were dispersed among other nationalities, their crafts are certainly noticeable in provincial life.

Tartans are worn in men's shirts and women's skirts and dresses. Many a woman boasts that the suit she is wearing was made of the tartan of her mother's or father's clan. Handicraft displays feature hand-woven paisley shawls, very fine lace cloths, tartans, different kinds of embroidery, hand-woven tweeds, and the traditional Fair Isle knitting. Scottish foods cooked chiefly on special holidays such as Bobby Burns day include bannock, scones, haggis and oat cakes.

A thrifty, intellectual people with a determination to succeed, our Scots have contributed much to education in Saskatchewan. Certainly national sports, golfing and curling, are very much a part of Canadian life today.

THE IRISH

Over-population and the complete failure of the potato crop in Ireland led to the first migration to America in 1847. The Irish did not settle in colonies but were sewn broadcast and soon were associated intimately with other Canadian settlers. Some came to western Canada by way of the United States; others came directly. Protestants and Catholics were fairly well balanced. Any appraisal of the Irish which does not make reference to the humour they contributed would be sadly incomplete, and Irish wit made a much needed contribution to the bleak days of homesteading.

The early Irish settlers were their own architects, masons, smiths, carpenters, farmers, and gardeners. They have kept up many of their native crafts, excelling in linens. Cut-work cloth, Irish hand woven tweed, tea cosies, sweaters made of the virgin wool from Arran Island, are still much in evidence.

AMERICANS

The Americans came to Saskatchewan mainly in the early 1900's. Dr. Oliver, in his analysis of settlement in Saskatchewan, estimates that about one-third of the American immigration consists of North Europeans of the second generation. Their fathers came from Northern Europe to central United States. Their descendants pushed northward to the prairies. Another third are of Yankee stock, belonging to the westward American movement that came from New England and other eastern sections of the usa, via the Ohio and Mississippi to the American Northwest and thence to Canada. The other one-third of the American immigration consists of British and Eastern Canadian folk who were repatriating themselves, some in the first, some in the second generation.

The building of the prairie section of the cpr was allotted to an American firm, and labour was recruited from the usa, thus helping to advertise the plains of western Canada. Demand for farms in the

United States was great, prices rose and the European immigrants who settled there saw that their sons could do better for themselves if they went north to the virgin lands of the Canadian prairies.

CHINESE AND JAPANESE

Although very few Japanese or Chinese settled in Saskatchewan, those who did have made a definite contribution to the arts, and the cuisine, of the province. While many Chinese citizens have made their native dishes well known to other Canadians, their handicrafts have brought them attention. Among the most beautiful crafts are embroidery on velvet, embroidered pictures and Chinese fans.

Embroidery is the favourite handicraft of the Japanese; however they are also famous for flower arranging and for the development of landscaping and miniature flowers suitable to our climate.

SASKATCHEWAN'S TARTAN

The richness of golden ripe prairie wheat immortalized in prose and poetry has been captured in strands of wool in the background colour of Saskatchewan's new tartan, designed by Mrs. Lillian M. Bastedo, wife of the Lieutenant-Governor of Saskatchewan. Only one other province, Nova Scotia, had an officially recorded tartan at that time. Unless officially recorded, the design remains merely a plaid.

Mrs. Bastedo planned the design on a drawing board, not on a loom where most wool designs originate. Samples of the design were then handwoven. The colours chosen are described as gold for the golden ripe prairie wheat, brown for the summer fallow, green for the Saskatchewan forests, red for the Saskatchewan lily, yellow for the rape seed flower and sun flower, white for the snow, and black for oil and coal.

The tartan is intended for use when no other tartan is applicable. It is also available to residents of the province where there is no hereditary claim to a clan or family tartan, but it will not supersede the traditional tartans. Wool colours for the tartan were developed by a Canadian wool manufacturer and the fabric is being produced in Canada. The design is very colourful and is to be seen in skirts, dresses, shirts, and men's hats.

In 1949 the Saskatchewan Government acknowledged the need of special attention to the arts by the creation of a body named the Saskatchewan Arts board to deal with them. The Board has encouraged drama, visual arts, ballet, literature, music and crafts in a variety of ways. Among these are the Arts Festivals sponsored in conjunction with local organizations such as Homemakers, IODE, Hospital Guilds, Home and School Associations and Co-op Guilds. By providing an opportunity to exhibit craft charactcristic of ethnic groups along with modern adaptions of these, almost forgotten skills have been revived, and pride in work with needle, loom and tool has been fostered.

During the Festivals, recognized artists in crafts and other arts have instructed those interested in improving their understanding and skills. Pottery making, weaving, wood working and Indian handwork have been among the crafts encouraged in this way. Saskatchewan residents interested in handicrafts have thus had the opportunity of meeting and seeing the work of craftsmen from all parts of the province, of receiving evaluations and instruction from recognized men and women in the field and of learning about the crafts peculiar to the varied backgrounds.

9 ✎

Alberta

IN THE MEASUREMENT OF YEARS, Alberta's documented history is a short one. It is only a little more than two hundred years since the first white man gazed upon this beautiful land and less than two hundred years since the first permanent structure was built.

The fur trading era, 1778-1874, is well documented through the journals and diaries of the early explorers and missionaries, who vividly picture the hardships and perils on the frontier. But they were mostly men of vision who realized the important role they were playing in wresting a new land from the wilderness. If any of these men could gaze upon the Alberta scene of today, they would realize that even their greatest hopes had been realized.

Modern railways and automobiles have replaced the old Red River carts; cities have grown from stockaded trading posts; beautiful churches have replaced the crude log missions; and industry and agriculture are providing a bountiful living for more than a million people.

That Alberta boasts one of the highest living standards in the world can be credited in a large respect to the oil boom. Prior to the oil strike at Leduc in 1947 the economy of the province was on a level with other provinces, but with the influx of people after 1947 the economy rose particularly for those with education and training, and still more for specialized technicians. Advanced technology and good highways has brought more leisure time, with the result that crafts (and arts) are becoming increasingly important to the Albertan way of life. This interest has been created and fostered by competent instructors and is to be found in practically every area.

BLACKFOOT INDIANS

The Blackfoot Indians, comprising three tribes, the Piegan, the Blood and the North Blackfoot, lived near the eastern base of the Rocky Mountains. They were typical nomadic Plains Indians dependent for a livelihood on the great herds of buffalo that darkened the broad expanses of their country until they were exterminated in 1880-1881. Their life was attuned to a hunting existence, a life of movement. Their villages were composed of portable, skin-covered lodges that could be quickly dismantled and easily transported to new and distant localities. The Blackfoot were not only the most numerous and powerful Indian people of the region but also the most aggressive. Through a hundred years of conquest, the Blackfoot drove back their enemies until they were able to claim a vast area east of the Rockies.

Early fur traders and explorers described the love of the Blackfoot for ornamenting their native costumes and equipment with simple but colourful and attractive designs; of their painstaking care in manufacturing the most common household objects with the most primitive of tools; and of their ingenuity in utilizing native materials in their decorative arts. Out of stones and woods they carved axes, knives, spears and arrows; from shells were fashioned hoes; from bones fish hooks. Wicker was twisted into traps and nets were woven from fibre and willow bark. Cooking utensils, dishes and woven baskets also appeared. Early in the nineteenth century, they learned to adapt some of the European-made materials from the trading posts to use in a traditionally Indian manner. The primitive Blackfoot who hunted the wandering buffalo required durable material for clothing and shelter that could be easily transported. They found that the skins of the larger animals – the buffalo, deer, elk, antelope and mountain sheep – admirably met these conditions. Lodge covers of buffalo cow skins could be folded tightly and packed on a travois when being moved from one temporary camping place to another. The travois consisted of two long poles fastened to a saddle and dragged behind.

A frame or platform was built behind and provided a place for a family's meagre belongings.

SEWING

The hard work of skin preparation and sewing was woman's work, and the need for many helping hands to dress the hides required by a family is cited as one of the reasons why hunters usually took several wives. Dressing the skin involved many tasks: first the fleshing to remove fragments of tissue, fat and blood; then scraping to obtain even thickness; tanning by working it over with a smooth stone and then drying in the sun. As this shrunk the skin, it must now be stretched. Finally it had to be softened. Skins to be used for making clothing often were smoked after being dressed. This smoking enabled them to dry soft and pliant after the garment had been exposed to rain or snow (the smoking odour that permeated the skins was considered a means of repelling mosquitoes and moths).

For thread, broad bands of sinew were cut from the legs and neck of the buffalo or deer. Shreds were pulled off with the teeth, softened in water or in the mouth, smoothed with the fingers and twisted by holding one end in the mouth and rolling the sinew between the palms of the hands. This sinew thread was passed through holes punched in the skins with a sharp pointed bone awl. Four different stitches were used – an over and under stitch, the running stitch, a mending stitch and an ornamental stitch. The women exhibited their skill as seamstresses and in dressing the skins.

PAINTING

Next to the dressing and sewing of the skins, painting is probably the oldest of the major crafts of the Blackfoot. Numerous and ingenious native paints were derived from animal, vegetable and mineral sources. Earth paints were the most common – here they obtained the reds, yellows and whites; charcoal and black earth furnished the black paint. The native pigments were ground to a powder in small stone mortars, and each color was kept in a skin bag closed at the neck with a buckskin drawstring. To use they were mixed with hot water in a clam shell cup, or mixed with the glue extracted from the tail of a beaver boiled in water or the white, clean under-scrapings from a hide. The Blackfoot artist's kit also contained a number of straight, peeled, willow sticks of different lengths which served as rulers in marking or painting straight lines on rawhide or soft skin. Every outfit also had a number of bone paint brushes for applying the colour. These brushes were cut from the porous edge of a buffalo shoulder blade or the end of a buffalo hip bone. The honeycomb composition of these brushes enabled them to hold the paint which flowed smoothly onto the surface of the skin. Some brushes were pointed for painting fine lines, others were rounded for spreading colour over larger areas.

The articles usually decorated with painted designs were parfleches (folded envelope-like, rectangular cases), tubular cases, shields and drum-heads – all of rawhide. Soft skin robes, men's shirts and leggings, lodge linings and lodge covers were also often painted, as well as such objects as the tripods, supporting back-rests used inside lodges, arrow shafts and war clubs and dance paraphernalia.

As a rule the women were the painters of geometric designs on rawhide cases, robes and lodge linings; the men used human and animal forms. They painted devices on their shields and drums, the religious symbols on their lodge covers and covered their robes with picture writing extolling their deeds of bravery in war.

Many of the lodges were decorated with animal paintings as well as geometric designs. In the animal figures on lodges we find the finest expression of Blackfoot religious art and the highest achievement of traditional Blackfoot painting.

Even today, painting in oils on buckskin is a Blackfoot speciality, with themes by Gerald Tailfeathers of the reserve near Cardston being particularly fine examples of this unique craft.

QUILLWORK

The Blackfoot Indians have a beautiful legend explaining how the first porcupines were given to one of their ancestors by the powerful Thunder Spirit. The same legend states that Thunder taught this person how to do quillwork. Quillwork was a decorative art of the Indians before the white man came, and usually done by women. Porcupine quills are of a whitish colour with black tips and range in length from one to five inches. Some were used in natural colour, others dyed to make attractive designs. The dye plant was dampened with water and a number of quills placed on top, wrapped in buckskin. This package was placed under the women's bed on the ground where it was pressed by the weight of her body for a couple of nights. The pine tree lichen supplied the yellow dye, a red water plant supplied the red and a blue coloured plant the blue dye. Quills were also dyed by boiling them in water with a quantity of coloured trade cloth.

Quillwork was regarded as a sacred craft which the girls and young women were taught by the older women. Quills of the same size in assorted colours were kept in long, cigar-shaped bladder containers until ready for use. The quillworker's kit also included some bone or metal awls for making holes, a quantity of sinew thread and a bone or horn instrument for pressing or flattening the quills after they had been sewn on.

Today quillwork is almost a lost art. Prior to 1870 women's dresses and moccasins were decorated with quillwork, but by 1880 beadwork had become so popular that quillwork was almost abandoned. However, there has been a slight revival of quillwork of late due to some difficulty in obtaining beads and also to the interest and encouragement of leaders working with the Indians.

BEADWORK

Blackfoot bead embroidery is of comparatively recent origin. The little glass or china beads, made by Venetian craftsmen in Italy, were introduced by the white fur traders. For ways to use these beads the native women turned to their traditional Indian craft of quillwork and followed the same designs on the same areas of decoration as the older craft.

There are different periods of beadwork: the Real Necklace, the Real Bead and the Seed Bead. A large bead of varying colour was used in the Necklace period. The Real Beads were smaller than the necklace beads but larger than the small seed beads used for embroidery. Real beads were applied to articles of clothing in narrow bands — women's dresses, men's shirts, leggings and moccasins. We find some costumes decorated with beads, some with quills, both being used in relatively simple designs, the older abstract geometric elements and the decorative flower and leaf patterns. The beadworkers used the simple methods employed by their mothers and earlier ancestors until

1870. Moccasins and leggings received the most decorative designs. Everyday clothing was trimmed only with fringes, while the ceremonial clothes were elaborately decorated.

Now we find that an outlet for authentic native crafts has been opened in Edmonton — Team Products Ltd. — which gives the shopper an opportunity to buy something that is truly Canadian. At the same time qualified workers are assisting and encouraging the Metis and Indians to do their native crafts and preserve their cultural heritage. At Team Products Ltd. a shopper will find decorative footwear in traditional designs of precise beadwork for the whole family for many occasions – low moccasins or slippers in numerous styles trimmed with fur from mink, coyote, lynx, beaver, muskrat, fox or rabbit. Some have solid beaded vamps, some open beaded design, some colourful and ornate and others subdued and simple.

The costumes of the Slave Indians of the Northwest Territories are depicted in replicas of dolls in beaded outfits trimmed with fur complete with mukluks and mittens; or dolls dressed in white caribou trimmed with Arctic hare, brown smoke caribou edged with beaver. Also to be found are mittens and gloves, purses, bolo ties and brooches of solid beadwork, bows and arrows, caribou bone knives for letter openers and many other fascinating bits of Canadiana.

TEAM PRODUCTS LIMITED

Teamwork is not a new idea among the Indians. Survival itself has depended on it. While fathers were hunting, grandparents took care of the children. When the meat was brought home, women took over with their skills. The children were always there to run errands – so, as a team, they survived.

This way of life is still important even though many changes have taken place. Survival still depends on teamwork and a better life can be earned by working together.

Indian craft had been steadily diminishing in many areas of Alberta in recent years, but with a co-ordinated marketing service and a Teamwork purchasing advantage, the art is being revived. Many younger women are once again learning the art of beadwork, birchbark crafts, porcupine quillwork, moosehair embroidery, leather tanning, and others.

All Teamwork crafts are marked with a tag showing the Indian Arts trademark.

In Calgary the Indian Friendship Centre was opened in 1964. Both Indians and non-Indian groups have assisted to establish this centre in order to give all forms of assistance to the Indian people living in Calgary and to those moving in from the reserves. The craftroom is also an outlet and a revival centre for Indian crafts. The articles are brought in from the five Reserves: Sarcee, Stony from Morley, Blood from Cardston, Peigans from Brocket, the Blackfoot from Gleichen as well as those living in Calgary. There is jewellery of all kinds from lovely modern beaded necklaces and earring sets to the old authentic sets. There are exact copies of war shields, spears, tomahawks, pemmican pounders, axes, and knives. Chicken dance costumes and feather head-dresses, buckskin purses, hackets and leggings all beautifully beaded are to be found there.

The same can be said of the Old Cabin Crafts in Calgary. This is a non-profit organization that is a very important outlet for Indian crafts in Calgary.

BRITISH

The largest ethnic group in Alberta at the last census was the British. Many of the early fur traders were British and the early police force was made up of soldiers from eastern Canada. Then came the immigrants from the British Isles and Ireland, and from eastern Canada, especially Ontario, and they settled in the towns as well as on homesteads. There were only two group settlements, the Barr Colonists at Lloydminister and the Parry Sound colonists from eastern Canada.

In 1903 the Barr colony of over fifteen hundred men, women and children was established in the Lloydminister area. They sailed out of Liverpool Harbour in March 1903 with two thousand on board, having staked their future on the promise of new opportunities in a new world.

The Parry Sound colonists, one hundred settlers and their families totalling three hundred, left Ontario in April 1892 and came to Fort Saskatchewan, Beaver Hills, Ardrossan and Lamont. They brought with them some sheep, the spinning wheels and looms – to bring one without the other would be folly. They clipped the wool, washed, carded and spun it into yarn. All the woollen clothing for those early years was knitted or woven from this yarn; the whole family participated in the routine of making clothes. The looms were in constant use as they were loaned to other settlers. The only time a lamp was used was when visitors came. When the coal oil supply was exhausted tallow dip was used, usually made of twisted rag submerged in a vessel containing oil. Another article in demand was a candle mould which would make five candles at a time when tallow was available.

FRENCH CANADIANS

The most important aspect of French-Canadian influence in the development of Alberta was the coming of permanent settlers, largely from eastern Canada, to make themselves a new home in a new land. Life was very primitive and the women spun wool and knit mitts, caps, socks, sweaters and other necessities. The missionaries had already tested the soil and climate for agriculture as each mission was dependent on its own efforts to exist. The community life centred around the mission while the church was the dominant factor in bringing in French Canadians and settling them in group settlements. French was and still is the language spoken in many settlements, although it is slowly changing as the young people mix with neighboring comunities in sports and other activities.

UKRAINIANS

Alberta can boast that the first Ukrainian settlers to arrive in Canada in 1892 settled in Alberta north of Lamont. They arrived from Western Ukraine which was then a part of Austria. The general heavy influx of settlers followed from 1896 to 1913. The reason for this migration was oppression, overpopulation and lack of land resulting in poverty as families increased.

These settlers brought many thing with them, such as scythes, flails, implements, utensils carved of wood, looms. The women brought feather beds, pillows, beautiful hand-woven tapestries, colourfully decorated sheepskin coats and jackets, and, of course, their beautifully decorated linens embroidered in flat stitch, cross stitch, drawn work and others.

In Ukraine, the women were very versatile in all forms of handwork. To own a large stock of linens was an indication of good housekeeping. Upon migrating to Canada, they found conditions very different. They soon learned it was no longer necessary or practical to make everything by hand, when inexpensive factory-made articles were available. In her rapid adjustment the Ukrainian woman quickly discarded the hand tools and the loom, but not her embroidery.

In the years that followed, it became apparent Ukrainian crafts were deteriorating, and they realized that if something were not done, their traditions and crafts would soon be dying out and their cultural background would disappear. The Ukrainian Women's Association of Canada was organized in 1926, and one aim was to revive Ukrainian arts and crafts and to preserve them. After collecting thousands of old and new articles a museum was opened in Saskatoon in 1941. In 1944 branch museums were opened in several cities, including Edmonton. Undoubtedly these will continue to expand as the women and men continue to hold classes for Ukrainian crafts and to hunt for heirlooms. Older women are teaching the younger ones the art of making the traditional bread called *paska* and *babka* and the Christmas *kolach*.

One of the most beautiful of all Ukrainian traditions is the decorated Easter egg with artistic designs of a symbolic nature. In the Ukraine the decorated eggs are called *pysanky* which means to write. The design is actually written on the egg with a special stylus dipped in beeswax, after which follows a series of dye baths. Some *pysanky* are not eaten but kept as keepsakes and even framed.

The origin of this art is ancient and obscure. Archaeological excavations in Ukraine show that it was practised several thousand years before the Christian era. Originally *pysanky* symbolized the release of the earth from the shackles of winter and the coming of spring with its promise of new hope, new life and prosperity. After the advent of Christianity, the decorated eggs took the new symbols of the Resurrection – the promise of eternal life. A painted egg may well be called a miniature mosaic.

Most of the homes decorate many Easter eggs during Lent, when it is traditional to give an egg to one's friend with the greeting, *Khrystos Voskres* (Christ is Risen) to which the reply is *Voistyno Voskres* (He is risen indeed!). It is a beautiful custom as these eggs are kept as souvenirs for years, and it is common to hear someone say, "I received this ten years ago from a friend."

GERMANS

The settlement of the German immigrants took place after the construction of the Canadian Pacific Railway during the years 1885-1890.

186

From that time until 1911 over 140,000 Germans, of which about one third were born in Europe, settled in the prairie provinces and British Columbia, mostly on farms. Only a small percentage were skilled workers. Together with other nationalities the main contribution made by the Germans was in agriculture. They were industrious people, carded their own wool, knit, hooked mats and were good dressmakers.

ICELANDIC

In March 1888 a group of fifty Icelandic settlers from North Dakota decided to emigrate to Canada. After making investigations, they began the arduous journey by rail to Calgary, and then by horses and wagons to an area west of Innisfail. They settled in a wilderness, penniless and entirely dependent on their own resources. The next Spring a further influx of settlers came from North Dakota. To help out financially the men sought work in Calgary while the women looked after the children and livestock. Everyone had a flock of sheep and after shearing, the women washed the wool, then spun and knit it into warm clothing. Extra socks and mitts were traded at the stores in Innisfail for groceries. The women were proficient at handicrafts of all kinds — embroidery, knitting, crochet, and hardanger, as well as making quilts and comforters and clothing. At first they had neither time nor materials to work with, but later the arts were revived. When time and money were in supply, all top sheets and pillow cases were embroidered in hardanger.

SCANDINAVIAN

The original settlers in the Burnt Lake area were Scandinavian, chiefly Swedish and some Icelandic. The majority arrived after the Calgary-Edmonton railroad was built in 1891.

Their crafts too were based on necessity of survival. Although many of the men had trades in the old country they came here to farm. They became excellent axe-men as the area was wooded and the homes and all the buildings were constructed of logs. The women carded and spun wool and dyed some of it. Knitting seemed to be

187

done by all, and a few had looms on which they wove fabrics for clothing needs, mats and blankets. Some of the women tanned sheep hides and made shoes for the children. This was an Icelandic craft. There are still a few spinning wheels and candle moulds in the area as evidence of their efforts, but the women of this generation sew and knit the modern way.

Some of the furniture was fashioned by hand; a table and benches was made without nails. The only imported items were the pots and pans. The spinning wheel and the ability to use it was most important in this young country.

DUTCH

In Alberta there are old Dutch settlements at Monarch, Granum, Nobleford and Neerlandia; and new settlements in central Alberta and other areas and in the cities. These new Dutch settlers are enriching Alberta life through their gay, immaculate shops specializing in Holland cheeses, chocolates and bakery products, a Marionette Theatre which requires the utmost skill and imagination to operate, fine craftsmen, geologists, and farmers who maintain a high standard of workmanship. The embroidery of the Dutch women is distinctive and becoming more evident as they join with craft groups. They have interested many women in their cross stitch by counted threads, knitted lace, drawn fabric and other embroideries and have raised the quality of workmanship of groups they have joined.

HUTTERITES AND MENNONITES

As well as racial group settlements, there were religious group settlements who obtained large tracts of land. One of these group settlements is the Hutterites, who emigrated to Canada about 1902 when Canada promised them exemption from bearing arms. Although they do not join in community activities, they are industrious and peace loving and in many places they have turned poor land into a pleasant place. They are not aliens, as all but a few very old members were born in Canada.

Mennonite immigrations to Canada fall into four definite periods:

188

the first was the movement to Upper Canada from United States in 1786 after the American Revolution; the second was from Russia in the 1870's; the third was in 1923 to 1930 from Russia; and the fourth were the displaced persons after the Second World War.

All these migrations have given Alberta new settlers, and their chief crafts are connected with their work, their homes and surroundings.

While the settlers brought their crafts with them, the promotion of arts and crafts in Alberta dates back to sometime previous to the formation of Alberta as a province.

We find that the first Exhibition of the Edmonton Agricultural Society was held at Edmonton House on October 15, 1879. The Hudson's Bay Company kindly offered the use of two rooms in the Fort, one for vegetables and one for ladies' work. Attendance was large, and the ladies' department was well represented with some beautiful work in silk, wool, worsted and leather which was displayed and entered for competition. This Exhibition served as an impetus to more work in the future. These annual events were a highlight in the new country and did much to stimulate interest in needlework.

Today Alberta is fortunate in having several provincial agencies promoting handicrafts by various means of assistance to the general public — from the amateur to more advanced groups with instruction available on the professional level.

HOME ECONOMICS EXTENSION SERVICE

(ALBERTA GOVERNMENT)

The first Women's Extension Service Program in Alberta took place in a tent. At the Summer Fairs in the year 1906, the Alberta Department of Extension welcomed women and girls to lectures and demonstrations in Domestic Science. The program included such topics as "Science and System in Housekeeping" and "Rational Furnishings." In the following years instructors from Macdonald Institute, Guelph, Ontario, conducted Domestic Science Short Courses. It was during this period that the Alberta Women's Institutes were organized and Women's Institutes branches were being formed at various places in the Province. These women were requesting courses in home economics.

An interesting project began in 1913 when "The Mixed Farming

Special" toured the province, carrying as many as twelve cars, two of which were devoted to domestic science. Many more Women's Institute branches were organized and the Department of Agriculture assumed responsibility for their supervision. Women travelled long distances to attend the Short Courses which featured topics on home sanitation and disease prevention, as well as foods.

In 1916 the Alberta Women's Institute Act was passed by the Alberta Legislature and more Short Courses were started due to their great popularity. Provincial Schools of Agriculture and Home Economics trained the young men in the fields of agriculture, horticulture, farm machinery, and woodcraft. They gave instruction to the young women in all phases of domestic science, homemaking and crafts. There were originally six of these schools, but at the present time there are three, now known as the Alberta Agricultural and Vocational Colleges, and the school term has been lengthened. The Schools continue to instruct young women during the winter months in the fields of clothing, home furnishings and crafts. For the young men they are stressing agriculture and vocational training and are rated as Junior Colleges. At the Old School there is a specialized clothing course which trains girls to take positions with commercial firms.

For the first time in the history of Alberta Extension work, a number of handicraft short courses were given to Girls' Clubs in 1921. In a number of communities suffering from drought conditions, this instruction proved a means of enabling some of the Club members to earn badly needed money.

One of the features of the Biennial Convention of the Alberta Women's Institutes held at the University of Alberta in 1921 was a Handicraft Exhibit. This featured many beautiful articles made by New Canadians from Russia, Sweden, and other lands. A very fine collection of articles, made by the Doukhobors in the Cowley vicinity, included fine towels and lace made from flax, and some very beautiful rugs. Provost Girls' Club contributed basketry; Strathcona Hospital loaned a display of articles made by soldiers. A Swedish exhibit was sent from Coronation. The Edmonton Handicraft Guild also contributed.

During the 1920's interest was shown in practical handicrafts and courses were given in Basketry and Millinery. The basketry course aimed at having women develop their work along lines which would enable them to go into the making of small articles of household furniture for their own use. The Department of Agriculture Annual Report states:

Many of our people have come from countries where arts and crafts are a well organized and paying industry. Through time we should discover those skilled and, using the law of demand and supply as a basis, bring people wanting such goods into contact with those who have the training to carry out the specialized work here, rather than having them send to the old lands. It is an important factor in our development as a province that we get to know the possibilities that are within our own territory.

ALBERTACRAFT EXHIBITIONS

It is difficult to assemble facts and figures in connection with early Albertacraft Exhibitions. They were started in 1953, with the primary objective to display craft work from Alberta, but interest has been so keen that many exhibits from groups and skilled individuals outside the province have been invited to display exhibits.

In the beginning these exhibitions were held in such centres as the Edmonton Art Gallery and Calgary Coste House. Because of the lack of facilities they were limited in size and scope. After the Auditoriums were built, in Edmonton and Calgary, Exhibitions were held in them on alternate years.

The 1963 Albertacraft entries in ceramics and weaving were outstanding. Never before had Albertans been able to view such variety and quality in these two fields. The experimental weaving of students from Alberta College of Art illustrated ways of combining new and local materials with standard and traditional weaving approaches. Ceramics from students, Guilds, instructors, and professionals illustrated approaches to both functional and decorative ceramics. Clay bodies were used to set off simple glaze areas, and texture and form became the essence of nearly all the work exhibited.

Albertacraft 1965 can also boast of an excellent display of stained glass windows. This was the first time stained glass exhibits had been displayed.

BANFF SCHOOL OF FINE ARTS

One of the world's unique education centres is Alberta's Banff School of Fine Arts.

The University of Alberta was founded in 1908 and the first President, Dr. Henry Marshall Tory, realized the University would only thrive and prosper to the extent in which it became personally involved in the lives of the people in the province. To bring this about, he travelled to the remote parts of Alberta lecturing on such widely diversified subjects as English literature, evolution, philosophy, and science. This was the beginning of University Extension Work in Canada.

As Dr. Tory travelled, he was impressed with the great desire of the people for goods books, music, painting and craftsmanship. In the fields of painting and handicrafts an ingenious plan was devised. A selection of paintings from the National Gallery of Canada, supplemented by two collections of paintings by Alberta artists, print reproductions and lantern slides, were assembled and a qualified lecturer was engaged to tour the schools and communities. The next year a collection of 320 pieces of handicrafts of different types was also sent out on tour.

It became apparent that there was a need for a permanent school where arts and crafts would be taught. In 1933 an experimental school in the arts was set up in the Public and High Schools at Banff — which was the beginning of what is now known as the Banff School of Fine Arts.

It started as a school in the arts related to the theatre. The school has grown until today (1967), offering a wide selection of courses in painting, music, drama, ballet, playwriting, short story and radio writing and technique, handicrafts, oral French, applied arts, weaving and design, leathercraft, modelling, and pottery. From the beginning the most qualified instructors available on the continent have been secured. The School has been recognized by UNESCO (United Nations Education, Scientific, Cultural Organization). Each year one or more UNESCO Fellows are in attendance.

Courses may be taken for credits leading to Banff Certificate or towards University degrees. Courses may also be taken by people who are studying professionally and by others who are taking the courses for their own recreation and pleasure.

From 1933 to 1946 the Banff School had no buildings of its own, but in 1965 was located on a thirty-acre site on Tunnel Mountain, across the river from the Banff Springs Hotel. The school provides excellent facilities including sleeping accommodation, dining space, class room space, an auditorium and permanent administration offices.

A strong force in the shaping of the crafts development in Alberta is undoubtedly the Provincial Government sponsored Recreation and Cultural Development Branch under the direction of Walter Kaasa. It includes drama, music, libraries, athletics, and visual arts.

The government began this venture in 1938, and an advisory board, made up of artists and craftsmen from various parts of the province, helped to form policy. In 1946 the department began awarding scholarships to worthy students and sending instructors to small centres where interested groups had asked for instruction. A bulletin called *Leisure* was published, giving news of activities in all the fields under the branch. Small booklets were published, which, in conjunction with display trays each graphically showing a craft, were circulated in the province. The booklets are free, on request. Some of the crafts so demonstrated were wood carving, lino block printing and batik.

Now the board is creating a library of slides for general circulation in the province. These have, as subject matter, crafts on all levels in the province plus national and international crafts.

The printed catalogue of available crafts' material (constantly revised) is invaluable, and free.

The Alberta Branch of Canadian Handicrafts Guild was formed in 1929 and is the link that joins all the Guilds that have been organized in this province. Its headquarters alternate between north, south and central in order to shorten travelling distances. The Alberta organization is affiliated with the Canadian Handicrafts Guild with headquarters in Montreal and is subject to the same constitution and by-laws.

Exhibitions are fostered and encouraged. Free use of halls and buildings is granted for this purpose by the government, businesses and other institutions, thus making a large contribution towards the furthering of interest in crafts.

WEAVING

This craft was brought to Alberta by the early settlers. It was a necessary part of their life and many of the older generation were skilled weavers. It cannot be said that any particular ethnic group brought this craft as women from many countries were experts with the spinning wheel and the loom when they settled here.

However, when manufactured material became available this time-consuming chore of carding, spinning and weaving became almost a lost art. The Searle Grain Company and the Canadian Handicraft Guilds did much to encourage weaving in the province. In addition the Calgary Guild purchased ten looms, which they placed in Coste House, and the Cultural Activities Branch gave assistance by teaching weaving courses in many centres. The weaving courses offered at the Banff School of Fine Arts gave further instruction and valuable help.

Today weaving is also taught to patients in Mental Hospitals, Rehabilitation Centres, and others, as occupational therapy and is a source of income.

Alberta can boast of the fact that in 1949 Mrs. R. B. Sandin of Edmonton was the second person in Canada to receive a Master Weaver's Certificate. Mrs. Frank Graham, Calgary, has also received this award.

QUILTING

Most Alberta homes boast one or more examples of the fine art of quilting which is closely entwined with the history of our country. Pioneer women were faced with the problems of creating with brains and fingers, needle and thread, the necessities of daily living. Quilts were essential for warmth, but they were also decorative.

The patchwork quilts of the early settlers developed into the pieced quilts. They were carefully cut out and pieced together to form large blocks which were joined to make the cover. The early designs were usually geometrical, but as the years passed and material became available, the "laid on" or appliqued type of quilt was developed. Many new and interesting designs were originated. It was, and is, a proud moment when a woman could boast of an original design.

In the early days "quilting bees" were one of the most interesting and entertaining events of the social life of the time. A bride's chest usually contained a baker's dozen — twelve for ordinary use and the thirteenth, known as the bride's quilt, was planned after her engagement had been announced.

Whatever the pattern of the quilt, whether decorated with designs of the quilting needle, richly appliqued with pieces of cotton, or in a crazy patchwork style, all were the product of a definite home craft which produced many useful, beautiful and lasting quilts. This is a craft that has continued down through the years. Patience in piecing and designing and the finest of stitchery go to make up this old-fashioned, useful type of work.

In 1959 the Federated Women's Institutes of Canada had as its Tweedsmuir Handicraft Competition, "Grandmother's Quilt Blocks," and branches of the Alberta Women's Institutes submitted patterns such as Lover's Knot, Optical Illusion, and Pinwheel. An Alberta entry won first prize from those entered across Canada.

This project required the inclusion of blocks that were pieced, appliqued, embroidered, quilted only, and original designs. Assembled in album format, each entry contained not only pieced blocks, but also quilting designs for each pattern, as well as scaled drawings in the colour of the finished quilt. The winning group was submitted by the Sunshine Women's Institute, of Coutts, Alberta.

More than twenty members were involved in the project. Of the original designs several are worthy of special mention. "Marion's Stripes and Squares" was designed by Mrs. Marion Macdonald Neilson in the early homestead era when she used tiny scraps of any length and width. With a gay solid colour for a diagonal stripe, through the middle of the block, she would piece the scraps in Roman stripes on either side, with a tiny black triangle at the corner. When set together the triangles formed a square, the solid midribs a larger square and the whole quilt an all-over geometric pattern. Thrift was the keynote; beauty the result.

Canadian Autumn is a colourful appliqed block in leaves of warm red, muted greens, falling past brown tree trunks. The whole is high-lighted with coloured embroidery. A moment of time on a lazy autumn day is captured in this naturalistic design.

Prairie Harvest has as its basic motif a conventionalized head of wheat made of yellow print on a tawny background. The blades of wheat are made of vivid gold and orange. Above the horizon a brown elevator thrusts its top upon the pale yellow sky. This is a handsome design for a master bedroom in a western setting.

The book of quilt blocks is covered in a beige textured cotton with an old-fashioned lady and her humble home embroidered in brown thread on the cover. It is on display in the Women's Institute museum cabinet in the Coutts Civic Centre where it may inspire future quilt-makers, both those at home and from farther afield.

RUGS

In the early days of our country's history, rugs of any kind were a hard-earned and welcome luxury protecting the feet from the dampness of crudely built houses. Hooked rugs were one of the oldest needle-crafts. The method was simple — nothing but drawing a little loop of rag or yarn through the mesh of a strong but closely woven fabric. Today we find a revival of hooking, and new designs and techniques.

Braided rugs were made by braiding the material which had been cut into strips, then sewing them with coarse, strong thread being careful to keep the rugs flat. Materials used can be cotton, wool, nylon, denim, or anything else available.

Crocheted rugs were done with a heavy crochet hook, a purchased steel hook or often a wooden hook fashioned by the man of the house. Materials were those available, but finer and closely woven.

Rag rugs or carpets made use of the discarded scraps of clothing. A sturdy type of mat was woven with a strong flax or cotton warp. The early colonists developed a reversible rug technique known as Summer and Winter — the dark side for winter and the light for summer. Rag rugs are cheerful and charming. They tell of the frugality of the early days when materials were scarce and everything was of value. They can now be woven on the simplest loom, as the weaving technique is one of the easiest to understand and the cheapest to do while offering a real colour harmony.

KNITTING, CROCHETING, EMBROIDERY

These were crafts which were a part of every early homemaker's life. The knitting provided the necessary articles of wearing apparel — socks, scarves, sweaters, toques, — and the crocheting and embroidery gave colour and beauty to the home. For a time home knitting machines were used but did not prove too practical. With all the new kinds of wool, from heavyweight of Siwash sweaters to fine baby wool, it is a challenge to knitters to try new wools, new patterns, and new designs.

Crocheting has continued to be a popular craft as it is easily learned, is not expensive and covers a wide range of decorative and useful articles. Efforts are now being made to promote interest in creating new and better designs.

Embroidery in simple, colourful stamped designs enhanced household linens down through the years. With emphasis on design and colour in recent years, the trend is towards the counted thread embroidery as proper materials are available. Specialized embroidery covers many different stitcheries: crewel work, drawn thread, drawn fabric, hardanger, creative stitchery, and others. Huck weaving could perhaps be included as well. Although the most popular type of embroidery traced on hot-iron transfer designs and has been used by the majority of women in Alberta from the earliest settlement, the women coming from many of the European countries had learned the art of embroidery by counted threads. Originality and creativeness in design can be achieved better on counted thread material as a design can be planned by working each stitch over the exact number of threads. Even weave fabric or canvas is essential, and is used for all drawn work, cross stitch, needlepoint, petit point, Assissi, and so on. During the past few years many women are embroidering this way.

Drawn thread embroidery, as its name implies, is carried out by withdrawing threads from the fabric and embroidering over the edges of the space of withdrawn threads. Decorative stitches are also worked over the loose threads. Drawn fabric embroidery is created by drawing together certain threads of the fabric. The actual stitching is not the main feature of this; it is the open pattern formed on the fabric by the pulling together of the threads of fabric.

Hardanger is a combination of drawn thread and solid embroidery and similar to cutwork except designs are suitable for counted thread material, while cutwork is stamped designs. The patterns are formed almost entirely of fairly elaborate openwork and completed by secondary motifs, executed in close or raised embroidery.

For centuries cross stitch has been used in embroideries in European countries. Each country had its own variation, and some countries had variations to denote the different regions in that country. Stamped cross stitch designs have been used since Canada was first settled; every little girl learned the art of making crosses, but now the European influence is being felt and the precise crossing of threads in good designs and colour combinations is gaining in popularity. The colorful Ukrainian cross stitch will always remain distinctive of the Ukrainian people and their traditions.

Needlepoint and petit point can be described as a half cross stitch, which should be worked in a precise pattern stitch to obtain a smooth front and back appearance. Petit point is worked on finer material which is the determining difference between these two. Beautiful pictures, scenes, designs and ear rings are worked in petit point. Needlepoint can also be used in pictures of larger size. Either wool or embroidery cotton is used, depending on the article. Using wool, durable chair seat covers, cushions, and wall hangings can be made.

Needle weaving, closely related to needlepoint but easier to work, had a spell of popularity a few years ago, when mostly cushion tops were made.

Crewel work is basically an English embroidery which is being revived. Its stitches are simple and so varied they are not monotonous. Crewel work itself is an antique needlecraft which gives scope for imagination with its freedom and grace and variety of colours.

Pillow lace making is, like knitted lace, one of the crafts brought here from Holland since the war, although it may have been done here years ago. It appears very intricate and time consuming, but the women who learned the craft when young still enjoy doing it. It was demonstrated at the Red Deer Handicraft Guild Display in October 1965 by Mrs. P. Winter whose nimble fingers tossed the bobbins back and forth creating the lace design.

WHEAT STRAW WORK

This was a craft of the depression years and was done in various areas of Alberta. Several articles were made but the most common were sun hats, jewel boxes, and carrying bags.

The straw was chosen when cut and graded into size of stems. The stems were stripped and soaked in water as the plaiting was done while wet. The plaiting or braiding was done with four or five straws around a central straw. A different weave was procured by using different sizes of straws and the number used. They were sewn together with stout string. Vegetable colouring did not take too well, but when left in natural colour, the straws turned a rich golden brown as they became older. Cardboard forms were used for the jewel boxes, which were lined with silk or other soft material. They were sturdy and attractive. The bags were often trimmed with raffia and would stand a certain amount of use. Several of these articles are still found in private collections.

HAIR WORK

Such items as watch chains and pictures were made of hair, and had a sentimental value. This was not a popular craft, but can still be seen in museums and as private keepsakes.

It was very fine work and required considerable skill to fasten the hair ends securely in the metal holders. A frame with weights was necessary as the working device. Five rows of numbers on the surface of the boards controlled the twists or cords that could be made. Each strand consisted of many hairs and was about the size of number ten thread. Several were loosely twisted together to form the watch chain, then clasps and fob were attached. Several colours of hair made an attractive chain. By using a variation of this work fancy woven belts were made from other materials. Horse hair was used for a coarser weave.

LAPIDARY

Originally, the cutting and polishing of stone was accepted as a minor part of jewellery making. From the crude beads made by prehistoric man down to the finely crafted stones made by the lapidarists today, this craft has a long history.

With the introduction of electrical tools, interest has been sparked in lapidary, for before this it was a very time consuming and drawn-out process. Lapidary is mostly a hobby of amateur craftsmen, who have little or no training in other craft areas.

The first gems were cut in convex forms and polished, but not faceted. These are called "cabochons." This is the popular form of cutting for the home lapidarist today. The scope of this craft is wide and varied. Besides the variety of jewellery that can be made, an imaginative craftsman can turn a few very ordinary stones into realistic looking insects, miniature furniture, pictures, and ornaments.

Lapidary came to the United States and Canada from Europe. The first clubs were formed in eastern Canada, then spread to the west. At present there are thirteen Rock and Lapidary Societies in Alberta, three located in the north and the others in central and southern areas. The objects of these clubs are to stimulate interest in the study of rocks and minerals and to encourage the pursuit of the lapidary craft by people of all ages. "Rockhounds" is a name given to members of these clubs.

Since equipment is expensive, most lapidary activity is confined to clubs. Many societies have purchased equipment for use by the members under the supervision of qualified instructors. Many families have their own shops set up in their basements.

Alberta is very rich in good polishing material. There is an abundance of petrified wood and some agatized wood. The bone beds of the Red Deer Badlands supply the rock hunter with agatized dinosaur bone, which takes a high polish and makes very beautiful and unique jewellery. These items make good souvenirs, representative of Alberta.

LEATHERCRAFT

In the early days harness making and repairing was important craft. Every settler and farmer learned the craft of repairing through necessity, but the craft of making a harness required the skill of the real craftsman who took justifiable pride in turning out a complete set of harness for heavy work, the light driving harness, or the fancy show outfit. Saddles and bridles have continued to be made as riding has become a hobby for many people — and there will always be need for the utility saddle and bridle.

Shoe-making and shoe-repairing is a craft and a business and one that will continue, but not in the home as it once was. Today the homemaker has found a new and satisfying way to work with leather through one of the craft courses that was made available to craft groups when the courses were first introduced. It is a craft that can be done at home once proper instruction has been given.

There is a large variety of leather for the craftsman to utilize. Leather is generally classified in three ways: the kind of creature it is taken from, the type of tanning process and the weight or thickness of the skins. Leather is a beautiful material and is usually thought of as being an already constructed material on which a craftsman merely tools, or carves.

POTTERY AND CERAMICS

One of the reasons for the interest and excellence in pottery in this province is that a ceramic division was included in the Alberta College of Art at its establishment. Alberta has abundant deposits of clay suitable for pottery and the availability of natural materials has thus made ceramics the major craft in Alberta today.

The first Potters Guild was orangized in 1950 in Edmonton. Interest spread throughout the province when courses were included in the craft program of the Cultural Activities Branch and instruction was given to craft centres. Centres were able to purchase kilns and other equipment through the Cultural Activities Branch and interest continued to grow as did membership. Craft Shops serve as outlets for all types pottery that is becoming known as typical of Alberta. It is more or less a group craft due to the equipment needed, although some enthusiasts have their own workshops.

RESIN WORK

A new craft that has not yet become general is resin work. Resin is a liquid plastic which is dyed to desirable shades and poured into moulds. It is expensive to buy, but it is possible to make some very lovely things inexpensively. The beginning project is always a picture or plaque on a fibre glass base. Such items as grasses, seaweed, small shells, and bits of lace can be used to make designs on the layer of black sand on the bottom; the color of the shells show up through the clear plastic on top.

WOODCRAFT

This covers many types of crafts dealing with wood, from the wood-turned articles put out by students taking shop at school to the wood carvers who create beauty out of old roots of trees and discarded bits of wood. Men are the main craftsmen in this art. Some are well known while many others work for their own creative pleasure.

Twisted, gnarled roots of the low-growing juniper, particularly those from the Alberta Badlands, have been shaped into carvings of weird beauty. The most desirable roots are to be found where there are high, steep hillsides where soil erosion occurs, or deep canyons, leaving the roots partly exposed to the elements. Many good sized roots are fifty years old before they are exposed and then often lie another fifty years before the juniper hunter finds them.

Juniper wood, when cleaned, shows quite a range of warm, beautiful shades, ranging from white, pale yellow, light to dark brown. The juniper carvers make lovely figurines, birds and animals, lamps, while some just clean and polish the twisted pieces to use as ornaments. In any case the finished product is a thing of beauty.

Mr. Wilfred Garstang Hodgson of Dorothy around 1920 realized the roots of the juniper might be carved. There is a strong imaginative quality to his figurines, partly due to the artist and partly due to the wood itself which lends itself to fantastic shapes, to symbolic forms that are quite distinct from the work of the artists.

In the Elnora district George Evans, C. Copeland, Don Ross and Andrew Thompson are carvers of juniper wood. Mr. and Mrs. R. A. Grant of Walsh both are interested in this craft. Mr. C. Copeland also works with diamond willow to make gavels, lamps, etc. Driftwood also lends itself to many interesting decorative items. Spruce, sanded and varnished, can also be used with effect. Sand-blasting technique makes lovely pictures, but one has to have the equipment and the knowledge for this type of wood craft. Mr. W. S. Wood, Red Deer, works on marble in the daytime and on wood for pleasure.

Another wood carver who has become known for his carving is Carl Antonson of Pibroch who carved a bust of all the Prime Ministers of Canada and the Queen as a Centennial project. His carving of Winston Churchill has drawn fine notices from the press. A native of Norway and now over eighty, he continues his hobby.

Still another wood crafter is Hobart Dowler who built log buildings that will stand as evidence of his craft for many years. Among the buildings he designed and supervised the erection of are the "Old Timers" lodges in Edmonton, Calgary and Red Deer, and the Rundle Mission Lodge erected as a Memorial Retreat for the United Church on the shores of Pigeon Lake. Each log building was first erected on Dowler's property. The logs were scribed while green, numbered, taken apart and shipped to their destination, where they were rebuilt.

CRAFT MOBILE

In 1964 the Craft Mobile — a travelling children's arts and crafts trailer — made its debut on the playgrounds of Lethbridge. The large friendly trailer, carrying craft materials and tools ordinarily not available on the playgrounds, rolled up and offered its treasures to the children wherever they played. For many children it provided a brand new, exciting and enriching summer experience.

Obtained from the Civil Defence Organization of the City of Lethbridge, and stocked and staffed by the Parks and Recreation Department, the Craft Mobile introduced an infinite variety of crafts such as mosaics, copper, basketry, leather, plaster of paris, puppetry, and paper craft. Youngsters made their own mosaic pictures from crushed rock and string, belts and keycases, copper pictures, baskets of many shapes and sizes, wall plaques from plaster of paris, paper mache puppets, murals in paint and paper crafts on the playgrounds.

With the establishment of craft centres and a mobile unit, the craft program opened a richer field for creative expression for all ages.

10 ✑

British Columbia

The handicrafts of the North West Coast Indians of the present age, and the portrayals of their history and tradition, were well developed when the Europeans arrived in the middle of the eighteenth century. Some of their artistic work and crafts have continued to this day, though modified by contact with European culture. Among the most popular of their arts have been the totem poles, depicting the mythical and heraldic figures belonging to various families. Fine examples of early totem poles are found in the Queen Charlotte Islands and at Sayward, but they are few. Many of the best poles have been moved to other sites where they are preserved as in Totem Pole Park, Victoria, at Prince Rupert, at the University of British Columbia, and in Stanley Park, Vancouver. Many people believe that the older totem poles which they see are examples of the art created before exposure to European culture, but according to the outstanding authority, Dr. Marius Barbeau of the National Museum in Ottawa, this is not the case. In his book, *Haida Carvers in Argillite*, (Bulletin 139, Department of Northern Affairs and National Resources, 1957), he says:

> They could not be; a red cedar, cut down when it is still green, carved a year or two later and planted without preservatives, is

highly perishable. Soon it begins to rot at the base, and its weight, together with the action of wind, storm and frost, brings it down within a fairly short span of years — often less than fifty years, particularly on the seacoast where the moisture persists the year round and the muskeg covering the ground and the lichen growth are corrosive. Up the Skeena and Nass Rivers, where the climate is dry and the soil may be gravelly, some of the oldest poles have stood unrestored for as long as seventy or, at best, a hundred years. They are the most archaic specimens of their kind. A systematic survey of all of them has made it clear that the totem pole carving evolved from humble beginnings after 1840.

It has been said that the art of totem pole carving was stimulated in its greatest period by the introduction of white man's iron tools, and that prior to this time, with dependence upon primitive stone tools the carving of poles and posts consisted of interior house posts and comparatively small, simpler memorial poles.

One of the best preserved totem poles today stands in the Queen Charlotte Islands at Skidegate Indian Village. It is carved from a huge cedar, and features the Eagle design at the top. The fine poles at H'kusam Village, Salmon River, near Sayward, now lie rotting on the ground, as in many other places along the coast.

The Haida Indians of the Queen Charlotte Islands were once a warlike race, and many tales are told of their fierce raids on the more peaceful tribes farther to the south. In their long, swift war canoes, they descended without warning upon an unfortunate community, and in some cases such villages were almost completely wiped out, or their inhabitants taken as slaves. But despite their ferocity, the Haida were a race richly endowed with artistic ability. Though their surviving totem poles appear to have been of late origin, their wooden ceremonial and other beautifully carved wooden objects are of much more ancient construction. Examples of their fine basketry, and some of their elaborate ceremonial robes, as well as carvings and artifacts have been preserved in museums and private collections throughout the world.

A fine example of one of their beautiful ceremonial rugs or blankets is highly valued in a private collection at Qualicum Beach. It is evidently one of the famous Chilkat or Tlingit blankets — once the most highly prized trade articles of the chiefs of various tribes of the Northwest Coast Indians. Closely and almost perfectly woven of mountain goat wool, as are most of these valuable old ceremonial blankets, it displays a balanced pattern of traditional motifs; two halves of the design from the central axis at the middle of the blanket being exactly alike. These blankets had their design drawn by a male artist of the tribe for the weaver's guidance, the woman weaver not daring to take liberties with the original pattern. It is now all but a lost art. The lower edge of the blanket is finished with a deep fringe of mountain goat wool and twisted cedar bark yarn.

Amongst the most highly prized examples of Haida Indian art is their argillite carving. Dr. Marius Barbeau states that white prospectors looking for copper and coal deposits first discovered the argillite bed on a mountain slope up Slatechuck Creek near Skidegate. A kind of slate, when found in the mine, it has a soft texture, but the argillite slowly hardens into beautiful black rock upon exposure to the air. The Indians carve it while it is still rather soft. Because of the high market value of genuine argillite carvings, the mine is carefully guarded for the exclusive use of the Indian artists. It is said to be the only site of such argillite in the world.

Carving argillite had its real impetus after the Indians had contact with the first white traders to the Islands. Dr. Barbeau quotes Francis Poole, who wrote of the subject in 1862:

> George Gunya, or perhaps his Connehaw uncle before him, must have been much impressed with the various tools, contrivances and instruments of the white traders on board ship. No doubt a sea captain played the flute before him, and he admired the white man's gifts and superiority. He went back home and tried his hand at the same achievement. Making his own flute and playing it seemed to have become his ambition. His keen observation and natural skill surmounted all difficulties. Soon he produced all sorts of curios for trade, among them ornate tobacco pipes, plates, and dishes as for the high table of foreigners . . .
>
> What materials could be used for such carvings was a question that found its own answer in the course of time — yellow and red cedar at first. Since there were no hard woods on the Island, Gunya used bone, whale's teeth, grizzly bear molars and walrus tusks. The natural resources of the country provided another medium, blue or dark slate; we now call it argillite. . . . It was his habit to work closely with the white adventurers. Soon he was certain that argillite could be worked like hard wood, and more easily than bone and ivory. So he carved a flute and a Pan pipe. To cap it all, he had the patience to learn how to play the flute.

Gunya's specialty was flutes beautifully decorated with floral and leaf designs, some with figures of frogs astride the flute facing the player, others with eagle, salmon or thunderbird decorations. Some of these flutes are still to be found in public and private collections. Other workers in argillite made plates and dishes, and among the artists was William Dixon. Figures of octopi, sharks, skates, sea-bears, killer whales and many other designs are carved on the plates, and the rims often inset with abalone shell, bone and opercula shell. The plates have a wide range of sizes and shapes. One beautiful oval example in the Detroit Institute of Arts is over eighteen inches long. Bowls in the shapes of beaver, frogs, ravens and other creatures; miniature chests and boxes, as well as model Indian houses were also carved. The development of the carving of miniature argillite totem poles, now probably the most popular form, seems to have come later than the other curios, beginning as late as the 1870's. Exquisitely carved, each small totem pole has its individual story. These are indeed treasures for collectors fortunate enough to own them. Unfortunately cheap imitations are now made of inferior materials, by unscrupulous imitators of this fine Indian art, for the tourist trade. The names of some of the argillite carvers are worthy of remembrance; Charlie Edenshaw, who lived from 1829 to 1924, is perhaps the best known. Amongst modern carvers Reuben Moody, son of Arthur Moody, who was also a carver, has a wide reputation.

The carving of wooden totem poles, both large and miniature, is carried on by Indians today in a number of places. As curios the miniature poles sell well, and larger poles are also in demand. The poles carved by Jimmy King of Campbell River, a native of Alert Bay and a colourful personality as well as a real artist with wood, embellish such places as the entrance of the Bayshore Inn in Vancouver, and Discovery Inn at Campbell River. The Comox band at Courtenay, under Chief Andy Frank, carved a number of totem poles for the British Columbia Centennial Year at their reservation. Similar projects are being undertaken by British Columbia Coast Indians in commemoration of Canada's Centenary.

Sam Henderson of Campbell River carves fine ceremonial masks as well as miniature totem poles. Dick Snow of the Anahim Lake Indian Reserve at Bella Coola does carvings, including totem poles. At Nanaimo the totem pole carving by Wilkes James has been carried on since his death by Stanley Bob; and Jimmy John Adams of Masset in the Queen Charlotte Islands uses traditional Haida designs in his carved and inlaid wooden trays.

The making of dug-out canoes from cedar logs was an important and most necessary skill of the Indians. In the Queen Charlotte Islands where some of the largest cedar trees grew, the Haidas made ocean-going crafts as much as seventy-five feet long. A very few dug-out canoes are still being made. When her Majesty, the Queen, and Prince Philip visited Nanaimo in 1958, Prince Philip made the first stroke of an axe into a huge cedar log that was later carved into an eleven-man canoe, christened *The Prince Charles*. This craft has won races wherever it has been entered in Canadian or international competition. The Indians at Clo-oose still make some dug-out canoes to ply the coastal waters, but this work is a dying art.

Basketry is a craft that the Indians inherited from their pre-historic ancestors, and which has continued among some of them to the present. The making of baskets by the Kwakiutl Indians is described in detail in the British Columbia Heritage Series, *Our Native Peoples*, Series I, Volume 7, published by the Department of Education, and procurable through the offices of the Provincial Museum of Natural History in Victoria. Here it is stated that "Kwakiutl basketry was confined almost exclusively to the 'soft' type, woven after the manner of matting, and the open 'bird cage' type."

At present there are a number of Indians who continue to make good baskets. The tribes at Clo-oose, Ahousat and Ucluelet keep the art alive, making multicoloured baskets of all sizes from grasses and the inner bark of cedar trees. Millie Jacobsen of Ahousat makes excellent baskets and mats. The Indians of Campbell River and Nanaimo also carry on the work. Baskets are still made at Masset in the Queen Charlotte Islands.

The art of weaving amongst the British Columbia coast Indians is of special interest and significance. The series of books relative to the native people of British Columbia (as mentioned above), describes this weaving at length.

A quotation from this source states:

The Kwakiutl had few needs for textiles. Nevertheless, they wove aprons, capes and blankets of goat wool and cedar bark, and hats of both cedar bark and spruce root. . . . All weaving was done entirely by hand without heddles or shuttles of any kind . . . Matting was woven on a crude loom consisting simply of two stakes driven into the ground with a horizontal crosspiece adjusted in height for the convenience of the weaver, who squatted on a mat before it. . . . For cedar bark and goat wool blankets a more elaborate loom was used.

The unique type of spinning of the mountain goat wool and cedar bark is also described in detail in the above mentioned manual.

In many parts of the province the Indians learned knitting from European settlers, and adapted it to their own use, spinning not only mountain goat wool, but sheep's wool, and even dog hair. Cowichan sweaters are made in a number of places on Vancouver Island. Also, in Bella Coola, on the mainland, Matilda Haas and Mabel Hill of the Anahim Lake Tribe, and in Clo-oose, members of the Nitinat Band spin wool for their originally designed knitted sweaters. Much of the same kind of work is done by the Indians of Nanaimo, who also continue the ancient method of making natural dyes for their crafts from plants and roots.

Leatherwork occupies some members of the Anahim tribe, who make buckskin jackets, belts, moccasins and gloves. Charlie Snow and Orden Mack of this tribe are skilled in silver and gold engraving for the making of jewellery.

Amongst the Indians of North Vancouver Island there are some of exceptional artistic talent. The work of Chief Speck of the Kwakiutl Tribe is becoming widely recognized in the perpetuation of beautiful traditional designs executed in exquisite wash and line drawings. The paintings of the late master-carver, Chief Mungo Martin, were also exceedingly fine. The silk screen printing, as well as the carvings of Ellen Neel, a niece of Munga Martin, are most praiseworthy. The painting of a former resident of Alberni, George Clutesi, is oustanding. Writing of him in *The Beaver Magazine*, (Spring, 1962), Ron Baird said:

> Clutesi carries a double yoke on his shoulders; a lifelong ambition to achieve complete recognition as a painter; and a second, even more compelling goal – to gain for his people the respect and understanding of their white fellow-Canadians. In both ventures, Clutesi has found the struggle a hard one and often a bitter one.

Born at Alberni, a member of the *Seshat* Band of Nootkas, he was sent to school at the United Church Residential School in Alberni, where his desire to become an artist was met with more discouragement than approval. Persistent in his ambition, however, he sketched on scraps of paper and cardboard. He left school at Grade 8, and turned to fishing; then became a labourer, and later a member of a pile-driving crew. A fall, in which he broke his back, laid him up for six years. Before he went back to heavy work, he opened a small variety store in Alberni, from which he sold his water colours and pastels.

Later he turned to oil painting. During his life there he gave much study to the traditions, customs and culture of the West Coast Indian tribes, and often staged Indian dances. During a visit to Canada by Her Majesty, Queen Elizabeth, Clutesi's troupe put on a full performance for the Royal party.

Though subjected to discouraging comments by the critics, his art found strong champions amongst prominent Canadians. Ira Dilworth, educator, broadcaster, and help to aspiring talent, gave him encouragement, and introduced him to Dr. Lawren Harris, the noted Canadian painter and member of the original Group of Seven. He was also encouraged by the the late Emily Carr who urged him to retain his unique style of forceful story-telling on canvas of West Coast Indian legends. Miss Carr willed to him her oil paints, a number of unused canvases, and nearly one hundred of her brushes. Besides his painting, Clutesi has given much time to lecturing on Indian lore, art and dances at the Victoria Art Gallery, the University of British Columbia Summer School, and Victoria Night School, and with these he has had outstanding success.

In recent years there has been a sincere effort on the part of both Indians and white people to preserve the culture of the Indians. With the efforts of Ellen White of Nanaimo, the wife of Chief Douglas White, and herself a Haida princess, ancient and modern crafts are taught and encouraged. The processing and preserving of foods and herbs, the manufacture of dyes from plants and roots, carding, spinning, weaving, needlework and wood carving are taught. To assist in fund raising for her numerous endeavours on behalf of her people, Mrs. White barbecues salmon, which is a special treat, in aid of church and social projects. The barbecuing is often done on the beach in the Indian fashion of long ago. She is interested in both the advancement of her race today as well as the preservation of the ancient culture. With the help of a recent Government grant she will be able to further this worthwhile work.

During the last visit of Queen Elizabeth and Prince Philip, the Indians formed a native village at Exhibition Park in Nanaimo. There various dances in costume were performed for the royal visitors. Foods were prepared in the manner of the early Indians, including a dessert resembling ice cream made from berries.

Efforts are made in many places to preserve the artifacts of the early Indians as well as examples of later work. In Campbell River, Mr. Ed. Meade, associated with the local museum, has done outstanding work in gathering and preserving many priceless Indian artifacts.

Many of the exhibits in the University of British Columbia collection were obtained through his efforts. In the Campbell River Museum potlach paraphernalia, costumes, ceremonial robes, noise makers and masks are all carefully labelled, and Mr. Meade has made tape recordings of the voices and stories of some of the historic figures in the Indian culture of the region. One of his most valuable pieces is a cedar bark costume which was preserved in an Indian home for many years because it had been carefully wrapped and placed in the attic of a dry house. The more usual fate of such valuable articles is their destruction by their owners through neglect from the ravages of mould or mildew.

Mrs. Lily Gray of Gabriola Island has an excellent private collection of Indian artifacts in her home – all found on the Gray farm at Degnan Bay. Dr. J. G. Macdonald of Qualicum Beach, whose mother – the daughter of Archdeacon Collison – was the first white child born in the Queen Charlotte Islands, has a comprehensive collection of Haida Indian art, including the ceremonial rug or blanket described earlier, some ancient masks, a beautifully carved chest, and examples of miniature argillite totem poles by noted Haida carvers.

The Museum in Prince Rupert preserves and displays Indian arts of many kinds. Bella Coola is building a similar museum. The Comox Band has preserved many examples of its arts and crafts. These are displayed at Centennial Park. During Fair Week these Indians perform dances and prepare barbecued salmon in native style. On Denman Island Mrs. Kirk has a small private museum of local Indian objects. Several collections of Indian arts are maintained in the Queen Charlotte Islands. At Ahousat there are Indian carvings to be seen in the cemetery. At Ucluelet some early fishing equipment is preserved, and some old style adzes are still used for the building of native canoes.

"Nanaimo has a fine collection of various Indian arts and crafts in its bastion." This historic building also houses relics of the city's pioneer past. Built in 1853 to protect the settlement, this famous landmark overlooks the harbour and Pioneer Rock, where the first settlers landed from Britain – a large number of them Staffordshire miners.

In the van of the revival of native arts and crafts in British Columbia have been such devotees as the late W. E. Necombe, Dr. Alice Ravenhill, Emily Carr, and Bruce McKelvie. Actively interested at present are Mr. Wilson Duff, until recently anthropologist at the Provincial Museum of Natural History, Victoria, and Dr. Clifford Carl, Director of this world-recognized Department of the Provincial

Government. The Indian Arts and Welfare Society of Greater Victoria has done a great deal to encourage the present generation of Indians to study and preserve their heritage, and provide financial assistance to promising native artists so their talents may be developed.

On the East Saanich Indian Reserve, Chief Edward Underwood and his wife operate a shop for the display and sale of Indian goods, while the Cowichan and Koksilah Bands near Duncan market their now world-famous Cowichan sweaters through a shop, The Canoe, on the Island Highway, south of Duncan. The knitting process employed in producing the Cowichan sweaters seems not to be truly an Indian aboriginal craft. Reputedly it was taught to the Indians by a Scottish woman. But the spinning process is said to be unique throughout the world, in its original form. Now, because of the increase in demand for these sweaters, mechanical devices are used to process the yarn. However, the final product is equally authentic and handsome. The wool is produced locally, given only the necessary minimum of preparation, retaining remarkable weatherproof qualities which are greatly appreciated by outdoor workers and sportsmen alike. The fleece of black sheep provides contrasting colour to the natural shade of the wool to establish typical Indian motifs and symbols for the patterns used in the sweaters, creating a truly unique product.

Spinning was formerly done with the use of a spindle, a rod three or four feet long placed through the centre of a spindle whorl. This was a disc of wood, eight or nine inches in diameter, that fitted tightly on the spindle, two-thirds of the way down the shaft. The loom consisted of two horizontal rollers supported in slots cut in wooden uprights set firmly in the ground. Warp was passed around these rollers in a continuous thread so that the web could be pulled around to a convenient position for the wearer, who always wove the fabric from the top downwards.

Successful attempts have been made to revive the Indians arts and crafts, particularly in the Okanagan and Hopeline Districts. At Osoyoos, under the guidance and leadership of Anthony Walsh, a stimulating teacher, the Inkameep Indians were inspired to again produce creative work in native plays, dances, and art forms that astonished the critics by their degree of excellence, as indicated by the winning of many prizes at the Royal Drawing Society in London, England, in 1936, 1937, and 1938. The work of these Indians was again exhibited at the Royal Drawing Society War Competition in London in 1943, and many more awards were received. Press and art critics highly commended the entries for originality of subject and fine workmanship.

The pictures submitted by these Indians were drawn and painted on home-tanned leather, and there were also excellent pencil, and pen and ink sketches. The subjects included war dances, games, hunting with bow and arrow, rock paintings, and drawings — horses, birds, bears. Reproductions of these pictures are being used as stationery for sale in support of the Osoyoos Museum, where the collection of fine Inkameep Indian original paintings and drawings are now on display.

A similar renewal of interest in the Indian arts and crafts is also taking place in the Hopeline District. Here, under the auspices of the Chilliwack Community Art Council, the Fifth Biennial Festival of Arts was recently held. Mr. Oliver N. Wells of Sardis has as his project: "To interest and encourage the Chilliwack Indians to re-establish some of those crafts which are their natural heritage." Among these arts are weaving, basketry, wood carving, bead and buckskin work, and more recently an interest has become evident in leather work, metal work, and sweater making. Arrangements were made to exhibit a display of thirty-nine items of native hand crafts, all made locally, consisting of small wood carvings, baskets, rugs, blankets and sweaters at the Dominion Handicrafts Guild Exhibition in both Montreal and Toronto in 1965. At both exhibitions the excellence of workmanship of all the Indian articles displayed was highly commended, and twenty-four of the thirty-nine entries were sold, realizing four hundred and twenty dollars for the craft workers.

OUR EUROPEAN HERITAGE

The pioneers who came to British Columbia brought furniture and personal articles with them that are treasured to this day by their descendants. At *Elkhaven*, the former Ormiston estate on Denman Island, one may see massive solid oak dining and bedroom suites, pictures, lamps, wardrobes, and a desk shipped around Cape Horn, all still in use. In other homes coffee grinders, flat irons, bedsteads, lamps, hand painted china, family Bibles and other books, cast iron pots and kettles, spinning wheels, guns, musical instruments, and grain grinders are prized as heirlooms today.

Arriving in the New World, many of these pioneers had to turn to new skills to survive. Boats and canoes had to be built for transportation. Hand-hewn shakes and shingles had to be made to roof the first cabins and houses. The art of splitting these with a "froe" came to Denman Island from New Brunswick. Much of the furniture was handmade after the settlers came – some of it beautifully crafted. Cattle and deer hides were tanned to make moccasins, gloves, pouches, and chair seats. The pioneer blacksmith was called upon to make many of the tools needed. Housewives saved fats to make their soap, using the ashes of hardwood for this purpose instead of lye.

In the increasingly affluent society of today more people are using their leisure to develop new skills, to revive old handcrafts, and to express their emotions and talents in the creation of things of usefulness and beauty in various artistic mediums. So today we have an infinite variety of needlework, woodwork, leatherwork, and crafts being undertaken, all of them interesting to learn, and yielding satisfying results.

An unusual type of needlework, fascinating to watch, intricate to execute and beautiful in completion, is pillow lace. As its names implies, it is made on a cushion – a round, very firm pillow – using bobbins wound with linen thread. The intricate processes of the making of "bobbin lace," as it is sometimes called, and its historic background from Tudor times, interesting and instructive as it is, would prove too lengthy to give here. But it is significant that this fine old art is being carried on in British Columbia still. In the autumn of 1919, Miss Elsie Spencer of Morecambe, Lancashire, England, came to visit her brother on Denman Island. Lace-making was her hobby, and she brought the necessary equipment with her – pillow, pins, linen thread, bobbins and traditional patterns. In a short time Miss Spencer was instructing nine women in the art. From these first pupils the art of bobbin lace has spread up and down the coast of British Columbia and into the United States. Mrs. F. S. Graham, who was one of the original group, later moved to Courtenay and started a class there in 1942. From this beginning the Courtenay Lace Club was formed. In 1956 Mrs. Graham again moved, this time to Campbell River where she began the Campbell River Lace Club. Another of Miss Spencer's charter members, Mrs. Catherine Swan, now living in Courtenay, has taught lace-making to her daughters, granddaughters, and friends. Mrs. Swan has demonstrated lace-making at the Pacific National Exhibition in Vancouver. All in all, knowledge of this beautiful art of lace-making has already reached several hundred women through the efforts of the original teacher, Miss Spencer.

Another fine type of needlework was brought to the coast by Mrs. H. Hansen of Norway. She arrived at Port Neville on Johnstone Strait in 1903, bringing with her the knowledge of Hardanger embroidery. Named from the fjord in Norway where the art originated, this work was used to trim church altar cloths, fine costumes, curtains and table linen. The Norwegian communities of Port Neville and the settlement of Hardwicke Island kept the work alive for many years. Unfortunately there are few left who know this art, but examples of the work done in earlier days are treasured by those privileged to own them.

Many other types of needlework are carried out by British Columbia women. Outstanding in quilt making is Mrs. Mary McBeen of Comox who has won many awards. Indeed, most communities boast fine quilt makers. Weaving is also a popular skill. Mrs. Nora Bate of Gabriola Island is among the foremost spinners and weavers. She produces hand-woven fabrics of great beauty from yarn spun from the fur of her angora rabbits, as well as a variety of other yarns spun from the wool of local Cheviot sheep, Angora goat mohair, and even dog combings. Her hand-dyed fabrics are made up for sale into attractive stoles, ponchos, and yardage. Not only are Mrs. Bate's products marketed locally, but are now to be found in exclusive shops on Vancouver Island and in Eastern Canada. Mr. P. R. Blower of Parksville is also well known for his fine weaving.

Other types of handwork should be mentioned such as the embroidery of Mrs. Reg Goodman of Nanaimo, who has revived rare old designs for her work. Mrs. Violet Spreckley of the Gull Gift Shop in Parksville is known for her exquisite petit point. Knitting is also a most popular skill of British Columbia women. Settlers in Nanaimo, who came from the Shetland Islands, taught Fair Isle Knitting, using traditional patterns, to the Indians, when they first came to Vancouver Island. These designs have been adapted, along with the original Fair Isle technique, in the making of the popular Indian sweaters of today. Newcomers from the Orkney Islands brought similar patterns to Denman Island. Crocheting and tatting are also done by many women, and rugmaking of various kinds is a favourite avocation in many homes.

The coast offers raw materials for many fine crafts. Driftwood, shells and semi-precious stones are to be found on many beaches, and these materials are used in the manufacture of decorative and pleasing articles by many enthusiasts. Hobbyists in Nanaimo, on Gabriola Island, and at Parksville work in all these mediums. At Denman Island agates are found on the beaches in considerable quantity suitable for making beautiful jewellery. Thunder eggs are also found. These apparently ugly stones are recognized by experts, and when properly cut reveal beautiful interior surfaces. Several residents of Juskatla in the Queen

Charlotte Islands have valuable collections of native stones, including opals, jade, agates and petrified wood.

Good pottery clay has been found in some areas to encourage the making of ceramics. Several women on Denman Island carry on this craft. Mrs. Zillah Clements of Gabriola Island produces individualistic pottery. The best English glazes are imported to give distinctive beauty to her mugs, pipkins, bowls, lamp bases, patio lights, tiles and plaques. She has her own Pot Shop for the display and sale of her products, and her pottery is also sold in other shops throughout British Columbia.

The carving of wood is a very old and satisfying art. Mr. P. Duchesnay of Gabriola Island does intricate wood carving, and also makes violins which he sometimes plays for old-time dances. Carved trays, bowls and tables are made by Mr. F. S. Henderson of Comox.

Two brothers, Thor Erickson and Carl Erickson, aged seventy-five and seventy-seven respectively, who retired to Campbell River, have created a wildlife museum in their home. Here are exhibited more than a hundred delicately carved wooden figures. These include tiny humming birds and life-size eagles. There are willow grouse, tern, pheasants, owls, sea gulls, ducks, and even an ostrich. Examples of marine life include whale, porpoise, shark and salmon. Animals depicted are buffalo, raccoon, weasel, skunk, moose, deer, and black bear. The brother Thor does the carving, using an ordinary sharp pocket knife to work driftwood, roots, pine cones, and pieces of yellow cedar and maple. Occasionally he uses mussel shells to give the birds' wings their life-like appearance. Carl helps Thor create the rough outlines for the finer carving, and helps prepare the exhibit of their unique collection.

Leather work and copper tooling is carried out by Peter Bell of Gabriola Island. Versatile Gladys Hammersley of Comox makes attractive book ends and lamp bases from maple burls, plaques of copper, and many articles from driftwood. She is also a taxidermist and a talented painter. Mrs. Greenard of Coombs makes plaques and trays from cones, seeds and other native plant forms. Mrs. Griffin of Denman Island collects Indian baskets, and this interest has stimulated night classes in basketry on the Island.

Royal Field, President of Field's Sawmill in Courtenay, has an interesting hobby. He has built a fifteen foot model of the mill that he and his brother operate. This model actually saws miniature logs when his display is shown at local exhibitions. His first effort was a demonstration model of the automatic unloader he designed and patented. He then decided to make a scaled-down version of the entire sawmill.

Mr. Field is now engaged in building other models of his industry for demonstration and educational purposes.

An interest in local wild flowers led to the collecting and painting of them with an unusual process by the late Mrs. A. E. Plante of Nanaimo. The beautiful landscapes and seascapes of Vancouver Island have inspired many artists. A number of communities have classes in art. As a result West Coast artists are receivng wider recognition. Audrey Young Oppel, a Courtenay housewife, specializes in pastel portraits of Indian children. Her work is being sold successfully throughout Western Canada, and some of her studies have been reproduced by lithographic process for correspondence cards. Kenneth Galloway of Campbell River has held one-man shows of his paintings in Toronto and in the United States. Mrs. Laura McLean of Comox paints the sea in all its moods, creating murals with sweeping vistas of sea and mountains.

Pioneer women undoubtedly brought with them their linens and embroideries for guest occasions, and do not seem to have developed a conscious trend towards beautification in this direction in the early period. Life was too serious a business at first for much creative leisure. However, rug-making was more or less prevalent, and quilts were a needed item offering scope for expression of the artistic urge. Many beautiful examples of early and later work in rug and quilt making are still in use. Woven rugs of wool, using the "roll-as-one-weaves" method learned from the Indians are still being made by Mrs. A. Ruckle of South Salt Spring Island and Mrs. A. Hunt of Cobble Hill, who use the wool from locally raised sheep.

The early settlers favoured woollen clothing and brought North Cheviot sheep to the new home. The excellent wool and meat of this hardy animal became an important part of the economy. Every homestead had its carders and spinning wheel. The wool was washed in large tubs of soft warm water with soap and soda added to cut the dirt and grease. When it was thoroughly clean it was rinsed and laid in the sun to dry. Carding was originally done by hand. Two flat boards covered with wire teeth served as a means of teasing the wool out, lock by lock, and fibre by fibre, until a perfect mixing of fibres resulted. The bats were then laid on a cheese cloth or old sheet, and tacked down to make a warm soft centre for a quilt. Beautiful quilts were made by covering this wool centre with patch work to make a variety of designs. The most popular patterns were Log Cabin, Wedding Ring and Star, with various interpretations of them.

The traditional spinning wheel was well known everywhere. The wool was attached to the bobbin of the spindle. The spinner gave a first movement of the fly-wheel with her hand, then activated the motion by using the treadle. The spinning of the wool then began with the worker pulling out or "drawing" the wool, and giving it a twist – wherein lies the whole principle of spinning. Using the spindle, two full bobbins were twisted into two-ply yarn. This was wound into skeins and dyed as desired.

The main use of raw spun wool was for knitting sweaters, socks and mitts. By using the natural black and white wool, the lanolin was retained, and the resulting garment shed moisture better than one made from dyed wool. Rugs from raw wool were made by braiding three strips of sheep's wool to form a long flat rope. Starting from the centre the braid was placed in circular or oval form, each round being stitched to the previous one, and continuing until the desired size of rug was obtained. Saddle blankets were either hooked on a suitable piece of backing, or felted. These raw wool saddle blankets were exceptionally good as they retained their softness and absorbed sweat, keeping the horses from getting sore backs when ridden hard and far. The base for hooked rugs was usually a sturdy piece of burlap stretched on a frame. The wool was hooked through the sacking, leaving just enough on the lower edge to keep it secure. The right side was left longer and was clipped after the rug was completed. Settlers in later days continued this old craft of rug hooking, which is believed to be of Scandinavian origin, in the practical use of discarded woollen materials. Strips about a quarter to half an inch wide were cut – depending on the thickness of the materials – and hooked into colourful designs. Articles of attractive hue were greatly prized, and it behooved an uneasy father to keep close watch on his wardrobe at rug-hooking time!

Three types of handicrafts are predominant in the early days; patchwork and appliqued quilts, the wool-filled comforters, and the rag rugs – braided, hooked or woven from otherwise waste materials. The pioneer women were governed by three principles: necessity, economy and beauty. Perhaps beauty ranked last, since some of the pioneers regarded it as a snare of the Evil One, to be considered in much the same way as "dancin'," "spot keerds," and "novils." Dire necessity compelled our earnest, God-fearing grandmothers to save every scrap of material — linen, woollen, cotton. Silk was an almost unknown luxury, and every bit of available material of whatever kind had some use in the making of a comfortable and attractive home.

Through the long winter evenings the scraps of material were sewn into blocks or squares to become colourful, if sometime inartistic patchwork quilts. The more sombre-hued, heavier woollen scraps of cloth were made into floor coverings. Wool-filled comforters often had covers made of pieces carefully cut from the least worn woollen clothing and sewn into squares. These comforters were tied, not quilted. Generally speaking the elaborate patchwork quilts were made of new materials, of the scraps left over from women's dresses and men's shirts. After the blocks for the quilt were prepared, the best quilters were invited to come for an afternoon, and on such occasions as many as ten or twelve women would gather around the quilting frame to complete the quilt.

Materials for the braided rug were obtained from out-worn cotton and linen garments. These were cut into strips and braided in long plaits that were subsequently sewn into round or oval floor coverings. Later the hooked rug became a favourite. The hooking process was a variation of the Oriental tambour stitch, and consisted of pulling strips of woollen cloth through loosely-woven material, usually coarse linen or jute, with a metal hook. Another type of handmade rug was similar to those made in Quebec, when carefully cut strips of material were sewn together in long lengths and woven on a loom.

Many of these pioneer crafts have been popular to this present day throughout British Columbia. For example, at Hope, on the Trans-Canada Highway, Mrs. M. A. Barber established a Craft Cottage, and built up a centre where skilled workers wove woollen and linen fabrics on hand looms until recently. Here Mrs. Barber taught many different kinds of hand crafts, and created a good trade in genuine British Columbia crafts and souvenirs for sale to tourists.

In rug making, there are now rug looms available on which, by means of the "Ghiordes" or "Sehna" knot, strips of woven material can be used to create beautiful rugs. The elongated, curved crochet hook may be obtained with which beautiful, thick-pile reversible rugs may be made. Perhaps the most striking modern rugs are those hooked in wool. With good design and colouring, real works of art may be achieved with this technique. But perhaps the greatest credit still should go to those who, clinging valiantly to the old ideas of thrift and patient endeavour — the worker taking advantage of the wide range of good colours available from the proper blending of materials obtained from out-worn clothing — hooked rugs utilizing the beautiful traditional designs are achieved. The best of these can take their place proudly in any home as furnishings of use and distinction.

Pottery as a hand craft is among the most important in British Columbia. Great credit is due to the workers for creating a distinctive regional product with designs typical of the country such as the Dogwood, the Thunderbird, and other original motifs. Woodworking is also popular, with a ready market for well designed and carefully finished lamp bases, plates, platters, trays, candlesticks, and bowls. The most recent craft interest seems to be in the making of rock jewellery and the utilizing of driftwood.

Evidence of the vital, widespread and growing interest in hand crafts is found in the ever increasing number of Art Centres or Art Councils established or being established in communities throughout the province.

The Okanagan Summer School of Arts in Penticton, built around the theme "a holiday with a purpose," was founded in 1960 by a group of interested local citizens and representatives of the other Valley cities, with the help of professors from the University of British Columbia. The public response has been so great that from an original enrollment of 325, the number registered in 1965 for all classes – advanced, intermediate, and beginning – has almost trebled. This year a young people's hostel, with live-in accommodation and meals for those from thirteen to seventeen years of age, under a fully qualified House Mother and Recreation Director, has been made available at very low cost. Classes are held in the Penticton Senior Secondary School, but as many classes as possible are held out-of-doors, especially art and instrumental classes. The program features workshops in the arts and crafts – music, drama, and creative writing — with special emphasis on arts and crafts, where adult and teen-age classes are instructed in photography, painting, pottery, and batik. Musical and dramatic presentations take place throughout the duration of The Okanagan Summer School of the Arts, and a closing feature is an exhibition of arts and crafts, photography, painting, pottery, and so on, when a considerable number of sales are made.

Summerland, a sixty-year-old community, with a present population of about five thousand, has achieved a remarkable record with its arts and skills. Pottery was first made from local clay in 1922 when The Summerland Art League was organized. The pioneers in this craft were Marion Cartwright, Mabel Cordy and Doris Cordy who modelled miniatures of Ogopogo – the mythical monster of Okanagan Lake, frogs, and other animals, as well as totem poles, bowls, jugs and vases. This work has achieved an unusual standard of commercial excellence. Classes have been formed to teach ceramics, sculpture, wood carving and screen printing.

In Summerland needlework has always been of fine quality and wide interest. Several silver cups have been won by the Summerland Women's Institute. In 1957 First Prize was won in the Tweedsmuir Competition. Other national awards have been won for lace, and hooked rugs of original design. Needlework pictures executed by a native of Switzerland have won world acclaim. Classes in weaving, with instructors from the Extension Department of the University of British Columbia, have created interest in this art.

The Summerland Art Club was formed in 1950, and has secured instruction for its members from outstanding British Columbia artists. A high standard of artistry and originality have been achieved in creating pictures of merit in a number of mediums. In 1963 an exhibition was held in which about one hundred pictures were shown by forty local artists. One native son has had his pastels shown in art galleries and salons of England and France. A unique achievement of The Summerland Art Club was the creation of life-size figures for a Nativity Scene, which is displayed each Christmas season on a well-lighted hillside for the enjoyment of the entire community.

In the Hopeline District a similar revival of arts and crafts has taken place. Under the enthusiastic leadership of Mrs. D. C. Orme of Ryder Lake Women's Institute, The Community Art Council of Chilliwack came into being at a meeting attended by one hundred interested citizens, held in the City Hall in November 1958. As a result of this meeting the first short courses in painting, with instructors from the Extension Department of the University of British Columbia, were held in June 1959. In July of the same year the first week-long Festival of Arts and Crafts was held. As Director, Mrs. Orme arranged classes for the teaching of rug hooking, weaving from home spun wool and other materials, vegetable dyeing, and fabric painting. Instructive films on these subjects are shown as part of the instruction in the club's workshop.

This year, on May 29, the opening of the Fifth Biennial Festival of Arts and Crafts, called the Five Corners Showcase, took place in Chilliwack. A day-long street fair was held, and special window displays featured Indian artifacts, paintings, hand crafted articles, lapidary work, photographs, and even a demonstration of wine making. An emphasis was placed on youth, with bands, majorettes, clowns, a fire engine display, and other forms of entertainment. Children's films were shown, and a puppet show, entirely constructed and activated by local talent, was put on. Talented young people were encouraged to take part in a number of performances.

The story of the growth and promotion of arts and skills in Penticton, Summerland and Chilliwack are typical of the interest shown in many other parts of British Columbia. This enthusiasm has come about through the sincere efforts of men and women recognizing the value of occupational recreation rather than activities carried on for amusement only, with rewarding results to show for the time spent on the endeavour. This worthwhile urge accounts for the ever-increasing interest in rock hunting for the making of jewellery and other ornaments, since there is such an amount of valuable material to search for. With this has come an interest in creating beautiful objects in metalcraft. Native clays provide a medium for attractive and original ceramics; and there is an abundance of wood to stimulate artistic carving.

All in all, there is no province in the Dominion where the interest in crafts is any keener that it is in British Columbia. And nowhere are there more beautiful materials to work with.